MW01035498

Suffering and t

Suffering

and the

Nature of Healing

Daniel B. Hinshaw

ST VLADIMIR'S SEMINARY PRESS
YONKERS, NEW YORK
2013

Library of Congress Cataloging-in-Publication Data

Hinshaw, Daniel B.
    Suffering and the nature of healing / Daniel B. Hinshaw.
        pages   cm
    Includes bibliographical references.
    ISBN 978–0–88141–473–8
        1. Suffering—Religious aspects—Orthodox Eastern Church. 2. Healing—
Religious aspects—Orthodox Eastern Church. I. Title.

    BX384.S5H56 2013
    233—dc23

                                                            2013007407

ST VLADIMIR'S SEMINARY PRESS
575 Scarsdale Road
Yonkers, New York 10707
800–204–2665
svspress.com

Suffering and the Nature of Healing

ISBN 978–0–88141–473–8

Printed in the United States of America

For my physician father, David,
who inspired me to begin my journey into the
world of healing;
for Fr John Breck,
who gave direction and purpose to my wanderings;
for Fr Roman Braga,
who taught me to search for healing in the midst
of suffering;
and finally for my fellow pilgrim and wife, Jane.

Contents

Introduction

Today the Virgin gives birth to him who is
  above all being,
and the earth offers a cave to him whom
  no one can approach.
Angels with shepherds give glory,
and magi journey with a star,
for to us there has been born
  a little Child, God before the ages.[1]

THIS VERY POPULAR Christmas hymn within the tradition of the Eastern Church highlights the profound paradox inherent in the incarnation. God for whom no boundaries exist, who is not circumscribed in any way, willingly chooses to assume the flesh of his creature and be contained in the womb of Mary. It is by this deepest of mysteries that God brings healing to his broken creation in the second Person of the Holy Trinity, the God-Man. In the words of the great fourth-century defender of Christian orthodoxy, St Athanasius the Great (+373 AD), bishop of Alexandria, "[Christ] rightly took a mortal body, that in it death might henceforth be destroyed utterly and human beings be renewed again according to the image. For this purpose, then, there was need of none other than the Image of the Father."[2]

From very early within the Christian tradition, many names within the Scriptures were understood to refer to the second Person of the Trinity. St Gregory, bishop of Nyssa (+395 AD) writing in his *Life of*

---

[1]St Romanos the Melodist, Prelude "On the Nativity," from *On the Life of Christ, Kontakia*, trans. by Archimandrite Ephrem Lash (San Francisco: Harper Collins, 1995), 3.

[2]St Athanasius, *On the Incarnation*, trans. by John Behr, Popular Patristics Series 11b (Yonkers, NY: St Vladimir's Seminary Press, 2011), 63.

Moses[3] gives a long list of names which he identifies with Jesus Christ that are taken from primarily the Old but also the New Testament. The many names, in their own unique ways, illuminate by their highly descriptive character as metaphors different qualities of the God-Man. An example of one of these names whose meaning has been transformed by the incarnation is the "Land of the Living" taken from Psalm 27.[4]

This book is an attempt by an Orthodox Christian physician to explore the central relationship between the incarnation of the Word of God as Jesus Christ and the nature of healing within the understanding of traditional Christianity. It is precisely because "the Word became flesh and dwelt among us,"[5] that St Gregory could speak of him in such material, physical terms as *Land*. The remainder of the epithet, *of the Living*, is equally crucial for understanding the story at the heart of this book. The reason for God's infinitely gracious condescension to become part of his creation is what is revealed within the second part of this name of Christ. For the divine became human in order to heal a broken and dying creation and to re-create and give it new *life* through the conquest of sin and death. With his resurrection from the dead, Christ did indeed become the *Land of the Living*.

Eastern Christianity has always emphasized the role of Christ as the Healer. Romanos the Melodist, the great sixth-century Byzantine poet and hymnographer, in a stanza of one of his *kontakia* (hymns) describes how Christ through his crucifixion and death heals his wounded creatures in very direct, physical, and medically graphic terms. The hymn is in the form of a dialogue between Christ on the cross and his mother who cannot bear to see her Son suffer so terribly. It epitomizes the critical importance of the physical incarnation of Christ in the healing of the human person.

[3]St Gregory of Nyssa, *Life of Moses*, trans. by E. Ferguson and A.J. Malherbe (New York: Paulist Press, 1978), 118.
[4]Psalm 27.13 (RSV) "I believe that I shall see the goodness of the Lord in the land of the living!"
[5]John 1.14.

Be patient a little longer, Mother, and you will see
How, like a physician, I undress and reach the place where
    they lie
And I treat their wounds,
Cutting with the lance their calluses and their scabs.
And I take vinegar, I apply it as astringent to the wound,
When with the probe of the nails I have investigated the
    cut, I shall
plug it with the cloak.
And, with my cross as a splint,
I shall make use of it, Mother, so that you may chant with
    understanding,
'By suffering he has abolished suffering, *my Son and my God.*'[6]

The traditional Christian understanding and teaching regarding sin, suffering, and death have had tremendous impact on the care of the sick. With increased secularization, the unique perspective of traditional Christianity is largely being lost from health care. There is much in modern health care that is very good and could be recognized and blessed as consistent with traditional Christian teaching and practice. There is much that is not. Thus, this book will review the relationship of modern health care practice to traditional Christianity and the Church's understanding of health, disease, and healing, in order to give a better sense of how traditional Christianity can more effectively interface with secular health care.

The book has been organized into three parts. The first part explores the human dilemma posed by suffering. The second part examines the nature of the encounter between the suffering person seeking help and the persons offering to help. The third and final part addresses the possibility of healing independent of cure, even in the context of death.

[6]St Romanos the Melodist, "On the Lament of the Mother of God," from Lash, *On the Life of Christ, Kontakia*, 148. The descriptions of medical treatment within this stanza of Romanos' kontakion reflect medical practice of his time. Apparently, physicians would sometimes undress or change their clothing to treat some types of conditions.

PART I

The Human Dilemma

"In Christ, history and eternity meet."[1]

I am God's wheat, and I am ground by the teeth of wild beasts that I may be found pure bread of Christ.... I do not order you as did Peter and Paul; they were apostles, I am a convict; they were free, I am even now a slave. But if I suffer I shall be Jesus Christ's freedman, and in him I shall rise free.[2]

---

[1]Roman Braga, "Indiction—The Beginning of the Church Year," *The Burning Bush: A Monastic Journal*, 24.2 (2011): 5.

[2]St Ignatius of Antioch, "Letter to the Romans," 4, 1, 3, Apostolic Fathers vol. 1, trans. by Kirsopp Lake, Loeb Classical Library no. 24 (Cambridge, MA: Harvard University Press, 1912, repr. 1985), 231.

CHAPTER I

From Caring to Curing

A SHORT STORY, *The Living Relic*, written in the mid-nineteenth
century by the Russian author, Turgenev, beautifully illustrates
the dramatic shift that was already taking place within medicine from
a focus on caring for the sick to curing disease.

The story is about a young woman named Lukeria, a beautiful peas-
ant girl who is robbed of her health at the bloom of youth by a freak
accident. She falls while dancing and develops a type of spastic paralysis, wastes away, and eventually ends up being placed in a back corner
of a wealthy landowner's estate. The son of the woman who owns the
estate is the narrator of the story. He has been out on a hunting trip
to various districts and relates the different experiences on his journey.
In this particular encounter he has come upon Lukeria who was lying
very still on a pallet looking like an icon. She had an other-worldly
appearance and was clearly suffering greatly. His first reaction was to
propose taking her to a hospital—"Who knows, perhaps you might yet
be cured?" Her response underscores how the dilemma that we often
face when we encounter the medical profession had already developed
in the mid-nineteenth century:

> Oh, no, sir, . . . don't move me into a hospital; don't touch me. I shall
> only have more agony to bear there! How could they cure me now?
> . . . Why, there was a doctor came here once; he wanted to examine
> me. I begged him, for Christ's sake, not to disturb me. It was no
> use. He began turning me over, pounding my hands and legs, and
> pulling me about. He said, "I'm doing this for Science; I'm a servant
> of Science—a scientific man! And you," he said, "really oughtn't to
> oppose me, because I've a medal given me for my labors, and it's
> for you simpletons I'm toiling." He mauled me about, told me the

name of my disease—some wonderful long name—and with that he went away.[1]

That last statement, "he went away," is a reflection of a fundamental problem in the medical care of those for whom there is no cure: abandonment.

The conflict which this story typifies is characteristic of a dualism that has developed in our medical culture as well as in the greater culture of the West. Modern medicine essentially has a scientific-reductionist basis. Medical science is based on objective (quantitative) measures (e.g., blood pressure, white blood count, etc.). Although such an approach is critical to the diagnosis and treatment of disease, it has its limitations. By their nature, emotional, social, or spiritual experiences of the patient or caregiver are subjective and qualitative. Thus, in this model they are not "scientific" and therefore are basically suspect. Inevitably, the emphasis on the objective/scientific approach has shifted the focus of medical effort to disease as a target of treatment and away from the person. As a consequence, a mind-body disconnect has developed in Western modern medicine. Objectivity resides in treating the body. It can be seen. It can be measured. Something measurable can be done to it. Such empiricism is a fundamental part of daily practice in the medical profession. A focus solely on the purely physical ("objective") aspect of illness contradicts the traditional Christian teaching on the psychosomatic unity of man. By way of contrast, St John Climacus in speaking of his own body emphasizes the inherent unity of body and soul. "How can I hate him when my nature disposes me to love him? How can I break away from him when I am bound to him forever? How can I escape from him when he is going to rise with me?"[2]

Recently, Susan Ashbrook Harvey has explored the understanding of the body in ancient Syrian Christianity. She notes that for early Syriac Christian writers, "Christianity was located in the body because

[1] Ivan Turgenev, "A Living Relic," chapter 18 in *A Sportsman's Sketches*, vol.2, trans. by Constance Garrett (New York: Macmillan, 1916) 243–244.

[2] St John Climacus, *The Ladder of Divine Ascent*, trans. by C. Luibheid and N. Russell (Mahwah, NJ: Paulist Press, 1982), 185.

the body, in the most literal sense, was what God had fashioned in the beginning and where God had chosen to find us in our fallenness. This was why God acted through the incarnation."[3] She goes on further to quote St Ephraim, the Syrian (writing in the fourth century), to great effect "Glory to You who clothed Yourself with the body of mortal Adam, and made it a fountain of life for all mortals! . . . Though the soul exists of itself and for itself, yet without its companion, the body, it lacks true existence . . . For it is through the senses of its companion that it shines forth and becomes evident."[4] St Ephraim, speaking metaphorically to Christ about his relationship to the human person, describes the intimate union of soul and body: "The soul is your bride, the body your bridal chamber."[5]

One might wonder whether there has been a parallel concern regarding medical dualism in the secular world. George Engel, a professor of Psychiatry and Medicine at the University of Rochester, has examined the phenomenon. Writing prophetically in 1977, he addressed the problem of Biomedicine (i.e., the reductionist approach to medicine) wherein an illness becomes a disease that has specific biological and ultimately molecular causation.[6] Fundamentally, in Biomedicine if it can be seen, touched, defined, and better yet *measured*, then something can be done about it. Psychological, emotional, and social issues are too soft, squishy, and ill defined and thus are excluded—again fostering the mind-body dualism.

Interestingly, Engel blames the Church for creation of the mind-body dualism in modern medicine. He uses as justification for his assertion the permission that was granted by the Western Church to scholars like Vesalius at the time of the Renaissance to perform human anatomic dissection. The implication was that the body was now ceded to physicians as their responsibility but the mind and spirit were still

[3]Susan Ashbrook Harvey, "Embodiment in Time and Eternity: A Syriac Perspective," *St. Vladimir's Theological Quarterly* 43.2 (1999): 105–130, at 114, 115.

[4]Ibid. 115, 124.

[5]Ibid. 110.

[6]George L. Engel, "The Need for a New Medical Model: A Challenge for Biomedicine," *Science* 196 (1977): 129–136.

the property of the Church. With this mind-body dualism in place, the anatomic approach that came out of the Renaissance helped create the idea of the body as a machine, which breaks down. The physician's responsibility is, like a mechanic's, to fix the machine.

One of the stimuli for Engel to write his essay was from the provocative discussion that occurred at a medical meeting he had attended. He quotes a particularly pungent remark from a participant who represented the reductionist perspective, a remark that underscores the distance modern medicine had already traveled down the dualistic path by the late 1970s. "Medicine should concentrate on the real diseases and not get lost in the psychosociological underbrush. The physician should not be saddled with problems that have arisen from the abdication of the theologian and the philosopher."[7] The attitude expressed in this remark represents one extreme. Unfortunately, it has been the dominant extreme.

Engel makes an interesting comment in response to this. "The historical fact we have to face is that in modern Western society, Biomedicine not only has provided a basis for the scientific study of disease, it has also become our own culturally specific perspective about disease—that is, our folk model."[8] Even for the least sophisticated members of our society, the expectation remains that it is merely a matter of time before science will find a solution for every disease and health problem. The ultimate health problem in Biomedicine is death. As a logical progression of the extreme reductionist approach of Biomedicine, "Death is now no longer the locus of sin and salvation but a graphic image on the screen of a brain-monitoring machine."[9] As a counterpoint to Biomedicine, Engel proposed a bio-psycho-social model for health care to acknowledge and embrace the larger universe of psychological and social factors that impact health and define illness.[10] More recently, with the development

[7]Ibid.

[8]Ibid.

[9]Jeffrey P. Bishop, Philipp .W. Rosemann, and Frederick W. Schmidt, "Fides Ancilla Medicinae: On the Ersatz Liturgy of Death in Biopsychosociospiritual Medicine," *Heythrop Journal* 49.1 (2008): 20–43.

[10]Engel, ibid.

of the new medical specialty of palliative medicine, the model has been extended to become a bio-psycho-socio-spiritual one, in which spiritual needs of those with life-threatening illnesses are also acknowledged. The dualism still persists, however, in that disease-oriented approaches drive the processes of care and the psychosocial and spiritual aspects of the human experience are often exploited in a utilitarian manner to manage distressing symptoms. "Where once medicine served as the handmaiden of charity, being situated within the field of faith and spirituality," faith has now become the handmaiden of medicine.[11]

The Roots of Christian Philanthropy[12]

At this point, it may be helpful to review from a historical perspective the approach of the Church to Medicine and care of the sick. Such a study might begin with an examination of the Greek word, *philanthropia* (i.e., philanthropy) in its pre-Christian as well as Christian usage. In the early pre-Hellenistic meaning of *philanthropia*, even though the word literally means "the love of mankind" as a broader construct, it had a narrower meaning in everyday speech. It was more equivalent to being kind, friendly, or courteous—being a proper gentleman, in essence. In the Hellenistic context it took on a more general meaning, closer to the Christian understanding with some significant differences. It is very compelling to realize that even in the matter of linguistics Christ came truly in the fullness of time. A context had been prepared prior to the incarnation even for the transformation of language—the transfiguration of words.

Thus, even in the pre-Christian Hellenistic sense of *philanthropia* there was a feeling of concern for others, but this was typically in the context of the relationship between a social superior and inferior. There was condescension, a condescending benevolence, which usually did not extend to a particular concern for the poor and needy. Their fate

[11]Bishop, ibid.

[12]Darrel W. Amundsen, and Gary B. Ferngren, "Philanthropy in Medicine: Some Historical Perspectives," in *Beneficence in Health Care* (Dordrecht, The Netherlands: D. Reidel Publishing Co., 1982), 3.

was established. There was much more *philanthropia*, or concern and anxiety, on behalf of prominent peers who by a reversal of fortune had lost their wealth and power, because of their own class's sense of vulnerability.

Pagans pitied those rich who had lost their fortune or power. Since the poor were already poor, they did not deserve pity. Pity was essentially on a quid-pro-quo basis with "an eye to reciprocity. One might someday require similar assistance, perhaps, even from the person one had helped in the past."[13] Public philanthropy was another common means of obtaining honor and public recognition. Frequently, prominent physicians or other public leaders were memorialized on stone monuments for their donations to a city or local community. Typically, the donation would be given in support of the needs of the entire community with no regard for social status. The philanthropist actively sought public recognition for service to the whole city or community.

Another important concept that went hand in hand with *philanthropia* was *philotimia*, love of honor. Love of honor in pre-Christian Hellenistic culture, particularly for professionals like physicians, took precedence even over money. Such a prioritization is not really very different from the present. The temptations of honor and glory still exceed wealth in many quarters today (particularly in academia).

In stark contrast to the pre-Christian use of *philanthropia* is the emergence of the word, *agape*, which had been used relatively infrequently before its adoption by Christians. *Agape* was embraced by early Christians and given the radical meaning of freely given, unlimited, unconditional, self-sacrificial, or *no-strings-attached* love. It is an active love, active in the sense of the *Last Judgment* in Matthew 25 or in John 15.12 "Love one another as I have loved you"—something that was heretofore unknown and unappreciated in the world. Within the postapostolic period, the word *philanthropia* began to appear in the writings of the church fathers. However, not until the fourth century did *philanthropia* begin to be synonymous in Christian liturgical usage with *agape* where Christ becomes *ho philanthropos*, the lover of man.

[13]Ibid.

The incarnation redefined love and most emphatically gave a new definition to the kind of *philanthropia* that could motivate Christians to do things (e.g., caring for lepers and plague victims) that their pagan forebears would not have been able to comprehend. From the fourth century on, the meaning of *philanthropia* was also translated into the founding of charitable institutions (e.g., orphanages, hospitals, old age homes, etc.) to physically incarnate the Christian understanding of *philanthropia* within the empire.

Within the ranks of clergy in the early Church this practical, *hands on* Christian ministry or *diakonia*, was accomplished by the diaconate. The diaconate was directly involved in caring for the needy and the sick. Many of the clergy were physicians, particularly deacons. The Rule of St Benedict emphasizes the fundamental necessity of caring for the sick and unfortunate for the serious Christian who by virtue of the incarnation desires to serve Christ in an intimate and personal encounter. "Before and above all things, care must be taken of the sick, that they be served in very truth as Christ is served; because He hath said, 'I was sick and you visited me' (Matt 25.36). And, 'As long as you did it to one of these my least brethren, you did it to me (Matt 25.40).'"[14] It is important to note here that Christ said, "I was sick and you visited me"—not *cured* me.

The Christian focus in the Church's healing ministry has always been on caring for and attending to Christ in the suffering one. There has been an ambivalence about cure—truly wonderful if and when it happens, but real healing, salvation, is what is to be sought. This tension exists in the early Christian use of the Greek word, *sōzō*. It has the same root meaning as *Soter* (i.e., both healer and savior).[15] Modern medicine in its devotion to the biomedical reductionist model has focused on the cure of disease(s) as the real end or purpose of medicine. If a modern

[14]From "The Rule of St. Benedict," Chapter 36: "Of the Sick Brethren," accessed at: http://rule.kansasmonks.org on 2 June, 2012.
[15]William F. Arndt, and F. Wilbur Gingrich, *A Greek-English Lexicon of the New Testament and Other Early Christian Literature* (University of Chicago Press, 1969), 805, 808.

physician can't see (or preferably measure) a tangible result of therapy directed at a specific disease, s/he may feel that the patient's problem is either unreal or beyond the help of medicine. Such is the mentality of many modern physicians. The meaning and power of "I was sick and you visited me," has been almost entirely lost. It has no real meaning for many modern physicians.

Furthermore, if modern physicians cannot cure or control a disease, this implies that they have failed, or worse yet, their patients have failed medical treatment. Unfortunately, the implication is that somehow it is the patient's problem or fault. *Caring* for the sick comes almost as an afterthought during the victory celebration following a cure. Usually it comes as a congratulatory comment with minimal or no recognition of the pain and suffering the patient experienced during treatment. But what comfort does the biomedical reductionist model have for one who is not cured?

The Byzantine Roots of Medical Education and Practice

In the Byzantine model of medical education, there were a number of differences from modern practice. A formal process for certification of medical professionals did not exist. The educational process itself was less structured. The Hippocratic writings, which presented a predominately naturalistic approach to medicine and care of the sick, were absorbed with few changes by the Christian empire. The naturalistic (and rationalistic) approach of the Hippocratic tradition was in tension with a popular piety coming out of paganism, a healing piety, which was reflected in the cults of the healing gods Asklepios, Serapis, and Isis.

An examination of the cult of Asklepios may help clarify the tension that existed between the understanding of illness in popular pagan piety and the more rationalistic ('scientific') approach practiced by the Hippocratic physician.[16] The 'baptism' by the Church of much from both of

---

[16]For a detailed discussion of the Asklepian healing rituals, see "Chapter 1: Pre-Christian Healing Places," in Guenter B. Risse, *Mending Bodies, Saving Souls: A History of Hospitals* (Oxford: Oxford University Press, 1999), 15ff.

these pre-Christian traditions contributed to some of the ambivalence and conflict seen in subsequent Christian attitudes toward health care. The cult of Asklepios represented essentially the other extreme at that time from the naturalistic—what today would be called 'state of the art'—scientific medicine practiced within the Hippocratic tradition. In the Asklepian tradition, there were a number of resonances with later Christian practice—at least with popular piety. For example, in the cult of Asklepios, individuals seeking healing would go to the temple of Asklepios. They would experience a process known as incubation, during which they would stay overnight at the temple and sleep with the hope and prayer that the god would visit them in a dream. In the dream Asklepios would either heal them directly or give them directions as to how they should pursue the cure of their illness, perhaps even directing their use of a natural medicine. Within the hagiographical tradition of the Church, the saints, at times during their lives but more often after their death, have intervened through visions of the night in a manner similar to Asklepios, to bring healing or support to Christians.

In another pagan tradition that prefigured later Christian practice, small effigies of body parts (e.g., eyes, ears, hands, feet) specifically affected by various ailments would be hung before the statue of Asklepios. Such images would then serve as visible and tangible evidence of supplications and prayers for healing. The use of similar symbols persists in parts of the Orthodox world (e.g., Greece) where an image of the diseased part is now hung in front of a healing icon, particularly of St Panteleimon or one of the other 'unmercenary' healing saints (Greek *anargyroi*, lit. silverless ones, so called because of their refusal to receive payment for their services).

Just as Asklepios had been known as the Compassionate, the Caring One, so also Christ became known as the Great Physician. In identifying himself with the brass serpent raised in the wilderness by Moses,[17] Christ not only declared his messianic healing role within

[17]Christ in reference to Numbers 21.8, 9 states in his conversation with Nicodemus, "And as Moses lifted up the serpent in the wilderness, so must the Son of Man be lifted up, that whoever believes in him may have eternal life." John 3.14, 15.

the Jewish tradition but also in a very real sense he appropriated the staff of Asklepios[18] to himself, thus affirming the universal nature of his healing ministry. Perhaps Asklepios, like so many forerunners or types in the Old Testament, was a type or prodrome within the pagan world, preparing Hellenized Roman culture for its encounter with the real Healing God.

Early Christianity and the Development of the Hospital[19, 20]

A totally new and unprecedented form of *philanthropia* developed under Christian auspices in the fourth-century East Roman empire. The hospital, a new institutionalized expression of *philanthropia*, developed out of the Christian commitment to visiting and caring for Christ in the person of the sick. All modern hospitals really owe their essential elements to a number of innovations of St Basil the Great and Egyptian monastics beginning in the fourth century. Prominent patronage was given to medicine by major church leaders, such as St Basil, who had himself been trained as a physician in his youth in Athens. Medicine in the East was a highly respected professional activity, even in pagan times. However, in Rome and the western portion of the Empire it was almost always practiced by foreign (usually Greek) slaves. In the West it was not proper for a good Roman patrician to practice medicine. Such social strictures did not exist in the East. This major cultural difference between eastern and western attitudes to the vocation of caring for the sick antedated the state sponsorship of Christianity within the empire. From the perspective of many of the Church Fathers of the fourth century, Medicine, in its broadest context to encompass curing illness as well as caring for the sick, was viewed as the *perfect profession*. By virtue

[18]For a description of the staff of Asklepios see: http://drblayney.com/Asclepius. html; accessed on 5 January, 2013.

[19]Mary E. Keenan, "St. Gregory of Nazianzus and Early Byzantine Medicine," *Bulletin of the History of Medicine* 9 (1941): 8–30.

[20]Andrew T. Crislip, *From Monastery to Hospital: Christian Monasticism & the Transformation of Health Care in Late Antiquity* (Ann Arbor: University of Michigan Press, 2005).

of the incarnation, it became the perfect profession, in as much as it was modeled after the healing ministry of the Great Physician, who also became the patient in the person of those who suffer.

Christianity was seen primarily as a healing religion. After the legalization of Christianity, there was a great emphasis on healing, both natural and miraculous. Interestingly, a contemporary and fellow student with Sts Basil and Gregory (Nazianzus) in Athens during their youth was the future apostate emperor, Julian (361–363 AD). He was a strong adherent of the cult of Asklepios. He even complained and raved at his own priests of Asklepios for not following the Christian example of selflessly caring for anyone, regardless of their religious faith, pagan or not. Julian recognized the potential of Christian *philanthropia*, as incarnated in the care of the sick, as a powerful weapon for winning souls, and desperately wished to emulate it in his attempts to restore pagan worship in the Empire. Thus, much of the Christianizing of the Roman Empire after Constantine, at least in the East, occurred in no small part as a result of large scale charitable activities initiated by Christian bishops and other church leaders, both lay and clergy.

What was St Basil's unique contribution to the evolution of Christian *philanthropia* and the emergence of the hospital? He did not consider his practice of medicine to be incompatible with his vocation as a bishop of the Church. He founded what has traditionally been referred to as the first hospital, although there were Egyptian antecedents developed earlier in the fourth century to serve the unique health care needs of monastic communities. It was known as *hē kainē polis*, *The New City* because it was so large. It was also known as the *Basileias* in honor of St Basil, its founder. It was physically located outside the walls of Caesarea, the seat of his diocese. In the nine years of his service as a bishop, Basil built a large complex to serve the major needs of the poor and dispossessed of Caesarea. The amazing accomplishments of his short tenure as bishop of Caesarea reflected this profound concern for the poor. He was driven by a very strong sense of social justice implicit within the theology of the incarnation: "For if we all took only what was necessary to satisfy our own needs, giving the rest to those who lack, no one would be rich, no one would be poor, and no one would be in need ... You are thus guilty of injustice toward as many as you might have aided, and did not."[21]

The Basileias included a large variety of social institutions dedicated to caring for the needy. The elderly poor were provided care and a home (*gerokomeion*). Foreigners, strangers, and the destitute (beggars) were given a place to stay. Orphans were raised in a supportive environment and educated for a trade. His hospital offered care for the soul and body with the hope of cure wherever possible. Finally, he also provided a hospice for lepers, which offered both a home and loving care for the ultimate outcasts of the ancient world until their death. What were the specific aspects and goals of the medicine practiced in the hospital of the Basileias? To gain greater insight into the character of that medical care, we must examine the nature of Byzantine medical practice from a later, better documented era.

The Pantocrator Xenon[22]

The *typikon* (rule) for the Pantocrator Monastery, founded by the Emperor John II Komnenos in Constantinople in the early twelfth century (1136), also describes the organization of the hospital or *xenon* attached to the monastery.[23] Although some evolution would have occurred with respect to the form and function of hospitals in the East Roman empire between the prototype founded by St Basil and the opening of the *Pantocrator Xenon* in 1136, it is reasonable to assume that some constant features would be present in the organization of the *Pantocrator Xenon* that should give some insights into the character of earlier hospitals within the Eastern Empire. Within the

[21]St Basil the Great, *On Social Justice*, (Crestwood, NY: St Vladimir's Seminary Press, 2009), 69, 70.

[22]Timothy S. Miller, *The Birth of the Hospital in the Byzantine Empire* (Baltimore, MD: Johns Hopkins University Press, 1997).

[23]Pantokrator *Typikon* of Emperor John II Komnenos, Monastery of Christ Pantokrator in Constantinople, October 1136, trans. by Robert Jordan, at: http://www.doaks.org/resources/publications/doaks-online-publications/byzantine-studies/typikapdf/typo38.pdf; accessed March 2013.

Pantocrator Monastery, there were a number of social institutions (e.g., old age home, orphanage), in addition to the *xenon*. A striking feature of the *Pantocrator Xenon's* mission was to provide curative medical therapy (state-of-the-art twelfth-century healthcare) similar to a modern hospital (at least in intent). A brief review of the *xenon's* organization and function will help to illustrate the similarities and differences with modern healthcare.

The hospital had 50 beds. This may appear to be a trivial number, but it is important to emphasize here that there was one bed per sick person. In the Christian West, sometimes as many as five people were placed together in a bed. If they were contending with an epidemic illness in the West, they of course died more quickly, as infectious diseases would be more efficiently spread among the patients and staff. The beds in the *Pantocrator Xenon* were arranged into five *ordinoi* or wards. Thus, the modern model of hospital beds being organized for care (using the ward or *ordinos* as the structural and functional unit) was already present.

One of the wards was for patients with wounds and fractures (i.e., a trauma ward), one with eight beds for diseases of the eyes, intestines, and other serious illnesses, and one with twelve beds for women. The two remaining wards were made up each with ten beds for males presenting with other illnesses. The wards were heated. There was a conscious effort made to keep the temperature regulated and to maintain a warm environment for the patients in the winter. Genders were segregated. There were bathing facilities present for a bath at least twice a week. The diet was balanced and vegetarian. The *xenon* was governed by the abbot, thereby demonstrating integration with the monastery, at least at the administrative level. Four *oikonomoi*, who were monks, were household managers. At this point a brief discussion about the Greek word, *xenon*, and how it came to be used to define hospitals may help illustrate the nature of these institutions within the context of the Christian empire.

In its earliest usage, the word *xenon* was used to identify mobile people (refugees) who were foreigners or strangers on the borders of the empire. The earliest charitable organizations that began to look like hospitals were more like hostels for people who were dispossessed and needy—refugees from the chaos in their world. Of course, some of them were also ill when they arrived. That the usage of *xenon* evolved to eventually mean an institution for caring for the sick is fitting in that everyone who becomes sick essentially is like a stranger (in some sense isolated from their fellow human beings by their illness). This is as true for our current culture as it was in the East Roman empire.

Staffing for patient care was highly organized and hierarchical, thus not unlike that of modern hospitals. There were two physicians or *iatroi* attending on each ward. There were three medical assistants. Women also served on the medical staff of the Pantokrator Xenon: There was a female physician who worked with the other physicians, particularly on the women's ward. In addition, four female assistants and other women provided care for the sick. An outpatient clinic was a relatively new feature, since the earliest hospitals actually did not have outpatient clinics. Originally, monks combed the streets looking for the sick, whom they would drag back to the hospital. The monks of the *Pantocrator* monastery were treated separately in their own infirmary. The *xenon* was for the use of the lay public. As much as possible, in the hospital the care of sick monks was kept separate from that of the non-monastics.

The two house physicians who were most senior in authority and status were known as *primikerioi*. They would alternate duty by taking a month of service at a time and then would be off for a month. A similar pattern of medicine is practiced today by hospitalists in many large tertiary hospitals. The wages the *primikerioi* were paid were minimal, if not "unmercenary," by the standards of the day. If they made decent wages, they probably did so by having a private practice during their months off. The *primikerioi* were responsible not only for overseeing all of the care, but they had a major teaching responsibility as well. So another major part of the mission of the *Pantocrator Xenon* (like many modern hospitals) was to provide teaching and training for the next generation of healthcare providers.

The integration of all aspects of treatment provided at the *Pantocrator Xenon* was in many ways in stark contrast to the fragmentation of care seen today. The first and primary action taken in the treatment of patients was confession and prayers, particularly at the time of admission. Confession occurred so that, "they might not die a truly ruinous death, a spiritual one, leaving this world without confession."[24] The Divine Liturgy was offered in two chapels, one for men, and one for women, each of which was staffed by a priest and a reader on Wednesdays, Fridays, Saturdays, and Sundays, as well as on major feast days. This was all an integral component of the treatment regimen. It has been estimated that the vegetarian diet consisted of as much as 3,300 calories a day. It represented quite a carbohydrate load, with bread and mixed vegetables, dressed with olive oil. In essence, patients admitted to the *Pantocrator Xenon* were entering a modified Lenten experience (i.e., a fasting diet) during their hospitalization.

In conjunction with the spiritual medicine described above, internal and external medicines (salves, plasters, etc.) such as the Hippocratic tradition had developed by that time were used extensively. Surgery was also employed (some of it fairly crude) for various conditions, including wound care, setting of fractures, treatment of hernia, and bladder instrumentation for stones. Bathing was a major component of care as well.

The Emperor John II Komnenos identified the sick as "the special friends of Christ."[25] While they were in the hospital, it was the responsibility of patients to pray for the emperor, including participating in liturgical services for him and his ancestors.

What was the goal of care in the *Pantocrator Xenon?* It was curative. Physicians in antiquity could ethically excuse themselves or refuse care to "hopeless" cases in order to protect their professional reputation. This attitude persisted even to some extent among Christian physicians and represented an ethical problem for them. For the physician (Christian or not), the practical problem was retaining the ability to

[24]Miller, ibid., 19.
[25]Ibid.

attract patients to one's practice if one cared for many patients who died while under treatment. One could easily acquire a reputation as a "bad" doctor. This same problem has been pervasive in medicine through the centuries and is still with us, now in the form of some procedural specialists who are reluctant to provide care to high risk patients to avoid poor outcome statistics. A real fear relates to the possibility that their personal statistics may be reported to state licensing boards or the media, and so lead to public embarrassment or censure. This, in turn, can result in limiting access to care to those who have the greatest risk of poor outcomes but who may also have the greatest need.

The monastery also had a *gerokomeion* (i.e., a home for the elderly, a nursing home) for up to 24 elderly men, which was distinct from the *xenon*. This is further evidence that the *Pantocrator* monastery provided other kinds of care that were not focused specifically on curing disease. The hospital (*xenon*) component, however, was really focused on cure. There is an interesting instance reported in the hagiographical literature that probably occurred about a century or two prior to the founding of the *Pantocrator Xenon*. It reflects the fact that there was something equivalent to hospice work going on at that time but underscores the fact that the hospitals (*xenones*) were not places where care of the dying would normally occur. If a patient was diagnosed as being "hopeless," the patient would be shunted elsewhere. The story is of a certain Sergios, who had been severely beaten and "was found sometime later by those assigned the task [of searching out the sick]. Sergios was lying as though dead, scarcely breathing. Sadly, they lifted Sergios up, and carrying him in a litter, they left him at the hospital called *Euboulos*. There, those learned in the medical art consulted together and examined his condition carefully from the first day to the seventh, but seeing that the injury was greater than any medical study or therapy, they completely gave up and abandoned hope for his life. Moving on, they left him unattended and urged those in charge of his care to make preparations because of this ... The people who were responsible for taking care of him received this painful news; they picked up the hopeless Sergios in a litter and carried him to a home in a holy house nearby, which was named after the martyr of God, Nicholas, and located next to the place called the *Tyche* of the City. Here they placed him to breathe his last according to the situation."[26] The story goes on to relate that after this transition in care he was actually healed miraculously. This is also a reflection of the great ambivalence that has existed throughout the history of Christianity regarding conventional medical care.

What was the ancient Christian model for the care of those who could not be cured?

St Basil and Lepers

As noted above, physicians in antiquity would not treat "hopeless," incurable cases for fear of damaging their professional reputation. A patient with leprosy was the "hopeless case" par excellence. In addition to its apparently hopeless character, leprosy carried with it a terrible stigma (not unlike HIV/AIDS today). St Basil helped leprosy replace epilepsy as the "sacred disease." Leprosy had been viewed up till that time, even by many pious people, as a curse from God. St Basil's ministry to lepers really changed that attitude dramatically within the Christian context. Lepers, who had once been viewed as objects of divine wrath, were now viewed as objects of divine preference.[27]

According to St Gregory of Nazianzus, concern for lepers in the Basileias was a radical departure from prior precedent and was St Basil's most amazing achievement, greater in ultimate importance than any of the great monuments or prior achievements of their civilization. "He did not therefore disdain to honor with his lips this disease [leprosy], noble and of noble ancestry and brilliant reputation though he was, but saluted them as brethren ... Basil's care was for the sick, and the relief of their wounds, and the imitation of Christ, by cleansing leprosy, not by a word, but in deed."[28] Most significantly, St Basil personally

[26]Ibid., xxviii, xxix.

[27]Keenan, ibid.

[28]St Gregory of Nazianzus, "Oration, Panegyric on St. Basil," 43.63, in *Cyril of Jerusalem, Gregory Nazianzen*, Nicene and Post-Nicene Fathers (NPNF), vol. 7, ed. by Philip Schaff and Henry Wace (Peabody, MA: Hendrickson Publishers, Inc., 1994), 416.

cared for lepers in his *kelyphokomeion*. The terminally ill are, in many respects, the lepers of today.

Was this attitude of deep concern for the suffering of the dying unique to St Basil? Prior to the legalization and state sponsorship of Christianity in the Roman Empire, Christians were well known for their fearless demonstrations of compassion in the face of almost certain death, gestures which were bestowed upon their neighbors, whether friend or foe. Eusebius, the fourth-century church historian records a much earlier dramatic instance of such compassion that was shown to the victims of a terrible plague in Alexandria in the mid-third century. The plague occurred immediately following the violent persecutions of Christians in that same city under the Emperor Decius:"But when the briefest breathing-space had been granted us and them, there descended upon us this disease, a thing that is to them more fearful than any other object of fear, more cruel than any calamity . . . Yet to us it was not so, but, no less than the other misfortunes, a source of discipline and testing . . . Most . . . of our brethren in their exceeding love and affection for the brotherhood were unsparing of themselves . . . visiting the sick without a thought as to the danger, assiduously ministering to them, *tending them in Christ* . . . drawing upon themselves the sickness from their neighbors, and willingly taking over their pains. And many, when they had cared for and restored to health others, died themselves, thus transferring their death to themselves . . ."[29] This is a crucified love made possible through the incarnation, i.e., tending them in Christ (*therapeuontes en Christo*), so that "many, when they had cared for and restored to health others, died themselves, thus *transferring their death to themselves.*"

---

[29]Bishop Dionysius of Alexandria (mid 3rd century), quoted in Eusebius, *Ecclesiastical History*, Loeb Classical Library, vol. 2 (Cambridge, MA: Harvard University Press, 1994), 185–7.

Christian Ambivalence to Medicine

Should a believing Christian rely on the skill and judgment of physicians and other healthcare providers or should the believer rely solely on the mercy and providence of God, seeking healing through prayer? In his tenth Catechetical sermon, St Cyril of Jerusalem, writing in the fourth century, emphasizes the central importance for believing Christians of relying upon the mercies of God, without specifically condemning standard medical practice. "If, therefore, anyone is suffering in soul from sins, there is the Physician for him . . . If any is encompassed also with bodily ailments, let him not be faithless, but let him draw nigh; for to such diseases also Jesus ministers . . ."[30] There were others who were clearly not mainstream Christians, like Tatian (who later became a Gnostic) who promoted dualism and emphasized that all material means were essentially evil. Thus, herbs and other material medicines should not be used and only spiritual means of healing should be sought. Even in the Gospel of Mark, when the writer gives the account of the woman with the flow of blood, there is a negative emphasis placed both on medical greed and incompetence: "[She] had suffered many things from many physicians. She had spent all that she had and was no better, but rather grew worse."[31] On the other hand, St Ignatius of Antioch in the early second century could strongly affirm that the spiritual can act through material means to bring healing: ". . . breaking a single bread, which is the *medicine of immortality*, an antidote which prevents death, yet enables us to live at all times in Jesus Christ."[32] His use of the word 'medicine' to describe the Eucharist (communion) clearly transcends mere metaphor and provides a great corrective to much of the dualism expressed by other early Christian writers.

Sometimes, apparent ambivalence toward consultation with physicians was a reflection of personal modesty. In his *Life* of his sister St

[30]St Cyril of Jerusalem, "Catechetical Lecture," X.13, NPNF, vol. 7, 61.

[31]Mark 5.25–34.

[32]St Ignatius of Antioch, "Letter to the Ephesians" 20, 2; Alistair Stewart, tr. and ed., *St Ignatius of Antioch: The Letters*, Popular Patristics Series no. 47 (Yonkers, NY: St Vladimir's Seminary Press, forthcoming).

Macrina, St Gregory of Nyssa in the fourth century records how he discovered after his sister's death that St Macrina had earlier been healed
of a probable breast cancer miraculously while preserving her modesty.
" 'This [scar],' she replied, 'has been left on the body as a token of God's
powerful help.' For there grew once in this place a cruel disease, and
there was a danger either that the tumour should require an operation,
or that the complaint should become quite incurable, if it should spread
to the neighbour-hood of the heart. Her mother implored her often
and begged her to receive the attention of a doctor, since the medical
art, she said, was sent from God for the saving of men. But she judged
it worse than the pain, to uncover any part of the body to a stranger's
eyes. So when evening came, after waiting on her mother as usual with
her own hands, she went inside the sanctuary and besought the God
of healing all night long. A stream of tears fell from her eyes on to the
ground, and she used the mud made by the tears as a remedy for her
ailment. Then when her mother felt despondent and again urged her
to allow the doctor to come, she said it would suffice for the cure of her
disease if her mother would make the holy seal on the place with her
own hand. But when the mother put her hand within her bosom, to
make the sign of the cross on the part, the sign worked and the tumour
disappeared."[33] Interestingly, as elements of the miraculous cure of her
breast cancer, St Macrina combined the tears shed as part of her fer-
vent supplication to God with the dust of the ground and applied this
poultice to the tumor. The material was combined with the spiritual in
her healing.

In contrast to the dualists, St Basil the Great, being a physician himself, had a more balanced view regarding the role of medicine in the
healing of believers. "[W]e should neither repudiate this art [medicine]
altogether nor does it behoove us to repose all our confidence in it; but,
just as in practicing the art of agriculture we pray God for the fruits, and
as we entrust the helm to the pilot in the art of navigation, but implore
God that we may end our voyage unharmed by the perils of the sea,

[33]St Gregory of Nyssa, Life of Macrina; accessed at: http://www.fordham.edu/
halsall/basis/macrina.asp on 5 January, 2013.

so also, when reason allows, we call in the doctor, but we do not leave off hoping in God."[34] His great friend, St Gregory of Nazianzus had a brother named Kaisarios, who was an important court physician in Constantinople. St Basil was confident that God's grace was as evident in natural healing with medicinal herbs and plants as it was also in miraculous healing. Other bishops, such as the fourth-century bishop Basil of Ankyra and the priests Zenobios and Dionysios, were also physicians. Another strong tradition that developed within the Church was that of the *Anargyroi*, the "silverless ones" or unmercenary saints—Sts Cosmas and Damian, St Panteleimon and others, most of whom were practicing physicians. They would treat/cure diseases both by conventional medicine and miraculous means without charging patients for their services.

St Basil in a letter to a physician named Eustathios most clearly articulates a vision of the ideal Christian healer/physician. "With all of you . . . who follow medicine, philanthropy is a practice. And it seems to me that he who should place your science above all things that are pursued in life would hit upon the proper judgment . . . the dispenser of health is your profession. But, in your hands the science is especially expert, and you extend the boundaries of your philanthropy, not limiting the favour of your profession to bodies, but taking thought also of the correction of spiritual infirmities."[35] Thus, the ideal healer and physician would be one who cares for body and soul.

The wedding of holy orders with the practice of medicine did persist for some time within the East Roman empire. A later patriarch of Constantinople, Photios, was fascinated with medicine and at least treated his close friends. But, Lukas Chrysoberges, a patriarch in the twelfth century not long after the founding of the *Pantocrator Xenon*, actually

[34]St Basil the Great, "Question 55" in "The Long Rules," *St. Basil: Ascetical Works*, trans. by M. Monica Wagner, The Fathers of the Church: A New Translation, vol. 9 (Washington, DC: Catholic University of America Press, 1962), 351. Accessed online at: http://archive.org/stream/fathersofthechur027835mbp#page/n351/mode/2up/ search/medical+care on 5 January, 2013.

[35]St. Basil, "Letter CLXXXIX. To Eustathios, Chief Physician," from *St. Basil, The Letters*, trans. by R.J. Deferrari, Loeb Classical Library, vol. 3 (Cambridge, MA: Harvard University Press, 1986), 49.

forbade the open practice of medicine by physician clergy. He would not allow them to join the physician's guild. His reasoning for this prohibition is not entirely clear. However, despite his efforts the tradition has continued into the modern era. Recent examples include the medical practice of Metropolitan Anthony Bloom and the hospital/nursing work of the New Martyr Elizabeth in Russia at the time of the Bolshevik revolution. Perhaps the crux of the matter lies in understanding the full meaning of St Cyril's teaching, that Christians with strong faith should seek ultimate healing from diseases in Jesus Christ who is the source of all healing. With the incarnation, all material means have been touched and blessed by the Incarnate One, such that the material is now permeated with the spiritual. The incarnation itself should liberate the believing Christian from this ambivalence regarding healing, since Christ made it possible that great healing can come by means of the tangible, whether it be in the consecrated Bread and Wine or the *touch* (e.g., medications, massage, surgery) of a healer/physician received in the context of faith and prayer.

The Impact of Christianity on Medicine

What have modern historians of medicine said about Christianity and its impact on medicine? According to one prominent medical historian of the first part of the twentieth century, it led to the "most revolutionary and decisive change in the attitude of society toward the sick ... The social position of the sick man thus became fundamentally different from what it had been before. He assumed a preferential position which has been his ever since."[36] Adolf Harnack maintained that Christianity, "deliberately and consciously assumed the form of the 'religion of salvation or healing' or of 'the medicine of soul and body,' and at the same time it recognized that one of its cardinal duties was to care assiduously for the sick in body."[37] A more recent historian,

[36]Henry E Sigerist, *Civilization and Disease* (Chicago, IL: University of Chicago Press, 1943), 69–70.

[37]Adolph von Harnack, "The Gospel of the Savior and of Salvation," in *The Mission and Expansion of Christianity in the First Three Centuries* (n.2) 1:121–51.

Gary Ferngren, has insisted, however, that early Christianity was not a religion of healing, if healing means cure of disease. Rather, "it was not curing but caring that constituted the chief ministry of the early Christian community to the sick."[38] This is a critical distinction that will be explored more fully later.

A sociologist of religion has made a careful study of the growth of Christianity within the Roman Empire based on the historical records available.[39] Stark has made a compelling case from his study of the rate of growth of modern religious movements like the Mormon church when compared with the best estimates of early Christian demographics, that modern rates of growth (~40% per decade) may also have defined the pattern of growth of the Church in the first three centuries.[40] He has emphasized the great importance of social networks in conversions. In other words, a prospective convert to a faith is more likely to be recruited by social contacts (e.g., family, friends) who are already believers. Thus, one need not invoke imperial patronage by the Emperor Constantine as the cause for the rapid growth of the Church by the mid-fourth century (approximately half of all people within the empire). The trajectory of growth was already in place to make it happen. Some of the factors that he cites as likely contributing to the rate of growth of the early Church include the respectful treatment of women within the Christian community, which fostered a higher rate of female conversions, greater fertility, and respect for the lives of unborn and newborn children among Christians, the courageous witness of Christian martyrs, and the early Christian approach to caring for their neighbors (both Christian and pagan) during times of epidemic illness.[41] When Christians did not abandon their neighbors but stayed with and cared for them through the illness, many would die but some would survive and acquire immunity. Good basic nursing care

[38]Gary B. Ferngren, "Early Christianity as a Religion of Healing," *Bull. Hist. Med.* 66 (1992): 1–15.

[39]Rodney Stark, *The Rise of Christianity: A Sociologist Reconsiders History* (Princeton, NJ: Princeton University Press, 1996).

[40]Ibid. 6, 7.

[41]Ibid. 103–115; 115–128; 179–189; and 82–94, respectively.

would also help both pagan and Christian plague victims have a better chance of survival. This devotion and courage in the face of death was noted by Bishop Dionysius in mid-third-century Alexandria.[42] They resulted in higher survival among the Christians and those they cared for, and that was seen as nothing short of miraculous. This witness would in turn increase the number of converts through an expanding social network generated during the time of the epidemic that now extended to the pagan neighbors of Christians.

It may be helpful to reflect for a moment on the meaning of the Greek word *semeion*, so often translated as *miracle*. Its meaning may also be highly colored by the dramatically altered context in which the Church found itself in the fourth century: it had suddenly become an object of imperial patronage and yet had been so recently the target of violent persecution. Within the context of the Gospel, *semeion* often meant a *sign* (i.e., of the Kingdom or power of God at work in the world). Some of the most effective signs or miracles demonstrating the power of God acting in the Christian community during the persecutions of the first three centuries may have been the martyrs with their faithfulness unto death in the face of great trials and torture. Selfless ministry to those dying of epidemic illnesses represented another form of martyrdom, as well. As the whole cultural situation changed with the end of the formal persecution of Christians, the *sign* of Christian martyrdom became manifest in the lives and struggles of Christian holy men and women within the emerging monastic movement. In the monastics' radical commitment to live their lives in Christ, it should not be surprising if, by the grace of the Holy Spirit, some of the deeds of Christ were to be manifested in their lives (including miraculous healing of the sick). The one who follows Christ will do the things he does. Thus, supernatural activity should not be a major surprise, nor should care of the poor and sick. In the many accounts of miracles in the fourth century, miraculous healings occurred through a variety of means including: invocation of the name of Christ, prayer and fasting, the sign of the cross, the laying on of hands, unction (anointing

---

[42]Bishop Dionysius of Alexandria, ibid.

with oil), exorcism, and contact with relics of the saints.[43] The use and significance of these *means* persist within the piety and practice of the Church to this day.

Demonic Causation of Disease and Sickness

A review of early Christian perspectives on health and disease would be incomplete without some discussion of the role of demonic forces in the etiology of human disease and suffering. In general, as modern biological models of disease have so effectively explained many aspects of human illness, Christians have begun to think that even contemplating the possibility of diabolical influences on human health is a reflection of some type of primitive superstition. Certainly, the early Christians and traditional Christianity throughout its history has had no such qualms. There are many references within the Gospels of disease causation by demonic forces (particularly mental illness).[44] Modern historians have emphasized that in the question of demonic causation of disease the fundamental dichotomy within Christianity over the role of medicine is highlighted.

> "[M]ost Christians have seen no incompatibility with spiritual principles to assume that God can heal by means of physicians as well as without, and that physicians are ordained by God to relieve pain and sickness. *If, however, suffering and disease are caused by a demonic spiritual force rather than by God, a physician treating by ordinary means would be of little help, and healing must be sought from God directly.* A tension between those who see medicine as an aspect of God's common grace and physicians as instruments of God, and those who hold that medicine is unnecessary since healing comes by faith and special grace, has characterized Christianity in every age"[45] [my emphasis].

[43]Ferngren, ibid.
[44]Cf. Matthew 8.28–34, 12.22, 17.15–18; Mark 5.1–20, 9.17–27; Luke 4.33–35, 8.26–39, 9.37–42.
[45]Amundsen and Ferngren, "Philanthropy in Medicine," 13.

In defense of the demons, it may be useful to remember the book of
Job. In Chapter 1, Satan presents himself before God and God points
out his servant, Job. He says "Have you considered my servant Job, that
there is none like him on the earth, a blameless and upright man, who
fears God and turns away from evil?" Satan responds, "Does Job fear
God for nought? Hast thou not put a hedge about him and his house
and all that he has, on every side? Thou hast blessed the work of his
hands, and his possessions have increased in the land. But put forth
thy hand now, and touch all that he has, and he will curse thee to thy
face."[46] God gives Satan permission to take everything away from Job.
But Satan is not allowed to touch his person. In spite of great personal
losses, Job remains faithful to God, "Naked I came from my mother's
womb, and naked shall I return; the Lord gave, and the Lord has taken
away; blessed be the name of the Lord."[47] Thus, in the second chapter
God points out Job's continued trust in him, and Satan responds in
verse 4, "'Skin for skin! All that a man has he will give for his life. But
put forth thy hand now, and touch his bone and his flesh, and he will
curse thee to thy face.' And the Lord said to Satan, 'Behold, he is in
your power; only spare his life.' So Satan went forth from the presence
of the Lord, and afflicted Job with loathsome sores from the sole of his
foot to the crown of his head."[48] It is important to remember that in
the story Job was not aware that Satan was the cause of his affliction
and suffering. Satan afflicted Job spiritually, socially, and physically. Not
only did Satan deprive him of his family and position in society, but
he also made him physically ill (i.e., boils). Modern medicine might
successfully treat the boils using material means (e.g., antibiotics, etc.),
even though the boils were caused by demonic power. Current medical
technology (or ancient for that matter) might be able to help alleviate
the physical distress experienced by Job, but would be quite inadequate
to address the grief and spiritual pain he felt (and certainly could not
replace all his other losses).

[46]Job 1.8ff.
[47]Job 1.21.
[48]Job 2.4–7.

It may be helpful to examine two examples from cell biology to determine if a dichotomy need exist, as the historians have suggested. A topic of interest in cell biology has been the phenomenon of programmed cell death or apoptosis that is so critical to the health of each organism. *Apoptosis* is a word (from the Greek) that was coined about 40 years ago by a British scientist,[49] to portray a sense of falling away, like leaves falling from a tree in autumn or petals falling from a flower. It was originally a morphological description of how cells die through a process of dramatic alteration of the dying cell's shape prior to its fragmentation. There is an elaborate biochemical program within the cell that coordinates this process. The strange paradox is that for each creature to live successfully, some part of that creature is continually dying on a cellular level. At a cellular level, our bodies have put into action that ancient Christian precept of dying daily—in a quite literal manner!

Please consider two different images: one of *agape* love on a cellular level and one of diabolical causation of disease. Healthy fully differentiated cells respond to the program for apoptosis and undergo a dying process so that their host, the larger organism, might live, not unlike the self-giving, self-sacrificial love manifest in the Eucharist—'for the life of the world.'[50] Each human person is essentially a *mikrokosmos*, a small universe in which by virtue of the incarnation, the energies of God may be manifest through the Holy Spirit. Thus, at a cellular level, our members can demonstrate this self-sacrificial, *agape* love for the whole which is also a type of the Church as the Body of Christ. On the other hand, what happens when this natural process of cell death fails?

The normal fate of many different types of cells within the body is to live briefly after being formed through cell division, mature to the

[49]J.F. Kerr, A.H. Wyllie, and A.R. Currie, "Apoptosis: a basic biological phenomenon with wide-ranging implications in tissue kinetics," *British Journal of Cancer* 26(4) (1972): 239–57.

[50]Quoted from "The Anaphora of St John Chrysostom," *The Divine Liturgy of Saints John Chrysostom and Basil the Great and The Liturgy of Presanctified Gifts of Saint Gregory Dialogos: An Altar Server's Guide to the Liturgies* (Minneapolis, Minnesota: Cathedral of the Protection of the Virgin Mary, 1991), 21.

point of being fully differentiated as specialized cells within different tissues, and then either turn over (i.e., die by apoptosis) or in some cases like neurons in the brain actually live for the life of the organism. Cancer often represents a failure of the normal cell death pathway to occur. This, coupled with unrestrained signals for growth, can lead to rapid growth and division of cancer cells that are now 'immortal'. Thus, immortality in the fallen material world is cancer, and it is only immortal as a parasite feeding on the life of its host and ultimately destroying it. It is, at a cellular level, the antithesis of *agape* love. Is it so incredible, particularly with the Book of Job in mind, to conceive of the possibility that highly intelligent but evil spiritual personalities could influence the material creation, including the human body, to produce and/or influence the development of many sorts of human suffering, such as cancer, mental illness, and others? The fourth-century church fathers and others emphasized that conventional medicine is a gift from God just as is supernatural healing. What has been lost in recent times is a sense of awe and awareness of the direct spiritual struggles, good and evil, which are manifest in our flesh in the forms of clearly visible and measurable biological processes, both healthy—promoting life, and diseased or evil—promoting death. Physicians can, with varying degrees of success, treat the biological consequences of this struggle within our members. The Church, through the Sacraments (Greek—*mysteria*, i.e., mysteries), directly addresses the more fundamental struggle with the evil spiritual powers. It should be no surprise if sometimes physical healing occurs with the Sacraments, particularly with the Eucharist, in which we unite ourselves body and soul with Christ. Unfortunately, rarely is there a fully integrated Christian approach to caring for the soul and body in contemporary medicine.

Tension between Caring and Curing within the Christian Tradition

A tension has also existed within the Christian tradition between curing disease and caring for the sick. The healing (curative) miracles of Christ and his disciples were signs (Greek—*semeia*) of his Messiahship and the coming of the Kingdom of Heaven. The Greek words used to describe these activities include *therapeuō, iaomai*, and *sōzō*. *Sōzō* has a secondary or double meaning of salvation along with healing—of being well in the ultimate sense. In contrast to using words that explicitly refer to curing, healing, or treating disease, in the gospel account of the Last Judgment, the criterion by which we are all judged is different. It is stated in Matthew 25.36, "I was sick and you *visited* me . . ."[51] It could perhaps be translated better as, "you *cared* for me." This is the other meaning of the Greek word *episkeptomai*[52] that is used by the evangelist. Interestingly, a word was chosen that was distinctly different from those listed above, which are primarily used in the context of healing (curing) illness. The sense of visiting in this context is akin to a physician visiting his/her patients and does not necessarily imply therapeutic intent (i.e., cure of disease) per se. This action is at the heart of the *agape* love that ultimately saves the sheep redeemed in the Last Judgement.

To summarize the current dichotomy in modern health care between treatment focused on cure and the older tradition of caring in medicine, "Cure is equivalent to the eradication of the cause of an illness or disease; the radical interruption and reversal of the natural history of the disorder. Treatment then is directed toward the underlying cause of illness rather than its outward manifestations. The curative approach views patients in terms of their component parts or as repositories of disease. Where the only goal is cure, facts become differentiated from feelings, and the body becomes dissociated from the mind."[53] Once a diagnosis is made, instead of determining the patient's goals of care, the curative approach demands that diseases be treated. On the other hand, the caring or palliative tradition within medicine has a different focus. The focus is on a person and the relief of that person's suffering, including control of symptoms, and whenever possible, restoration

---

[51]Matthew 25.36.

[52]Arndt and Gingrich, 298.

[53]E. Fox, "Predominance of the curative model of medical care: a residual problem," *Journal of the American Medical Association* 278 (1997): 761–763.

of function. Caring does not depend so much on complete medical knowledge, but more on a relationship. Caring takes time and often is at odds with the demands for efficiency and rapid patient turnover of the acute care setting. Fundamentally, at the heart of caring for the sick is relief of suffering.

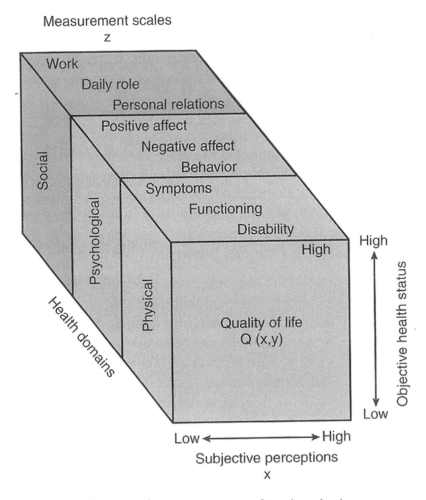

Figure 1: Schematic Depiction of Quality of Life

CHAPTER 2

Suffering and the Human Condition

If there is a meaning in life at all, then there must be a meaning in suffering. Suffering is an ineradicable part of life, even as fate and death. Without suffering and death human life cannot be complete.[1]

COMING FROM A SURVIVOR of the Holocaust, these words of the twentieth-century Viennese psychiatrist Victor Frankl acquire a credibility and authority born of intense personal experience. But how is one to understand this seemingly paradoxical character of suffering? Perhaps it would be helpful to look at recent attempts to define both quality of life and suffering in the context of modern medicine and then examine the nature of suffering within the larger context of the incarnation.

In the context of research in health outcomes, quality of life has been defined as "a multi-dimensional patient-centered outcome."[2] What does this actually mean, and who decides what the dimensions should be? Typically, scientific definitions of quality of life have included different aspects of the human experience that can even be depicted graphically in three dimensions (Figure 1).[3] What factors define quality of life, and are they equivalent to those which define a good life? Factors that are thought to impact quality of life in clinical-outcomes research have generally been separated into non-health-related and health-related categories. Examples of commonly measured non-health-related

[1]V. Frankl, *Man's Search for Meaning*, trans. by I. Lasch (Boston: Beacon Press, 2006), 67.

[2]L. Temple, S. Fuzesi, S. Patil, "The importance of determining quality of life in clinical trials," *Surgery* 145(6) (2009): 622–6.

[3]M.A. Testa and D.C. Simonson, "Assessment of Quality-of-Life Outcomes," *New England Journal of Medicine* 334(13) (1996): 835–840.

factors affecting quality of life include financial status, location of residence, and time available for leisure activities. Of note, all of these are materialistic factors. Are there no other non-health-related factors, outside the material realm, that might also contribute to quality of life? Health-related factors that are thought to affect quality of life include physical (e.g., the presence or absence of pain), psychological (e.g., one's emotional and cognitive state), and social (e.g., the ability to perform one's duties in society) factors.[4] A number of instruments have been developed that are intended to provide more objective and reproducible means of measuring the subjective patient experience, especially in the context of clinical trials of different therapies. The various types of instruments include:

1) *Generic*, which facilitate comparisons across broad categories of illnesses and thus may have limited utility for assessing specific diseases like cancer (e.g., Short Form 36-Item Health Survey);

2) *Disease-specific*, which assess health-related quality of life in populations with specific diseases like cancer (e.g., Functional Assessment of Cancer Therapy—General [FACT-G]); and

3) *Symptom-specific*, which provide detailed measurement and assessment of symptoms (e.g., pain, nausea, etc.) associated with a given disease process (e.g., McGill Pain Questionnaire).

All of the instruments are notable for their lack of measures of the spiritual domain of human experience. With its various limitations such an approach may be useful in clinical research, but is this what quality of life means to us individually? Eric Cassell has noted that "medical science, like all science, is concerned with generalities. Patients, however, are not generalities, they are necessarily individual—but there is *no* science of individuals."[5] Another way to approach the question of what is a good life or perhaps even addressing the problem of defining

[4]B.S. Langenhoff, P.F. Krabbe, T. Wobbes, T.J. Ruers, "Quality of life as an outcome measure in surgical oncology," *British Journal of Surgery* 88(5) (2001): 643–52.

[5]E.J. Cassell, *The Nature of Suffering and the Goals of Medicine*, 2nd ed. (Oxford University Press, 2004), 91. By permission of Oxford University Press, USA.

quality of life is to invert the question. In other words, what is a 'good death'? What are the attributes or components of a good death? In a focus group study[6] the following components of a good death were identified:

1) Effective pain and symptom management;

2) The ability to maintain clear decision making;

3) Being prepared for death;

4) Having a sense of completion;

5) Contributing to others; and

6) Being affirmed as a whole person.

It is interesting to note that more than half of the components identified by the focus groups are spiritual issues (i.e., preparation for death, completion, contributing to others, and affirmation of the whole person). Even the other two (i.e., pain and symptom management and clear decision making) are spiritual in that they impact the whole person. In a random national survey that followed up on these observations, the importance of forty-four attributes of quality at the end of life were rated by patients, bereaved family members, physicians, nurses, social workers, chaplains, and hospice volunteers.[7] Similar to the results of the initial focus group study, twenty-six items were rated as important across all groups including pain and symptom management, preparation for death, achieving a sense of completion, decisions about treatment preferences, and being treated as a whole person. However, issues that were very important to patients and all others surveyed except physicians were:

[6]K.E. Steinhauser, E.C. Clipp, M. McNeilly, N.A. Christakis, L.D. McIntyre, and J.A. Tulsky, "In Search of a Good Death: Observations of Patients, Families, and Providers," *Annals of Internal Medicine* 132(10) (2000): 825–832.

[7]K.E. Steinhauser, N.A. Christakis, E.C. Clipp, M. McNeilly, L. McIntyre, and J.A. Tulsky, "Factors considered important at the end of life by patients, family, physicians, and other care providers," *Journal of the American Medical Association* 284(19) (2000): 2476–2482.

1) Being mentally aware;

2) Being at peace with God;

3) Not being a burden to one's family;

4) Being able to help others;

5) Being able to pray;

6) Having funeral arrangements made;

7) Not being a burden to society; and

8) Feeling that one's life is complete.

Why are physicians apparently out of step with their patients, families, and other health care colleagues? Physicians by virtue of their training and licensure wield enormous authority and influence over the fate of patients who come to them for help. When the very professionals upon whom the public depend to act in their best interests are unable to perceive the importance of such fundamental aspects of quality at the end of life, serious questions should also arise about their ability to prioritize with regard to the general needs of their patients. Such disconnects between physicians and their patients may underlie much of the suffering that is so prevalent in the health care setting.

Eric Cassell, in a now classic paper defined suffering as "the state of severe distress associated with events that threaten the intactness of the person ... Suffering is experienced by persons ..." and he says that suffering "occurs when an impending destruction of the person is perceived; it continues until the threat of disintegration has passed or until the integrity of the person can be restored in some other manner." It "can occur in relation to any aspect of the person, whether it is in the realm of social roles, group identification, the relation with self, body, or family, or the relation with a transpersonal, transcendent source of meaning."[8] Dame Cicely Saunders, the founder of the modern hospice and palliative care movement, coined another expression

[8] E.J. Cassell. "The Nature of Suffering and the Goals of Medicine," *New England Journal of Medicine* 306 (1982): 639–645.

to embody the full experience of suffering she witnessed among her patients with terminal cancer. 'Total Pain' was her term to recognize the multiple domains in which pain can be experienced: physical, psychological, social and spiritual.[9] It is precisely the fact that pain can be experienced not only in a physical sense but also as psychological, social, and even spiritual distress that makes Total Pain come close to approximating Cassell's definition of suffering. In Total Pain, the whole person is engaged in the experience. Not only is one's physical well-being threatened but so also are one's psychological (emotional) health, social relationships, and spirituality at risk. Spiritual pain in this context is something experienced by all persons. It is the experience of a threat to one's source(s) of meaning, whether religious in nature or not. Just as there may be psychological, social, and spiritual aspects that accompany each physical form of pain or distress, so also there may be specific pains that primarily affect one or more of the four domains that make up Total Pain without having too much impact on the others. Nonetheless, the power of Cicely Saunders' concept is that one should always look for pain in the other three domains of Total Pain even when the most visible or obvious form seems to predominate. To underscore this further, a person is a psychosomatic unity. Thus, Eric Cassell emphasizes, "The understanding of the place of the person in human illness requires a rejection of the historical dualism of mind and body."[10] One cannot divorce physical distress from the other aspects of the person when suffering is present. When one attempts to cure disease without caring for the person (breaking up the psychosomatic unity), this attempt can cause suffering. This fact may help explain the precarious position in which would-be healers of today find themselves and also underscores the dangers inherent in the lack of understanding physicians have exhibited with regard to their dying patients' goals at the end of life.

[9]C. Saunders, and N. Sykes, *The Management of Terminal Malignant Disease*, 3rd ed. (London: Hodder and Stoughton, 1993), 1–14.
[10]E.J. Cassell, ibid.

The development of the modern hospice and palliative care movement has been in direct response to this perceived 'disconnect' between the suffering of the sick, especially that of the terminally ill, and the disease-focused, curative approach of modern health care, which may ignore, neglect, or even exacerbate suffering. The World Health Organization has defined palliative care as "an approach that improves the quality of life of patients and their families facing the problem associated with life-threatening illness, through the prevention and relief of suffering by means of early identification and impeccable assessment and treatment of pain and other problems, physical, psychosocial and spiritual. Palliative care:

+ provides relief from pain and other distressing symptoms;

+ affirms life and regards dying as a normal process;

+ intends neither to hasten or postpone death;

+ integrates the psychological and spiritual aspects of patient care;

+ offers a support system to help patients live as actively as possible until death;

+ offers a support system to help the family cope during the patient's illness and in their own bereavement;

+ uses a team approach to address the needs of patients and their families, including bereavement counseling, if indicated;

+ will enhance quality of life, and may also positively influence the course of illness;

+ is applicable early in the course of illness, in conjunction with other therapies that are intended to prolong life, such as chemotherapy or radiation therapy, and includes those investigations needed to better understand and manage distressing clinical complications."[11]

[11]*National cancer control programmes: policies and managerial guidelines*, 2nd ed. (Geneva: World Health Organization, 2002); Accessed at https://apps.who.int/dsa/justpub/cpl.htm on 23 June, 2011.

Philosophically, there is no fundamental difference between hospice and palliative care. In the United States, hospice is defined by the Medicare Hospice Benefit which is a covered benefit under Part A of Medicare. To be eligible for hospice under this benefit, a patient with a terminal illness and a projected survival or prognosis of less than six months may be enrolled after certification of the terminal diagnosis and limited prognosis by two physicians. Ideally, hospice care is provided in the patient's home but can be provided wherever the patient is residing (e.g., nursing home, residential hospice, etc.). The care is holistic in nature and team-based. Thus, it depends on the participation of many different disciplines (e.g., nurses, social workers, chaplains, physicians, complementary therapists, pharmacists, psychologists, volunteers, etc.) with the patient and family (loved ones) being the most important members of the team. Palliative care has extended this approach 'upstream' into the acute health care system, so that any patient with a life-threatening illness who is experiencing suffering may receive palliative care regardless of prognosis. Figure 2 depicts the relationship of palliative care to cure-oriented care and the place of hospice within this process.

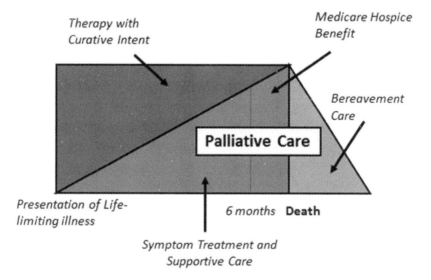

Figure 2: Schematic Depiction of Hospice and Palliative Care

Persons and Suffering

Although it seems quite clear that the organs and organ systems which harbor disease do not suffer, what then are the unique characteristics that constitute the person who can and does suffer?[12] A person is more than a mind. The "I think therefore I am," of Descartes is not sufficient, although the mind is (can be) a part of the person. Self (self-awareness) is not the same as person, although an important, perhaps essential part. There are aspects of the self known only by others. Persons acquire their personhood within community, in connection with other persons. Indeed, "Suffering . . . often can only be understood, in the context of others."[13]

This raises several questions. Is a new-born infant a person? Is a severely mentally handicapped child or adult a person? How and when do we become persons?

"Persons have personality and character. A person has a past."[14] We are to some extent narratives. We each have our own story. "A person has a family."[15] Our close relationships are critical determinants of who we are as persons. "A person has a cultural background."[16] Our culture will influence, even define our experience of illness and also influence how others treat us as sick persons.

"A person has roles."[17] A serious illness threatens this aspect of the person directly; especially to the extent a person may no longer be able to fulfill one's roles. Like a rock thrown into a pond, the ripple effect of a constriction of one's roles, whether they be at home, at work, or in the larger community, will be felt by others and add a communal aspect to the suffering. Thus the intensity of suffering is reflected by the degree to which a serious illness threatens relationships.

[12]For this discussion of the characteristics of a person, I am much in debt to Professor Cassell's excellent discussion in *The Nature of Suffering and the Goals of Medicine*, 34–41.

[13]Ibid. 34

[14]Ibid. 36

[15]Ibid. 37

[16]Ibid. 38

[17]Ibid. 38

"A person has a relationship with himself or herself."[18] Serious illnesses may significantly alter this relationship (for the better or worse). "A person is a political being."[19] Debilitating illness may create a sense of powerlessness in this context. "Persons do things."[20] They create and they destroy. "Persons have regular behaviors."[21] We are 'creatures of habit'. When serious illness destroys this basic, anchoring characteristic of the person it can be very disorienting, disrupting the essential rhythm of one's life.

"Every person has a body."[22] The person suffers as a result of the disintegration of the body. This may be experienced as the visible changes of progressive illness or aging as well as in deteriorating function with increased debility and dependence.

"Everyone has a secret life."[23] Disease and impending death may threaten the person's ability to address unresolved issues, 'unfinished business' in this realm. At the same time, increasing awareness of the imminence of one's death heightens the sense of urgency associated with unresolved issues and conflicts. This in turn may exacerbate the threat to the person who may feel impotent to address the issues, thereby increasing the suffering.

"Every person has a perceived future."[24] Hope often resides in that perceived future. Life-threatening illness 'robs' persons of their future and may create intense suffering when there is an anticipated future that includes unrelieved physical distress.

"Everyone has a transcendent dimension—a life of the spirit . . ."[25] The ability to connect with or bond to others beyond the self, to a cause, to something or Someone bigger or greater than oneself is often critical to the relief of suffering.

[18]Ibid. 39
[19]Ibid. 39
[20]Ibid. 40
[21]Ibid. 40
[22]Ibid. 40
[23]Ibid. 40
[24]Ibid. 41
[25]Ibid. 41

How are the person and human suffering perceived within the incarnational theology of traditional Christianity? Contemporary western culture is focused on individual autonomy. Individual choice, desires, and perceived rights are omnipotent and are subjects of marketing strategies. The American (Western) ideal of "life, liberty, and the pursuit of happiness" is primarily focused on self, the ego. In Christianity, the focus is not on the first person singular but the second person, the other—ultimately the Other, transcending self and ego.

When God assumed human nature, he entered into the whole of human experience from conception through death, except for sin. Every aspect of human existence takes on new meaning in light of this understanding. Our suffering acquires meaning because he suffered. Each human person is an icon (image) of the Crucified One. Thus, every human relationship has within it the full potential of an ever deepening relationship with the Ultimate Other.

In a very real sense, God 'knows' us into becoming real persons. "Before I formed you in the womb I knew you."[26] By way of analogy, humans can in a similar, much less exalted manner endow beloved pets with many of the characteristics of personhood, such that a pet can become more than an animal companion and be even viewed and treated as a person. The ability to form relationships has to some degree the power to create persons.

What are important aspects of the person in traditional Christianity? Freedom of choice is a crucial aspect of the person for Christians, *but* only within a great paradox is it actually operational. For choice is only truly free in obedience to the Other—the way of the Cross. Fundamentally, Christians are persons to the extent that they live in relationship with God. This relationship has at least three foundational characteristics that define and nurture the human aspect of the relationship.

1) Eucharistic—giving thanks to God;

2) Doxological—giving glory to God; and

[26]Jeremiah 1.5.

3) Prayerful—cultivating the continual awareness of the Presence
of God in all places, situations, and other persons.

For a fuller understanding of suffering within the Christian tradition, it may be helpful at this point to explore the ironic history of the
word that is now used in medicine to define the disease-based, curative
approach of modern health care, i.e., *pathology*. The history of this word
embodies the tension between the ancient tradition of caring and the
modern quest for cure. It also bridges the gap between the modern concept of disease and the ancient understanding of suffering. The history
and meanings of two additional words will also be explored to place
pathology in its full context within the Christian tradition.

In classical Greek, *pathos* had the primary meaning of *"that which
happens* to a person or thing" (e.g., an incident or accident) or *"what
one has experienced*, good or bad" but more often bad (e.g., misfortune,
calamity). In the context of the soul, it also referred to the *emotions*
or *passions*. As a verb, *pascho*, it had a meaning of *"have something
done to one, suffer."*[27] Already in classical times it had begun to acquire
a negative connotation which developed further in later Hellenistic
usage. Within the early Christian tradition, *pathos* had acquired the
meaning of "that which is endured or experienced, *suffering.*"[28] It was
used extensively by the early Christian martyr and bishop Ignatius
of Antioch (+108 AD) in his letters to mean 'suffering' (or the Passion of Christ) and most significantly as a substitute for 'death': "...
unless we do choose to die through him in his passion [*pathos*], his
life is not in us."[29] The same *pathos* was also used by the early fathers
of the Church in reference to *passion* (e.g., pride, lust, etc.). Within
the early Church the verb form, *pascho*, now acquired a more distinct

[27]H.G. Liddell, and R. Scott, *A Greek-English Lexicon*, revised by H.S. Jones & R.
McKenzie (Oxford: Oxford University Press, 1968), 1285, 1347.

[28]Arndt and Gingrich, 607.

[29]St Ignatius of Antioch, "Ignatius to the Magnesians," 5, 2; *Apostolic Fathers*, vol.
2, trans. by Kirsopp Lake, Loeb Classical Library no. 24 (Cambridge, MA: Harvard
University Press, 1912, repr. 1985), 201.

meaning of "suffer, suffer death, be killed; [have to] die."[30] Variations of *pathos* found prominent usage in the New Testament (e.g., "we see Jesus, who for a little while was made lower than the angels, crowned with glory and honor because of the suffering (*pathema*) of death"[31]) and the ancient creeds of the Church (e.g., "suffered [*pathonta*] and was buried").[32]

Within the traditional Christian understanding of suffering two other words have been closely linked to *pathos*: *hamartia* and *thanatos*. *Hamartia* (noun) and *hamartano* (verb) in classical Greek meant to *"miss the mark* (especially of a spear thrown)" or *"fail of one's purpose, go wrong, mistake;* and rarely, *neglect."*[33] In early Christian usage, it meant *"do wrong, sin."*[34] Sin, in the ancient sense of the Greek word *hamartia*, is then a failure to be the way things should be, 'a missing the mark'. This is in contrast to the notion of sin so common in Western theology of being purely a volitional act where without a conscious engagement in evil, there is no sin. This approach is predicated on an emphasis in the West on responsibility for sin (guilt) which is in distinct contrast with the Eastern emphasis on viewing sin in a more 'medical' frame of refer-ence—diagnosing what is wrong that requires healing with less imme-diate concern about establishing blame. This approach is reflected in the prayers of the Eastern Church. For example, the prayer of Archbishop John Chrysostom of Constantinople (+407 AD) recited by the faithful in preparation for communion states, "I pray to you, have mercy upon me, and forgive my transgressions, those voluntary and *involuntary*, in word and deed, known and *unknown*"[35] [my emphasis].

---

[30] Arndt and Gingrich, 639.

[31] Hebrews 2.9. Greek text transliterated from *The Greek New Testament*, eds. K. Aland, M. Black, C.M. Martini, B.M. Metzger, and A. Wikgren, 2nd ed. (United Bible Societies, 1968).

[32] "The Nicene-Constantinopolitan Creed" in *Daily Prayers for Orthodox Chris-tians: The Synekdemos*, ed. N.M. Vaporis (Brookline, MA: Holy Cross Orthodox Press, 1986), 61.

[33] Liddell and Scott, 77.

[34] Arndt and Gingrich, 42.

[35] *Daily Prayers for Orthodox Christians*, 94.

In a very thoughtful and intriguing analysis, Daniel Sulmasy has highlighted the relational nature of matter throughout the entire cosmos, whether in the macroscopic realm of human interactions or at the most minute level of subatomic particles. He emphasizes the essentially dynamic rather than static character of matter that is attested to by recent work in particle physics and described by quantum mechanics."[O]nce one arrives at the particle level, a fundamental rule emerges that is really true about everything, no matter how big or small, namely, that relationality is ontologically prior to particularity, that the electromagnetic field is prior to matter. That is to say that what matter, or anything else, is, at its most fundamental level, is not a pile of unimaginably tiny bodies, but a set of temporary yet dynamic relationships in the electromagnetic field that is already given."[36] When *hamartia* occurs, fundamental relationships that are woven into our material world, even perhaps at the invisible level of subatomic particles, are disrupted. With this in mind, one can begin to understand the need for and the power of the Creator's uniting himself to his creation in order to restore the right relationship, to bring healing to the cosmos.

The final word in this discussion, *thanatos*[37] or "death" was even used as powerful metaphor by early Christian writers. Death is referred to as a person in Acts 2.24[38] in reference to Christ's overcoming death, "But God raised him up, having loosed the pangs of death" (*odinas tou thanatou*—'birth pangs' or better yet, labor pains of death). The second-century Church father Polycarp of Smyrna refers to death as Hades when quoting this passage, "whom God raised up, having loosed the pangs of *Hades*."[39] Thus in a very powerful use of metaphor early Christian writers emphasized the relational character of suffering and death. Christ became a human person to enter into all human relationships and transform them—including our captivity to death. By

---

[36]D.P. Sulmasy, *A Balm for Gilead: Meditations on Spirituality and the Healing Arts* (Washington, DC: Georgetown University Press, 2006), 21, 22.

[37]Arndt and Gingrich, 351.

[38]Acts 2.24.

[39]St Ignatius of Antioch. "Epistle of St. Polycarp to the Philippians," I:2, 201.

dying he caused death, our jailer, to die, "since it was not possible for the Author of life to be a victim of corruption."[40] Romanos the Melodist stated this most beautifully in another of his kontakia:

> Three crosses Pilate fixed on Golgotha,
> two for the thieves and one for the Giver of life,
> whom Hell saw and said to those below,
> "My ministers and my powers,
> who has fixed a nail in my heart?
> A wooden lance has suddenly pierced me and I am
>   being torn apart.
> My insides are in pain, my belly is in agony,
> my senses make my spirit tremble,
> and I am compelled to disgorge
> Adam and Adam's race. Given me by a Tree,
> a Tree is bringing them back
>   again to Paradise."[41]

Thus, in the ancient Christian understanding, sin (*hamartia*) is a break from the way things should be, as much in the natural world as the supernatural, affecting the entire cosmos most particularly in its relationships. As a result of sin, bad things happen, are experienced by persons, and suffering occurs. Sin and suffering are ultimately connected to/lead to death. But, dying has been transformed by Christ's victory over death into a passage through death to life.

On the other hand, *pathos* (suffering) in modern usage has been transformed into 'disease' as in *pathology*, the study of disease. "Doctors pursue symptoms because of the belief that they are the direct manifestations of disease. Diseases are the 'real' things—the things that count

---

[40]Quoted from "St. Basil the Great's Anaphora," in *The Divine Liturgy of Saints John Chrysostom and Basil the Great and The Liturgy of Presanctified Gifts of Saint Gregory Dialogos: An Altar Server's Guide to the Liturgies* (Minneapolis, MN: Cathedral of the Protection of the Virgin Mary, 1991), 30.

[41]St Romanos the Melodist, "Kontakion On the Victory of the Cross," in *On the Life of Christ*, trans. Archimandrite Ephrem Lash (San Francisco: Harper Collins, 1995), 155–6.

. . . Sick persons, as persons, are an agglomeration of 'soft' data—feelings, emotions, values, and beliefs—in these terms, not as real as their diseases."[42] As the focus in care of the sick has shifted to the diagnosis of diseases and their treatment, this larger, transcendent perspective of human suffering as a tragedy of cosmic proportions has been lost.

Since all of the ingenuity, skill, and techniques of modern medicine are focused on diagnosing diseases, how does one diagnose suffering? It will be very difficult, if not impossible, to relieve that which one is unable to recognize or 'diagnose'. Since suffering affects persons, the standard 'objective' measures used to diagnose physical ailments will not be helpful. Blood tests, CT scans, and other sophisticated imaging techniques may identify anatomic or physiologic abnormalities related to disease processes but are of little use in diagnosing suffering. Typically, suffering involves a symptom or symptoms that threaten the integrity of the patient as a person. The meaning that a given symptom has for the individual patient defines the nature of the suffering experienced (e.g., if cancer-related pain is progressing, the fear of impending death can cause intense suffering). Failure to recognize and treat suffering is often a reflection of the inability of the caregiver to focus on the person rather than the disease. To make a diagnosis of suffering, one must be actively looking for it; ask, "Are you suffering?"[43]

When one thinks of symptoms associated with suffering, physical pain is usually the first to come to mind. However, many other symptoms are capable of producing intense suffering in those with serious life-threatening illnesses. Nausea, vomiting, loss of appetite, shortness of breath, dizziness, sleeplessness, fatigue, anxiety, depression, even hiccups and itching are examples of some of the debilitating symptoms that, especially when intense and apparently unremitting, are associated with intense suffering.

Is pain equivalent to suffering? The International Association for the Study of Pain (IASP) has defined pain as "An unpleasant sensory and

[42]Cassell, *The Nature of Suffering and the Goals of Medicine*, 98. By permission of Oxford University Press, USA.

[43]E.J. Cassell, "Diagnosing Suffering: A Perspective," *Annals of Internal Medicine* 131(7) (1999): 531–534.

emotional experience associated with actual or potential tissue damage or described in terms of such damage."[44] Fundamentally, being a subjective experience, pain is whatever the patient says it is. Consistent with Cicely Saunders' concept of Total Pain, any form of physical distress (e.g., pain, pruritis [itching], nausea, hiccups, etc.) that is so dominant as to limit integration/expression of the other domains of personhood (i.e., psychological, social, and spiritual) may qualify as a cause of suffering. The experience of pain (or other distressing symptoms) has at least two characteristic features: intensity and unpleasantness. Intensity refers to the "strength" of the pain. How strong is it? This is the aspect of pain that is usually measured during nursing assessments in the hospital as the "fifth vital sign." Unpleasantness attempts to measure the emotional or affective aspect of the pain experience. How unpleasant is the pain? When used experimentally, these two features measure distinctly different aspects of the pain experience. The emotional aspect or unpleasantness of the pain is much more closely linked to the meaning of the pain to that person. Thus, it more closely approximates suffering than pain intensity, per se. The emotional context in which the pain is experienced will often define the intensity of suffering. For example, the pain of normal childbirth can be very intense but usually is not emotionally negative with the anticipation of a happy ending so that suffering is a minimal aspect of the experience. However, if signs of potential fetal distress are identified by the mother's obstetrician and there is a real concern for the safety of the baby, the mother's labor pains may then acquire a new meaning, one that is certainly "unpleasant" and deeply painful on an emotional level to the mother. She may now begin to truly suffer in her pain.

Another way in which the emotional aspect (unpleasantness) of pain can be triggered or intensified is by uncertainty. Not knowing the

[44]"Part III: Pain Terms, A Current List with Definitions and Notes on Usage," *Classification of Chronic Pain*, 2nd ed., IASP Task Force on Taxonomy, ed. by H. Merskey and N. Bogduk (Seattle: IASP Press, 1994), 209–14, online at: http://www.iasp-pain.org/AM/Template.cfm?Section=Pain_Defi...isplay.cfm&ContentID=1728; accessed 18 July, 2011.

cause of the pain is often a great source of suffering. More will be said about uncertainty later in this volume. Fear that the pain cannot be controlled also exacerbates the unpleasantness of the pain and in turn the suffering of the person. A close corollary of this is fear that the caregiver (e.g., physician) may abandon the patient. Indeed, when physicians do not have the skills or tools at hand to control pain and other distressing symptoms, the temptation to abandon the patient can be very great. Physician-assisted death (e.g., physician-assisted suicide, euthanasia) may represent an extreme form of such abandonment. Chronic unremitting pain (even of lower intensity which could be tolerated at any moment) by virtue of its persistence and seemingly endless nature can be a source of great suffering. Finally, pain observed by another can be a source of suffering in the other. If you love, you will suffer. When we take the risk of loving other persons, we also risk suffering with them and possibly because of them.

Can suffering be measured? The Comfort Assessment Tool is a two page instrument that represents an effort to extend the use of various scales that are commonly used to measure pain intensity and unpleasantness to the measurement of suffering.[45] The first page of the instrument is a detailed pain assessment including: a diagram for identifying the site or sites of physical pain, a rating scale for the pain, identification of the pattern of pain, quality of pain, rating of the acceptable level of pain, identification of other major symptoms (e.g., nausea, etc.), and numerical rating of how the symptoms have interfered with comfort in the last 24 hours. The second page represents an attempt to rate the individual's suffering on three levels:

1. Physical—how much is the suffering due to physical distress (rated using a numerical scale)?

2. Spiritual—how much is the suffering due to spiritual distress (using numerical rating scale plus other qualifiers)?

[45]B.K. Baines, and L. Norlander, "The Relationship of Pain and Suffering in a Hospice Population," *American Journal of Hospice and Palliative Care* 17(5) (2000): 319–326.

3. Personal/Social—several questions using numerical scales are posed related to loss of autonomy, "unfinished business", fear of the future, and finally assessing one's ability to cope with suffering.

Here are some examples of the types of questions used in the Comfort Assessment Tool:

+ How much are you suffering due to your symptoms? Rated on a 0–10 scale from No Suffering to Extreme Suffering

+ How much are you suffering due to unfinished business? Rated on a 0–10 scale from No Suffering to Extreme Suffering

+ How much are you suffering due to your fear of the future? Rated on a 0–10 scale from No Suffering to Extreme Suffering

Attempting to 'measure' suffering using an instrument of this type raises some concerns. Defining the boundaries of what is primarily spiritual versus other forms of distress is very difficult. Much of spiritual distress can come in terms of a loss of meaning or purpose without its being described in overtly spiritual or religious terms. The tool presupposes an ability to be introspective. This is a variable quality in the general population and may vary substantially in the same individual on the same day (e.g., waxing and waning delirium) when critically ill. Suffering is so complex and multifaceted that no instrument will explore it adequately for each unique individual. Administration of an instrument cannot substitute for being present and open to the other. However, it's much better than nothing and represents a potentially useful means of educating health care providers as well as patients and their families to think about and look for suffering *beyond* pain.

Because of the integration that exists within each person there is a great interdependence between the four domains that constitute the Total Pain of Cicely Saunders. Thus, unresolved spiritual, social, or psychological pain can cause physical pain to be unresponsive even to massive amounts of opioid pain relievers. On the other hand, integrity in the psychological, social, and especially spiritual domains of the person can minimize physical distress. This principle may best be illustrated by the story of one woman's response to intense suffering. 'C' was an elderly woman who presented to a hospice team with a locally advanced unresectable colon cancer which had replaced the lower half of her abdominal wall with a large, stinking, and fungating mass. Nursing staff at her nursing home noted that she rarely required pain medication and seemed to be 'meditating' a lot. When a member of the hospice team while dressing her wound asked her what she thought of her "unwelcome guest" (referring to the cancer), she responded by quoting the psalm, "Be still, and know that I am God."[46] She had transcended her suffering through achieving a continual state of prayer.

[46]Psalm 46.10.

CHAPTER 3

The Context of Suffering

Suffering is the source of culture.[1]

SUFFERING DOES NOT exist within a vacuum. It always has a context. The larger context of suffering is cultural. Indeed, a survivor of the horrors of the Romanian Communist Gulag has described the relationship between suffering and culture quite succinctly with the sentence noted above. This chapter will first explore the general relationship between culture and suffering, then examine the specific impact of the materialistic cultures of East and West on human suffering during the last century, and finally explore how individual narratives of human suffering in words and art can give expression to universal as well as individual characteristics of suffering.

Suffering and Culture

A primary dictionary definition of culture is "the integrated pattern of human knowledge, belief, and behavior that depends upon the capacity for learning and transmitting knowledge to succeeding generations."[2] The following are some other definitions that further illuminate the concept of culture as it relates to human suffering. "Culture ... consists in those patterns relative to behavior and the products of human action which may be inherited, that is, passed on from generation to generation independently of the biological genes."[3] "By culture we mean all those historically created designs for living, explicit and implicit,

[1]Father Roman Braga, personal communication from an interview, September 29, 2010 at The Dormition of the Mother of God Orthodox Christian Monastery, Rives Junction, Michigan.
[2]Merriam Webster online dictionary, online at: http://www.merriam-webster. com/dictionary/culture; accessed 1 November, 2010.
[3]T. Parson, *Essays in Sociological Theory* (Glencoe, IL: The Free Press, 1949), 8.

rational, irrational, and nonrational, which exist at any given time as potential guides for the behavior of men."[4] "The essence of a culture is not its artifacts, tools, or other tangible cultural elements but how the members of the group interpret, use, and perceive them. It is the values, symbols, interpretations, and perspectives that distinguish one people from another in modernized societies; it is not material objects and other tangible aspects of human societies. People within a culture usually interpret the meaning of symbols, artifacts, and behaviors in the same or in similar ways."[5] Thus, cultures develop a history, a tradition of beliefs, attitudes, and behaviors that are passed down to subsequent generations. Culture provides a collective perspective that guides individuals' interactions with and interpretations of their 'reality' including their experience of suffering.

What are some of the major characteristics of a culture?

1. Cultures are *learned*. The process of learning one's culture is called *enculturation*.

2. A culture is *shared* by members of a society or group. There is no 'culture of one'.

3. Cultures are *patterned*. People in a given society (culture) live and think in ways that form definite patterns.

4. A culture is *mutually constructed* through a constant process of social interaction.

5. Cultures are *symbolic*. Culture, language and thought are based on symbols and symbolic meanings.

6. Cultures are *arbitrary*. They are not based on "natural laws" external to humans, but are created by humans according to the "whims" of the society (e.g., the standards of beauty within a given culture).

[4]C. Kluckhohn, and W.H. Kelly, "The concept of culture," in R. Linton, ed., *The Science of Man in the World Culture* (Syracuse, NY: Syracuse University Press, 1945), 78–105.

[5]James A. Banks and CherryA. McGee, *Multicultural education* (Needham Heights, MA: Allyn & Bacon, 1989).

7. Culture is *internalized*. Culture has a characteristic of being habitual or 'taken-for-granted'. It is perceived as being natural, 'just the way things are'.[6]

8. Cultures are *continuously changing*, in a state of constant evolution. They are subject to external as well as internal forces driving change. The culture into which one's grandparents were born is quite different from that of their children which in turn is radically different from that of their grandchildren.

9. A culture is 'leaky' or *porous*. As a corollary of the evolving nature of cultures, they are not self-contained, closed systems but are in continuous interaction or dialogue with other cultures, both internal and external to a given culture.

10. *Individual personalities* can shape or dramatically change a culture (e.g., Emperor Constantine in the fourth-century Roman Empire, Napoleon Bonaparte and nineteenth-century European culture).

How then can suffering be the source of culture? Just as individuals struggle to understand and relate to a world where things are not the way they should be, where often the spear misses the mark, where sin leads to suffering, so also the larger society attempts in a collective manner to make sense of the human tragedy. Suffering may, in effect, be a powerful catalyst for the development of culture. Perhaps another way to better clarify this may be to invert the question. What aspects of culture have not been influenced by suffering? To what extent does suffering influence or stimulate the arts (i.e., literature, music, fine arts/monumental art, etc.) within a culture? Does it not provide the *chiaroscuro* that lends perspective to the arts within a culture? Is it possible to conceive of a culture without suffering? What would it look like? Would it really be without suffering?

[6]Online at: http://www2.eou.edu/~kdahl/cultdef.html; accessed November 1, 2010.

What are the most common forms in which suffering is embodied within a culture? Pain, sickness, and death, both in the direct experience of individuals and in the collective dread of the larger society that wishes to avoid the same experiences, are powerful drivers of culture. Cultural responses to the threat of pain, sickness, and death often come in various flavors of denial. Billboards with advertisements which provide comforting advice for those on their way to and from work, "If you had only come to our health system you wouldn't be in the terrible situation you now face," and images of youthful appearing elders without wrinkles vibrantly walking off the tennis court, speak volumes about our own culture's angst regarding these omnipresent harbingers of suffering.

Alternatively, rather than being overtly denied, these forms of suffering have been all too often trivialized within the media with many films being supersaturated with gory, even cartoonish violence or jaded cinematic antiheroes cynically expounding upon their boredom with the meaninglessness of life as they send more victims to their deaths. Stalin's famous dictum, "One death is a tragedy while millions are a statistic," almost sounds like the last cry for help of a struggling idealist when compared to the crass cynical brutality embraced as entertainment within the media. And yet this is another form of denial. However, when artists, writers and composers make a serious effort to directly face and struggle to interpret these fearful and awesome mysteries of pain, sickness, and death, the opportunity to create great art remains.

Other all too common forms through which suffering shapes culture include poverty, broken social relationships (e.g., divorce, unrequited love), oppression or loss of freedom (e.g., slavery or the effects of racism), and conflicts both individual (e.g., domestic violence) and collective (i.e., war). The peculiar and even startling aspect of how these different forms of suffering shape culture and its expression is the paradoxical manner in which human tragedy can sometimes be transmuted into the highest forms of beauty. It is precisely the capacity of the best art to express with compelling eloquence the poignant beauty hidden deep within suffering that underscores the power of suffering to define and shape culture. Michelangelo's youthful David, fresh from his conquest of the giant Goliath, embodies the Renaissance ideal of the perfect 'beauty' of youth; a youth that is untarnished with age or suffering, in control of its destiny, with the world at its feet. But, his Pietà, in spite of (or precisely because of) the intense suffering portrayed, in which the dead God-man is held in his mother's arms, achieves a beauty in its abasement, its humility that with all the beauty of form, his David cannot begin to express.

Within every culture there are many sub-cultures that are linked to suffering. Indeed, they magnify and focus suffering within the culture, creating unique ways in which segments of a society can experience an intensification of suffering while sometimes providing an apparent insulation for other elements of the same society from the experience.

A medical culture exists in the United States in which there is a tension between a culture of health and illness. Billions of dollars are spent annually outside the conventional health care system on complementary and alternative therapies, a reflection of the larger society's frustration with the limitations of the health care system as well as the desperation to survive, to match the image of youthful vigor smirking back at the public from every advertisement. America's fear of suffering and death is driving the cost of health care near the end of life to extreme levels which may eventually bankrupt the country.

The so-called 'drug culture' is another example of a subculture within the larger culture linked to suffering. The use of substances with mood altering properties, licit or illicit, provides at best (in a licit context with good medical support and supervision) a bridge to health and recovery for those suffering with incapacitating depression, chronic pain, or other forms of mental suffering, and at worst (under illicit circumstances) a temporary escape or 'anesthesia' from distress that often develops into the additional nightmare of suffering from chronic addiction that may also be associated with violent crime and prostitution.

Prison culture presents a paradox. Although the original intent of prisons was to reform and rehabilitate, i.e., to 'heal' the criminal, the opposite outcome may often predominate. Prisons may insulate the rest of a culture or society to some extent from criminals and their unique form of suffering. However, to the extent prisons fail in their purpose of reform and rehabilitation, their more limited mission of isolating the criminal will also eventually fail and the insulation from criminals they provide will be ephemeral. Rather, prisons will likely become (if they are not already) places in which the larger society's suffering will be concentrated and brewed to a new intensity to burst out in frightening and uncontrollable forms.

Military culture has a unique relationship to suffering. In its noblest traditions, military service is a self-sacrificial vocation dedicated to the defense and protection of the society from which its members are recruited. Unfortunately, its mission can also be distorted to make it become a weapon in the hands of a tyrant or a tool to serve evil interests (e.g., rape in the Democratic Republic of the Congo).

Ideologies can be powerful determinants of different subcultures of suffering. Terrorism is often justified by an appeal to injustice and suffering but usually perpetuates and creates more suffering. Nationalism is often pursued to achieve an enhanced sense of personal identity, value, and self-worth at the expense of other nations (i.e., enhanced self-esteem potentially through the suffering of others as with Nazi Germany). With political ideologies, ideas take precedence over persons, inevitably leading to suffering.

Religious faiths may be the most extreme and painful examples of subcultures where ideologies can cause suffering. Individual adherents or leaders may betray the very core of their faith through legalism, hypocrisy or intolerance, thus producing suffering by the way they treat others within or outside a given faith, i.e., using faith as the means to oppress rather than as a healing force.

Are humans programmed to suffer? When humans experience bereavement through the loss of a loved one, as in the death of a spouse, the bereavement itself can be associated with adverse effects on the health of the survivor, even an increased risk of mortality in the first year after the loss.[7] This well-known observation of increased morbidity

---

[7]N.A. Christakis, and T.J. Iwashyna, "The health impact of health care on families: a matched cohort study of hospice use by decedents and mortality outcomes in

and mortality in bereaved humans is mirrored in non-human primates, especially in the relationship between mother and infant. This special relationship between mother and infant among primates is known as attachment, "a special affectional relationship between two individuals that is specific in focus and endures over time."[8] Unfortunately "the most frequent consequence of the loss of a mother is the death of the infant."[9] Responses to the loss of the attachment figure range from death to redirection of the attachment to another member of the species. The original bond is strong, often surviving separation for long periods. Even separation of six month old baboon infants for six months from their mothers did not extinguish the attachment. The attachment is to an *individual* not just a source of food, warmth, or support.[10] A particularly poignant description of this phenomenon is of the grieving of a young chimpanzee named Merlin who lost his mother and literally died of grief: "Hunched up with his arms around his knees he often sat rocking from side to side with wide open eyes that seemed to stare into the far distance ... By this time Merlin was so thin that every bone showed ... Often he lay stretched flat on the ground while other youngsters played, as though he were constantly exhausted."[11] Thus, it appears that humans are not the only creatures that form attachments or relationships that are strong enough to transcend even death. They may, however, be the only creatures who can contemplate and anticipate their death. Perhaps for this reason, the human rituals associated with grief, more than any other form of cultural expression, illuminate the powerful impact of suffering on culture.

surviving, widowed spouses," *Soc. Sci. Med.* 57 (2003): 465–475.

[8]"Parent and infant attachment in mammals," in *Parental Care in Mammals*, eds. D.J. Gubernick, and P.H. Klopfer (New York: Plenum Press, 1981), 244.

[9]P.C. Lee, "Effects of the loss of the mother on social development," in *Primate Social Relationships*, R.A. Hinde (London: Blackwell, 1983), 73.

[10]A. Zeller, "The Grieving Process in Non-human Primates," in *Coping with the Final Tragedy: Cultural Variation in Dying and Grieving*, D.R. Counts and D.A. Counts, eds. (Amityville, NY: Baywood Publishing Co., 1991).

[11]J. Van Lawick-Goodall, *In the Shadow of Man* (Boston: Houghton Mifflin, Co. 1971), 230–34.

What are some of the characteristic features of grief rituals from traditional, pre-industrialized cultures and how do they compare with 'modern' cultural expressions of grief?[12] It has been noted that "mortuary customs, grief and mourning are structured expressions of a society's beliefs about what death is."[13] Traditional societies have viewed death as a process with stages as opposed to a single event (i.e., cessation of vital functions) as in the typical modern western understanding. Examples of cultures which have emphasized death as a process with different stages include the Huron Indians of seventeenth-century North America, the Maori of New Zealand, and the Toraja of Indonesia. A closer look at Huron culture may serve to more fully illustrate the concept of death as a process. Human life from the Huron perspective consisted of the following stages:

1. Being alive.

2. Dying—a period of time leading up to physical death, including a well-recognized set of behaviors in preparation for death (e.g., picking out one's clothes for burial, saying farewell to family and friends, and winding down one's life).

3. Being "just dead"—the dead person's soul/spirit remains in the village and continues to participate in the activities of the living for some period of time, usually while the flesh rots at a cemetery close to the village.

4. "Fully dead"—the final stage of joining other spirits of the dead to enter the "village of souls" their final resting place for eternity. In the "village of souls," they "live" a "mirror image" existence of that of their counterparts in the physical world. Marking this transition, skeletal remains are transferred further away from the village, mixed, buried together, and they are not moved.

[12]For the following discussion I am indebted to the excellent collection of essays in *Coping with the Final Tragedy*, ibid.
[13]P.G. Ramsden, "Alice in the Afterlife: A Glimpse in the Mirror," ch. 3 in *Coping with the Final Tragedy*, 40

The ideal pattern was a gradual predictable transition from being fully 'alive', aging towards dying, and with physical death moving through a process of decay or 'continued dying' to being 'fully dead' or 'living' as a member of the spirit community. This was reflected physically by the transformation to skeletal remains. Abnormal deaths—suicide, childhood or accidental deaths, and deaths in battle were an interruption of this process, and the burial rites for such individuals reflected this loss of continuity with the normal pattern.

In contrast, modern notions of death are typically of an abrupt transition between two separate states: from 'alive' to 'dead' with death as the 'leap' from one to the other. Typically, in Western societies such as the United Kingdom and modern North America, mortuary practices reinforce the absolute and abrupt change from 'alive' to 'dead'. Removal of the corpse from among the living both socially and physically, is as quick as possible and it is usually never to be seen again. The growing popularity of cremation is consistent with the "conviction that physical death brings an immediate end to social existence."[14] Thus, for a person from a 'modern' Western culture, life begins abruptly at birth and ends equally abruptly at death.

A modern example of the interface between death and grieving which retains some marked similarities with the pre-industrialized cultures is rural Brittany. For rural Bretons who often have to migrate to large cities (e.g., Paris) for work, "the truly meaningful periods of life" are childhood and old age, both spent in their native village. *Retour au pays* ("return home")—it is crucial in Breton culture to die and be buried in the place of one's birth and youth. There is an old Breton saying: "He who is born in a miserable country always returns."[15] Remembering the dead, through the tending of flowers cultivated on the gravesite, is a longstanding tradition within Breton communities. Funerals and the feast of all saints draw many back to Brittany to honor their dead loved

---

[14]Ibid. 38

[15]E. Badone, "Memories of Marie-Thérèse," ch. 13 in *Coping with the Final Tragedy*, 220–221.

ones each year." "The dead compel the living to return."[16] A "second" death occurs when no one visits or tends the gravesite any more. In effect, a person or family passes out of the memory of the living—another form of social death. Tombs are known as *les maisons secondaires*—"second homes" or "vacation homes for the future." Most rural Bretons prefer to know a terminal diagnosis. The 'good death' comes with forewarning. "More than a physical event, death is a long-term social process."[17] It is a procession of many smaller deaths (e.g., aging, retirement, loss, decrepitude, isolation, dependence on others, etc.). Nursing/retirement homes are considered the "antechambers of death."

Fundamentally, the work of grieving cannot be separated from ritual. Human beings have beliefs and rituals that are intended to give meaning to death. Ritual transforms grief through meaning. A hospital chaplain has suggested that "People will use rituals to make reality more bearable."[18] Different cultures have developed 'rules' about how to die and how to deal with death and bereavement. There is great variety in how humans understand death and respond to bereavement. Indeed, "The experience of pain which surrounds a death may be the only cultural universal in the field of death and bereavement and not the finding of a particular pattern."[19]

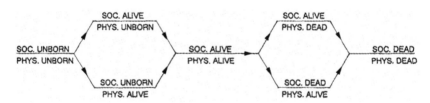

Figure 3: Distinction between Being Physically and Socially Alive and Dead

---

[16] Ibid. 227

[17] Ibid. 228

[18] J.A. O'Connor, "Good Stories from There Develop Good Care Here: A Therapeutic Perspective," ch. 15 in *Coping with the Final Tragedy*, 265.

[19] Ibid. 268

Figure 3 depicts the relationships between the physical and social aspects of life and death.[20] In traditional pre-industrial cultures, as an individual is conceived, is born, matures, grows old, and eventually dies, an initial transition to life and later to death on both social and physical levels occurs. Although modern secular culture in the West has tended to emphasize death as a very abrupt and distinct separation between being alive and being dead, this is not entirely true. When one considers such practices as prenatal ultrasound during which the developing fetus can be seen and even its gender identified, a social 'birth' has occurred. Indeed, this may have occurred earlier with the first perception of fetal movement or 'quickening' by the mother. By the same token, video images of loved ones when viewed after their physical death help perpetuate in some sense their social 'aliveness.' The heroes and heroines of secular society continue to be alive socially through the media, popular culture, and sometimes as cult figures (e.g., Marilyn Monroe, Michael Jackson, et al.). Even individuals of national historical significance continue to live socially in other institutions (e.g., past presidents depicted on currency or in public monuments).

When one considers the question from other perspectives, the vision of pre-industrialized cultures of social and physical living and dying as a process does not seem so strange. Earlier in this book apoptosis or programmed cell death was described as a phenomenon in which many different types of human cells undergo a process of division, maturation, and terminal differentiation which ultimately leads to their turnover or death. This highly choreographed process allows for the safe maintenance of healthy tissues. When the process fails, cancer may develop. If it proceeds too quickly or occurs excessively in response to external threats, it may cause other forms of serious damage or injury to the organism. In a very real biological sense, each human organism from the earliest period of development to the end of biological existence is at any moment experiencing this hidden process of being physically alive, yet also physically dying in some portion of its members.

[20]D.R. Counts, and D.A. Counts, "Conclusions: Coping with the Final Tragedy," ch. 16 in *Coping with the Final Tragedy*, 282.

For those Christian faithful whose belief and practice as Christians are rooted in the Church as the Body of Christ and communion of the saints, one can indeed be socially alive independent of being physically alive. The presence and veneration of the relics (portions of the physical remains) of Christian saints within many churches throughout the history of the Church are direct testimonies to this reality within Christian faith and practice.

How do these distinctions between physical and social death play out in western society and in particular, modern health care? Is a critically ill patient with limited potential for survival or recovery already socially dead? What about a patient with advanced Alzheimer's dementia or an individual with significant disabilities? What are the implications for the beginning of life? The examples identified in these questions underscore the many ethical challenges that are already present within modern health care. Conflicts arise to the extent that there is no clear consensus in the larger secular culture about the nature and significance of being alive and being dead, both from a physical and social perspective.

Materialism and Suffering—The Communist Totalitarian State

Now a large herd of swine was feeding there on the hillside; and they begged him to let them enter these. So he gave them leave. Then the demons came out of the man and entered the swine, and the herd rushed down the steep bank into the lake and were drowned. When the herdsmen saw what had happened, they fled, and told it in the city and the country. Then people went out to see what had happened, and they came to Jesus, and found the man from whom the demons had gone, sitting at the feet of Jesus, clothed and in his right mind; and they were afraid. And those who had seen it told them how he who had been possessed with demons was healed.[21]

Dostoevsky's great novel *Demons* begins with the above quote from the Gospel. His highly insightful and prophetic study of a revolutionary cell

[21]Luke 8.32–36.

in late nineteenth-century Russia explores the mindset and behavior of an intelligentsia whose parents had been nourished by the Enlightenment but who had themselves followed a natural progression to Nihilist anarchism. Unfortunately, unlike the man in the Gospel, the demons afflicting the souls of the Russian intelligentsia were not cast out and the horrors of the Bolshevik revolution proceeded with all their fury.

The twentieth century was witness to human suffering on an unprecedented scale. The major portion of the suffering and deaths in the twentieth century can be directly linked to communism and the totalitarian regimes it has inspired. One might ask what was the root cause of all these horrors? One survivor of the suffering caused by communism in Romania has indicated that "at the origin of all the tragedies the communist genocide had caused to this country lies the loss of a simple traditional value, which historically has been so deeply rooted in the Romanian soul—*the fear of God*."[22] What was the source of such a drastic change in the Romanian soul? The demons of nineteenth-century nihilist philosophy emerged in full force in communist ideology which became the poisoned nourishment offered to the captive peoples of Eastern Europe, Russia, and elsewhere. Formal definitions of nihilism are: "a viewpoint that traditional values and beliefs are unfounded and that existence is senseless and useless"; and "a doctrine that denies any objective ground of truth and especially of moral truths." These philosophical definitions have evolved operationally as: "a doctrine or belief that conditions in the social organization are so bad as to make destruction desirable for its own sake independent of any constructive program or possibility"; and in its sense as a specific political movement, "the program of a nineteenth-century Russian party advocating revolutionary reform and using terrorism and assassination."[23]

If the Party creates and defines a new reality, it is essential to assure that nothing (and no one) poses an effective challenge to the new reality.

[22]G. Boldur-Latescu, *The Communist Genocide in Romania* (New York: Nova Science Publishers, Inc., 2005), 1–2.

[23]Online at: http://mw1.merriam-webster.com/dictionary/nihilism; accessed 6 December, 2010.

The totalitarian communist state created a culture focused on control. Control was exerted through fear, loss of privacy, complicity, deprivation, loss of individuality, loss of personal responsibility, and lies, lies, and more lies.

Fear of arrest had a corrosive influence on society within the totalitarian state. According to Solzhenitsyn, those chosen for arrest and imprisonment in the Gulag were among the pure and good who could not remain in such a society, and with their absence from society it became more and more decrepit; their departures were hardly noticed, but they signaled the "dying of the soul of the people."[24]

Control could very effectively be exerted through complicity—the collective compromise of human consciences. In reference to the clear disconnect between students and university faculty created at the time of the 1989 revolution in Romania, Boldur-Latescu states, "[W]hat united them [i.e., the faculty] was the complicity in supporting the dictatorial regime from inside departments and from inside the leadership of the schools. They were united, not through their beliefs in the communist ideology—the majority did not believe in it, anyway—but through the guilt of lying to and intellectually oppressing their students. Oftentimes, the solidarity in wrongdoing is as strong, or even stronger, than the solidarity of goodhearted people."[25] Dostoevsky develops this concept of control through complicity further in *Demons* where the leader of the revolutionary cell establishes tight control over the souls of his comrades by making them all directly complicit in the murder of a colleague now arbitrarily deemed a 'traitor'.

> "[Y]ou united together into a separate organization of the free assembly of the like-minded, so as in the common cause to share your energy among yourselves at a given moment and, if need be, to watch over and observe each other. Each of you owes a higher accounting. You are called to renew the cause, which is decrepit and

---

[24]A. Solzhenitsyn, *The Gulag Archipelago*, vol. 2 (New York: Harper & Row, 1975), 642.

[25]Boldur-Latescu, *The Communist Genocide in Romania*, 115.

stinking from stagnation … In the meantime your whole step is towards getting everything destroyed: both the state and its morality. We alone will remain, having destined ourselves beforehand to assume power: we shall rally the smart ones and ride on the backs of the fools … This generation must be re-educated to make it worthy of freedom."

"Nobody will denounce us now. You won't either."

"And you?"

"No question, I'll have you all tucked away the minute you make a move to betray, and you know it."

"No, no one will denounce us," he said resolutely, "but—the crew must remain a crew and obey, otherwise I'll … What trash these people are though!"[26]

Communist culture of the twentieth century was also a culture of control through deprivation. Long queues for food and the basic necessities of life, chronic shortages, uncertainty regarding the availability of resources, fear that at any moment, one might lose the little one had, and the ever present fear of losing the family bread winner to the Gulag, all provided powerful disincentives to question authority or resist the ever tighter control of the state. Milos Forman, in an interview about his film, *The Fireman's Ball*, a thinly veiled satire about the communist regime in Czechoslovakia, expresses the poignant reality of deprivation under communism and its corrupting influence on morality by quoting a popular aphorism repeated among the people, "If you don't steal, you steal from your family."[27] Again, with prophetic insight, Dostoevsky identifies the fundamental tension between human freedom, predicated on an acceptance of suffering, and the desire for bread, i.e., material well-being, in the tale of the Grand Inquisitor, in his novel *The Brothers Karamazov*. "[I]n the end they will lay their freedom at our feet and say to us: 'Better that you enslave us, but feed us.' They will finally

---

[26]F. Dostoevsky, *Demons*, trans. by R. Pevear and L. Volokhonsky (New York: Vintage Classics, 1995), 607–609.

[27]Milos Forman, from an interview about his film, "The Fireman's Ball."

understand that freedom and earthly bread in plenty for everyone are inconceivable together, for never, never will they be able to share among themselves."[28]

The culture of control engendered by the totalitarian communist state promoted a loss of individuality. Better to not stand out from the crowd, even within the creative community. Thus, creativity was held captive to ideology; individual initiative tended to be stifled. Perhaps one of the most visible examples of the collective destruction of individual initiative and the individual was the phenomenon of 'systematization' in which large nondescript housing blocks were established in massive urban projects to replace individual family homes. Rather than creating a larger sense of community, these massive and truly hideous structures created a population of isolated strangers. Common areas in the buildings characteristically were left unfinished, in all their cold, concrete splendor. Only in crossing the threshold into an individual flat could one discover that a real person or family lived there. Even the very notion of the beautiful was controlled, held captive to ideology.

Loss of a sense of personal responsibility follows closely on the heels of losing one's individuality. Solzhenitsyn identifies as the chief dilemma of the twentieth century the question of whether one may deliver one's conscience into another's hands, and simply carry out orders, or whether one should be guided by one's own sense of right and wrong. Even the intention of oaths, meant to protect the people against evildoing, can be distorted and become tools in the hands of an evil government and its minions.[29]

Perhaps more than by any other method, control in communist totalitarian cultures was exerted by lies and plenty of them! Orwell in his novel 1984 describes the process by which language itself can be distorted as 'doublethink' to make lies become truth. "Whatever was true now was true from everlasting to everlasting. It was quite simple.

[28]Fyodor Dostoevsky, *The Brothers Karamazov*, trans. by R. Pevear and L. Volokhonsky, (New York: Farrar, Straus, Giroux, 1990), 253.
[29]Alexander Solzhenitsyn, *The Gulag Archipelago*, vol. 3 (New York: Harper Perennial, 2007), 224.

All that was needed was an unending series of victories over your own memory. 'Reality control . . .' in Newspeak, 'doublethink.'"[30] "Everything faded into mist. The past was erased, the erasure was forgotten, the lie became truth."[31] Newspeak—"It's a beautiful thing, the destruction of words."[32]

> WAR IS PEACE
> FREEDOM IS SLAVERY
> IGNORANCE IS STRENGTH.[33]

The very nature and integrity of a nation's literature is at risk under these conditions. Alexander Solzhenitsyn, commenting on this problem in the Soviet Union, stated that literature was non-existent there in the whole period from the 1930s to the 1950s, because there is no literature without the whole truth.[34]

In Romania during the early 1950s, the nephews of a man imprisoned for his faith were asked at their 'young pioneers' meeting: "Are you praying at home?" Their parents told them to keep the family prayer life a secret. They quickly learned that in their culture the truth could not be expressed. "This, also, is a form of suffering."[35]

A unique aspect of the communist totalitarian states is that they were so efficient at producing collective suffering of entire nations, and on such a grand scale. The effects of their program, the flavor of suffering experienced by their victims (i.e., their entire society) can be summarized as follows:

1. Dehumanization—diminution of the value of the individual person;

2. Denial of the person on a societal level—collective suffering;

[30]George Orwell, *1984* (New York: Signet Classics, The New American Library, 1961), 32.

[31]Ibid. 64

[32]Ibid. 45

[33]Ibid. 26

[34]Alexander Solzhenitsyn, *The Gulag Archipelago*, vol. 2, 632.

[35]Father Roman Braga, personal communication.

3. The state is everything—"Live through the leader";

4. Collaboration or moral compromise as the price of survival—society as a prison;

5. Fundamental values are inverted;

6. Suffering extends even to the environment (e.g., the destruction of Lake Baikal in the Soviet Union and the Danube Delta project in communist Romania); and

7. Paradoxically, prisoners have the greatest level of freedom as persons.

The amazing miracle is that for some, the suffering they experienced as victims of the communist totalitarian state was the catalyst for the transformation of their souls. Solzhenitsyn recounts that early on he realized that the Gulag was not a bottomless pit of despair for him, but he called it instead "the most important turning point" in his life.[36] When he let himself descend to rock-bottom he experienced a transformation that over the time of his imprisonment "put the finishing touches" on his character.[37] He then goes on to describe the profound opportunity that his intense suffering in the Gulag provided for personal spiritual growth, and he declares that as soon as one gives up the idea of survival at any cost, being imprisoned slowly transforms one's character in an awesome manner, in an unlooked-for direction. The formerly dry soul matures through suffering, blossoms forth, as it were, so that one learns to love one's neighbors, if not quite in the Christian sense, at least to love those who are near.[38]

Stalin's Soviet authorities directed an experiment in their new satellite, Romania, in the late 1940s to create a 'communist personality'. This model for communist prisons was developed at a town named Pitesti. An effort was made through the harshest forms of physical and mental torture including use of psychoactive drugs and attempted brainwashing

[36]Alexander. Solzhenitsyn, *The Gulag Archipelago*, vol. 1 (New York: Harper & Row, 1974), 187.

[37]Solzhenitsyn, *The Gulag Archipelago*, vol. 3, 98.

[38]Solzhenitsyn, *The Gulag Archipelago*, vol. 2, 610, 611.

to 'correct' the minds of young Romanian intellectuals. Everything that had been sacred in their lives prior to imprisonment was fair game for destruction. Religious rituals were revised by the communist directors of the 'experiment' with the gross distortion of symbols and use of foul words that were antithetical to their original use and intent. Father Roman Braga, one of the survivors from the hell of Pitesti summed up the 'experiment' of Pitesti in this way, "Man doesn't know who he is. Man has an abysmal region; the rational component is only a small part. I saw saints become criminals and those without spiritual formation become saints."[39] The only reason the Pitesti 'experiment' ended was that information regarding the extreme aspects of the prisoners' treatment was leaked to the West, embarrassing the Soviets.

There is a deep, almost unfathomable paradox associated with the great suffering experienced by so many of the prisoners within the communist labor camps. How could they suffer so greatly, especially in terms of physical deprivation and even torture, and yet describe their time as prisoners in positive terms? Perhaps, it is best explained by Solzhenitsyn's practical exegesis of the passage in Luke's gospel quoted at the beginning of this section: He says that the meaning of life on earth consists not in prospering, but in the maturation of the soul. And from that point of view, the torturers in the Gulag were most awfully punished themselves, because they were turning into swine, devolving from the human state into something less by inflicting torture on people whose maturation "holds out hope."[40]

The so-called 'politicals', the political prisoners in the labor camps, were predominantly Christians whose primary crime was to be sufficiently insolent to place service to God above service to the state. "The Christians were their principal contingent. Clumsy, semiliterate, unable to deliver speeches from the rostrum or compose an underground proclamation (which their faith made unnecessary anyway), they went off to camp to face tortures and death—only so as not to renounce their faith! They knew very well for what they were serving

[39]Father Roman Braga, ibid.
[40]Solzhenitsyn, *The Gulag Archipelago*, vol. 2, 613.

time, and they were unwavering in their convictions! . . . women among them were particularly numerous . . . we overlooked the fact that the sinful Orthodox Church had nonetheless nurtured daughters worthy of the first centuries of Christianity—sisters of those thrown to the lions."[41] Valeriu Gafencu, one of the young Romanian intellectuals who did not survive the rigors of the Romanian Gulag but whose spiritual life as a Christian flourished in the midst of intense suffering reflected on his experience before he died: "We are now living in an age in which Christians have found another path of confession: The madness of the cross, of sacrifice for the Truth. The enemies of Christ have unleashed the greatest and most cruel persecution of Christians. Today, anyone who believes must be prepared to die. This path is a spiritual privilege of great beauty . . . The tortures to which we are subjected are the doors through which Christ renews and raises up the Church and the world."[42] He boldly asserts the core of the paradox, the path of suffering as a *"spiritual privilege of great beauty . . . "* The tortures that he and his fellow prisoners experience become a means of healing for the Church and the world, a co-participation in a small way in the sufferings of their crucified Lord. They truly experienced the joy of taking up their cross and following him. Even with all that he also suffered, Father Roman Braga echoed Valeriu Gafencu's assessment of the meaning of the suffering under communism, "This suffering was a blessing. We couldn't understand a lot of things without this persecution. This suffering was for the redemption of the whole nation."[43]

How can such intense suffering bring healing to an individual person or to a whole nation? Perhaps, when all of the props of our existence are pulled away, when all of our fond illusions about life are stripped from us, when we fully experience a true kenosis, the substrate is exposed upon which real personal growth can occur. "Know thyself!" he says, quoting an aphorism from Greek philosophy. And he makes the point

---

[41]Ibid. 309, 310.

[42]Valeriu Gafencu, quoted in *The Saint of the Prisons* by the monk Moise, trans. by Monk Sava of Oasa Monastery (Sibiu: Editura Agnos, 2009), 222–224.

[43]Father Roman Braga, ibid.

that a sense of knowing everything is awakened in a person by that person's considering the ways he (or she) has missed the mark whether by what was done or what was left undone. So, when he considered the years of his imprisonment, he was able to say, often to the amazement of those who heard him, "Bless you, prison!"[44]

Materialism and Suffering—Western Secular Culture

As western life becomes more free and easy, western man becomes less prepared to fight for those who have allowed themselves to be exploited. Nevertheless, the time will come also for men of the west, because prosperity carries within itself a force for ruin; and to extend this perceived well-being for as little as a day, many a man will give up everything of his own and of others, even everything sacred.[45] How does our own Western secular culture that emerged 'victorious' out of the Cold War relate to suffering? If the communist totalitarian state could be characterized as creating a culture of control, what can be said of the West? The secular culture of the West is also concerned with control, but it is a control—or at least the illusion of control—exerted by the individual. It is a culture of individual autonomy. The western culture of autonomy is dedicated to a number of propositions:

1. "Life, liberty and the pursuit of happiness";

2. Personal fulfillment and material well-being;

3. Individual rights and personal freedom at all costs;

4. Privacy in everything (from one's home to one's faith);

5. Choice (whether for a new car or to abort a fetus); and

6. Accountability to no one (but one's self).

---

[44]Solzhenitsyn, *The Gulag Archipelago*, vol. 2, 616.
[45]Alexander Solzhenitsyn, *In the First Circle*, trans. by H.T. Willetts, (New York: Harper Perennial, 2009) 667.

"We hold these truths to be self-evident, that all men are created equal, that they are endowed by their Creator with certain unalienable rights, that among these are life, liberty and the pursuit of happiness."[46] But, are humans actually endowed with "certain unalienable rights"? Let's look more closely at how one group has followed the logical progression of these "Principles of a Free Society". The Ayn Rand Center for Individual Rights (named for the novelist of the same name) has articulated succinctly the position of extreme autonomy, so often in evidence in western secular culture:

- "Life, liberty, and the pursuit of happiness"—three basic rights identified in the U.S. Declaration of Independence

- The right to life is considered to be the only fundamental right, from which all other rights are derived.

- The right to life protects the individual's ability to take all those actions necessary for the preservation and enjoyment of his life. It is based on the idea that life is the standard of moral value.

- The right to liberty protects the individual's ability to think and to act on his own judgment. It is based on the idea that rationality is man's highest moral virtue.

- The right to pursue happiness protects the individual's ability to live for his own sake, rather than for the sake of society. It is based on the idea that the pursuit of one's self-interest is one's highest moral purpose. This is also referred to as "Objectivism and rational selfishness".[47]

In the totalitarian communist state, the locus of control was centralized to the government. In western capitalist states, the locus of control is at the level of the individual member of the electorate

---

[46] Accessed on 12 December 2010 at: http://www.earlyamerica.com/earlyamerica/freedom/doi/text.html.

[47] Ayn Rand Center for Individual Rights, accessed on 12 December 2010 at http://principlesofafreesociety.com/life-liberty-pursuit-of-happiness.

(theoretically); although quite often, the actual locus of control is centered in unelected elites.

Protagoras of Abdera (c. 480–410 B.C.) is credited with the statement, "Man is the measure of all things," which later became the ideal of the Renaissance. Thus, human beings in the West have acquired the illusion of autonomy and control over their environment. Solzhenitsyn spoke prophetically in his famous (infamous to some) Harvard commencement speech of the dangers of this deification of the individual:

> . . . there is a disaster which is already very much with us . . . an autonomous, irreligious humanistic consciousness. It has made man the measure of all things on earth—imperfect man, who is never free of pride, self-interest, envy, vanity, and dozens of other defects . . . On the way from the Renaissance to our days we have enriched our experience, but we have lost the concept of a Supreme Complete Entity which used to restrain our passions and our irresponsibility. . . . We have placed too much hope in politics and social reforms, only to find out that we were being deprived of our most precious possession: our spiritual life. It is trampled by the party mob in the East, by the commercial one in the West. This is the essence of the crisis: The split in the world is less terrifying than the similarity of the disease afflicting its main sections.[48]

The western focus on individual autonomy finds its practical expression in freedom of choice. Indeed, freedom cannot be true freedom without this inherent potential for choice. In western secular culture, the assumption, conscious or unconscious, has been that one can only demonstrate one's freedom by making autonomous choices. Unfortunately, many of the choices that are made are driven by individual desire or the ego, primarily from selfish motivations, and they are often defended as a demonstration of exerting one's 'rights'. The 'You Deserve a Break Today' advertising slogan is a symptom of this form of thinking.

---

[48] Alexander Solzhenitsyn, "Harvard Address, 8 June, 1978," in *The Solzhenitsyn Reader* (Wilmington, DE: ISI Books, 2006), 574–5.

It is interesting and may be instructive to examine the etymology of 'choice'. The ancient Greek word for 'choice' is *hairesis*, from the same root for heresy.[49] To choose, fundamentally, includes an element of creating division, of separating oneself from others. An ego chooses—but what motivates the choice?

It was noted earlier that nihilistic thinking was a very important impetus for the revolutionary movements leading to the 1917 Bolshevik revolution in Russia and the later practical expression of its ideology in communist totalitarian states. Rather than being the polar opposite of western secularism, nihilistic thought has found its own place in driving the secular mind in the West, only with a slightly different emphasis than in the communist East. In the West, the emphasis has been on the "doctrine that denies any objective ground of truth and especially of moral truths."[50] In other words, all values are relative and, in effect, each person a god. This is a major element in the intellectual foundation for much of what is aggressively marketed as 'diversity' on today's university campuses. Since there are no absolute truths (oddly this sounds like an absolute truth!) in Western relativism, everyone should exercise full tolerance for the individual 'truths' of each—the essence of 'political correctness'. 'Tolerance' does not allow for the possibility of a serious critique of another's 'truth', unless that 'truth' represents a manifestation of 'bigotry' and 'intolerance'. In this world view, 'intolerance' and 'bigotry' are often identified with serious religious faith or traditional ways of thinking.

Tolerance was once nearly synonymous with respect for the other and was reflected by courteous dialogue in which there might be mutual respect but also an acknowledgment of divergent views or opinions that might be incompatible. The 'new' tolerance immediately shuts down any real discussion and subjects those who seriously believe that their 'truth' might have universal applicability to open ridicule as 'intolerant' ignorant individuals. "Tolerance is the virtue of people who do

---

[49] Arndt and Gingrich, 23.

[50] Accessed on December 6, 2010, at: http://mw1.merriam-webster.com/dictionary/nihilism.

not believe in anything."[51] Charles Krauthammer in a very insightful essay suggests that Chesterton's pithy remark may need to be updated to keep pace with the current state of evolution of western culture. "At a time when religion is a preference and piety a form of eccentricity suggesting fanaticism, Chesterton needs revision: tolerance is not just the virtue of people who do not believe in anything; tolerance extends only to people who don't believe in anything. Believe in something and beware."[52]

In a universe where values are relative and individual autonomy reigns supreme, personal responsibility is a doubtful proposition. Responsibility implies accountability to a higher authority or set of values. But if, as the nihilist believes, there is no higher authority than the face in the mirror, there is no need for shame or guilt. Even if you get caught, it is always the fault of someone else: your parents, your teachers, the government, faulty genes (again your parents! and no need for repentance, if you can obtain the services of a clever lawyer!). Dr Victor Frankl was an admirer of the United States and the many freedoms enjoyed by its citizens, but with some caveats. "Freedom ... is a negative concept which requires a positive complement. And the positive complement is responsibleness ... [which] refers to a meaning for whose fulfillment we are responsible, and also to a being before whom we are responsible ... Freedom threatens to degenerate into mere arbitrariness unless it is lived in terms of responsibleness ... the Statue of Liberty on the East Coast [of the United States] should be supplemented by a Statue of Responsibility on the West Coast."[53]

The indictment of humanity by Dostoevsky's Grand Inquisitor applies with equal force, as much to the triumphant culture of the secular West as it did to the 'defeated' communist totalitarian states of the East, "in the end they will lay their freedom at our feet and say to us:

[51]G.K. Chesterton, quoted in C. Krauthammer, "Will it be coffee, tea, or He? Religion was once a conviction. Now it is a taste." *Time Magazine* 151.23 (15 June 1998): 92.
[52]Ibid.
[53]V.E. Frankl, *The Will to Meaning: Foundations and Applications of Logotherapy* (New York: Meridian, Penguin Books,1988), 49.

'Better that you enslave us, but feed us.' They will finally understand that freedom and earthly bread in plenty for everyone are inconceivable together, for never, never will they be able to share among themselves."[54] This is particularly true when 'bread' is understood in the broader sense of material well-being or the 'stuff' of modern western life (e.g., smart phones, MP3 players, etc.). The fundamental tension between real human freedom (with the implicit acceptance of suffering and self-denial) and the desire for bread (material well-being) remains.

The human obsession with acquisition of material goods and assuring one's well-being has come at a price. The historian, Arnold Toynbee, in assessing the angst of western culture regarding death, identifies the western person's flight from a deeper inner life as a pervasive symptom of the materialistic focus of the culture. "The typical Western man or woman has allowed one of the most characteristic and noble faculties of human nature to atrophy . . . the faculty . . . of communing with oneself and through oneself . . . with the Ultimate Spiritual Reality behind the universe. This faculty of spiritual contemplation is one of the features of human nature that make us human." But, "We turn sub-human if we lose this faculty or destroy it. Yet the average modern Westerner becomes uneasy if he is by himself . . . the time and energy that is not consumed in working, feeding, and sleeping is occupied in some form of 'entertainment' . . . Anything and everything is acceptable that will preclude 'the flight of the alone to the alone'. Confronted by death without belief, modern man has deliberately been clipping his spiritual wings."[55]

In fact, death has become the ultimate obscenity for westerners. "The word 'death' itself has become almost unmentionable in the West—particularly in the United States . . . Death is 'un-American'; for, if the fact of death were once admitted to be a reality even in the United States, then it would also have to be admitted that the United States is not the

---

[54]Dostoevsky, *The Brothers Karamazov*, trans. R. Pevear and L. Volokhonsky (New York: Farrar, Straus, Giroux, 1990), 253.

[55]Arnold Toynbee, *Man's Concern with Death* (New York: McGraw Hill, 1968), 130–1.

earthly paradise that it is deemed to be (and this is one of the crucial articles of faith in the 'American way of life')."[56] Of course, the obscene and frightening nature of death for human beings is nothing new. That humanity has been fleeing to material possessions as an escape from coming to terms with suffering and death is most directly addressed by Christ in the gospels, "Beware of all covetousness; for a man's life does not consist in the abundance of his possessions." And he told them a parable, saying, "The land of a rich man brought forth plentifully; and he thought to himself, 'What shall I do, for I have nowhere to store my crops?' And he said, 'I will do this: I will pull down my barns, and build larger ones; and there I will store all my grains and goods. And I will say to my soul, Soul, you have ample goods laid up for many years; take your ease, eat, drink, be merry.' But God said to him, 'Fool! This night your soul is required of you; and the things you have prepared, whose will they be?' So is he who lays up treasure for himself, and is not rich toward God."[57]

For the western secular mind, suffering and death represent rude interruption of "life, liberty and the pursuit of happiness." Alexander Solzhenitsyn reflects on this dilemma of western humanism, "If, as claimed by humanism, man were born only to be happy, he would not be born to die. Since his body is doomed to death, his task on earth evidently must be more spiritual: not a total engrossment in everyday life, not the search for the best ways to obtain material goods and then their carefree consumption."[58]

Is there room for suffering in western secular culture? Suffering and death are the very antitheses of "life, liberty, and the pursuit of happiness." Although death can sometimes be rationalized in abstract terms, the idea of suffering before death creates terror. Suffering implies a real loss of control—not a happy prospect for the autonomous man. Loss of control over the process, timing, and circumstances of death are a great source of suffering in Western secular culture. It is this fear of

[56]Ibid. 131.
[57]Luke 12.15–21.
[58]Solzhenitsyn, Harvard Address, 575.

losing control and the powerful desire to maintain control that more than any other motivating factors drive most requests for physician-assisted suicide. In the West, youth and external beauty are highly valued. The physical changes that frequently accompany advanced illness, e.g., weight loss and progressive cachexia, acquire an almost obscene quality like pornography—the pornography of dying. Since death is still unavoidable, suffering quite often becomes the ultimate enemy. Using "all means necessary" to end suffering thus can be seen as a viable option, even a noble act.

Frequently in the West, one suffers and ultimately dies alone. One's values define how one responds to suffering and how one dies. Individual needs and desires drive the pattern of care offered to those who suffer and can dictate how hospice and palliative care services are provided. The wide variety of religious faith and spirituality (or the lack thereof) in the West often results in a superficial approach to addressing the existential and spiritual distress that occurs. Even something as serious and fundamental to the human condition as preparation for one's death succumbs to consumerism—the "have it your way" death or death "on our own terms."[59] Death has increasingly lost its place in the communal experience of the West through the diminution of common forms of grieving. This is a reflection of the overall loss of any sense of community in the traditional sense. For the West, the burning question still remains unanswered by the secular culture: Is suffering the greatest evil?

"I slept and dreamt that life was joy. I awoke and saw that life was service. I acted and behold, service was joy."[60]

---

[59]References to a popular advertising slogan for the Burger King franchise and the title of a Bill Moyer's documentary series on end-of-life care in the United States, respectively.

[60]Rabindranath Tagore quote, online at: http://www.brainyquote.com/quotes/quotes/r/rabindrana134933.html; accessed 4 June 2012.

Narrative and Suffering

"In having no cure to offer, we actually had everything to offer. We discovered what the word 'healing' meant ... crossing the traditional threshold of a medical-industrial complex and beginning to engage with the patient, with their story."[61]

With his discovery of the limits of curative medical practice when confronted by the terminal nature of his AIDS patients' suffering in the early 1990's, Dr Verghese noted a realization that healing is a phenomenon that can be distinctly different from cure. More specifically, healing is integrally connected with patients' stories, the narratives of their illnesses, their suffering.

More often than not, the central element, the foundation of a great work of literature is a powerful and compelling story. Suffering is very frequently the theme, the underlying force driving such powerful stories. How do medical histories relate to patients' stories of their illnesses? Let us examine in more detail the nature of stories and their potential relationship to the traditional medical history. To highlight this, let us consider the following brief stories:

1. An 83-year-old woman presents to the hospital emergency department with complaints of increasing pain in her abdomen, nausea with bloating, weight loss, and increasing weakness and fatigue.

2. Old Mrs I__ is a favorite with all the children in her neighborhood. She is known among the children as 'the scolder' because she often comes to her door and scolds them when they are noisy or fighting. After the 'scolding' though, she always has a smile for them and invites them into her kitchen for a treat and a story from her youth. The children are upset when she hasn't come to her door for the usual 'scolding' for many days.

Is there any obvious relationship between the brief medical history in number 1 and the story about old Mrs I__ in number 2? If it became clear that the persons described in 1 and 2 above are actually the same

[61]A. Verghese, "The Physician as Storyteller," *Annals of Internal Medicine* 135(11) (2001): 1012–1017.

person, does not the story in number 2 create a much richer, more vivid image of the very ill individual described in number 1? Has she been transformed from being yet another 'repository of disease' in the description in number 1 to a person who is part of a community, rich with relationships which are now being disrupted by her illness?

What are the primary elements of a story? The essential or primary elements of a story include plot, characters, setting, and tone. Typically, a plot has a beginning and an end. There is usually a central element, i.e., a conflict, mystery, or problem to be solved that drives the story. The problem or conflict usually involves or engages various characters. A good plot will draw the reader into the story and create sympathy (or sometimes antipathy) for the characters as they struggle to solve or resolve the problem. Resolution of the problem or conflict is often central to a 'successful' end or completion of the story.

The sine qua non of a story is the cast of characters that populate it. It is their problem, their conflict, their suffering, and how they respond to it or resolve it, that captures the imagination. Characters may portray or embody the conflict at the heart of the story. They may cause or experience the suffering that is portrayed through them, and often develop in positive or negative ways. They can be the 'voices' of the storyteller who may need more than one 'voice' to explore the problem at the heart of a story.

The setting is the environment in which the action of the story takes place. It may be a major defining aspect for the characters and may even in some sense represent another character in the story. The environment or setting includes not only the location and physical conditions experienced by the characters, but also their social, cultural, and political context. Great or cataclysmic events (e.g., wars) may serve as powerful backdrops for stories. For a person who is ill, the setting (e.g., hospital, nursing home, home, cultural/religious background, level of education, presence or lack of a social network, poverty, wealth) may define behaviors, symptoms, hope, despair, etc. All of these factors experienced at the individual level may then be colored by a common experience of the larger community.

The tone of a story is the mood created or evoked in its telling. This can be influenced by the content of the narrative but also by the manner in which it is told. It may be dominated by a particular mood—happy, sad, angry, fearful, hopeful, humorous, etc., or it may represent a mixture of several moods/emotions. It is usually defined by the storyteller but can be modulated by the listener's (reader's) biases and interpretation. It may be a more powerful motivating element than content alone. It represents the synthesis of the artist's intent and the listener's (reader's) response and may produce new and unexpected meanings and reactions beyond the original concept of the author.

In what ways are people affected by stories, and how can they influence those who hear or read them?

A story uses words to create involvement and relationship. Stories take the stuff of our everyday lived life and carry us into the actions that constitute our experience: the people we love or hate, the jobs we do well or badly, the way parents and children behave, decisions that we face. If the storyteller is good, we often hear or notice something that is going on right now as I am living my life but that I had missed noticing. Now that I see it, I can live into it better—enjoy a pleasure more deeply, be wary of a danger more vigilantly, grasp an opportunity that I was unaware of, appreciate a person that I hadn't thought was worth spending any time with ... Sometimes a storyteller will recast what it means to be a man or a woman in such a way that we see ourselves and the people around us so differently that we get a fresh burst of energy to go back to the same old thing in a brand new way: We had concluded that we are at a boring dead end and the storyteller reveals love or conflict or values in a way that engages us at an entirely different level. Storytellers imagine alternate ways of living, wake up our imaginations to who we and our neighbors are in fresh ways. We are stimulated to live more intensely, more aware.[62]

[62]E.H. Peterson, "Fiction: A Cutting Edge Spiritual Discipline," speech presented at *The Christy Awards* (Orlando, Florida, 11 July 2003).

The stories embodied in great literature at their best are windows which can give us deep insights into the suffering of others, extending our own lived experience. Metaphors are important, if not essential elements, in storytelling. Metaphors are compressed stories. In literal terms, a metaphor is a lie. Sometimes the most effective way to tell the truth is the use of metaphor in which what is literally, concretely true is subordinated to a glimpse of a transcendent truth. Metaphors, by design, are not precise. They may have more than one meaning. Metaphors do not allow passivity. They force the active participation of the reader/listener by use of the imagination. At their best, metaphors actively involve us in the intricate connectedness inherent in the cosmos.[63]

Stories can be powerful pedagogical tools. Fables and parables are examples of stories that have been used throughout the ages to teach. A hallmark of a very good fable or parable is its ability to transcend time and culture and convey a message that still speaks to the audience at hand. But, can stories do more than teach? Can stories be the vehicle through which relationships are formed and developed? Is there a reciprocity between the story and the one who enters into its content?

Common themes in storytelling, both ancient and modern, have been war, love, death or loss, and conflict or struggle. Suffering is a common underlying motif for all of these powerful themes. That these themes have been so durable throughout history highlights the strength of the grip that suffering exerts over the minds and hearts of human beings.

It would be impossible and overwhelming to list all the great literature that draws its power from suffering, but the following are good examples: Homer's *Iliad* and *Odyssey*, the Old Testament story of *Job*, the passion accounts in the gospels of the New Testament, and more recently, Hugo's *Les Miserables*, Hawthorne's *Scarlet Letter*, Tolstoy's *War and Peace*, Dostoevsky's *Crime and Punishment*, and Solzhenitsyn's *Cancer Ward*.

[63]Ibid.

Within the Christian tradition, the mystery and story of the incarnation is experienced and celebrated in many forms. Some of these may be a part of the common or liturgical worship of the faithful and some may be experienced on a more individual basis, but always with the intent of nurturing a real relationship between the believer and God. Thus, the gospels, whether they are read during the corporate worship of the Church or during one's private prayer life, are an invitation to enter directly into the experience described in them—a direct encounter with the Crucified One.

Words are not the only means of telling stories. The icon in the Eastern Christian tradition is precisely a story in art, but not just any story. The stylized character of an icon is meant to draw the person who engages with the icon beyond the mere image of people and events that are portrayed by physical means into a relationship with the very person or persons depicted. Ultimately, an icon derives its authority, its authenticity from the reality of the incarnation. All icons should draw the viewer to Christ. In this case as with contemplation of the stories in the gospels, the story is more than good pedagogy. It becomes a pathway to a relationship with the Teacher, himself.

How do stories relate to the practice of medicine, to the care of the sick? "*Story* helps us link and make sense of events in our lives ... physicians create stories ... are catalysts in stories ... we are characters in various stories, walking on and off the stage in the tales that take place in our hospitals and clinics."[64]

Let us revisit the contrast presented in the two brief narratives at the beginning of this section and compare stories with medical history taking. History taking in medicine is centered on a 'chief complaint', usually a symptom or several symptoms causing distress to a person who now becomes a patient. As in a mystery story, the symptoms become 'clues' for the 'detective'—the physician who is in search of a disease (the central problem of the story)—to treat with the hope, cure! Other active illnesses or past history of diseases treated earlier become part of the evidence explored by the medical 'detective'. The 'story' is focused

[64]Verghese, ibid.

on solving the mystery of the disease that is assumed to be causing the symptoms. If the disease is not identified, it becomes an incomplete 'story', an unsolved mystery, which may lose the interest of the medical 'detective'. The role of the patient as a character within the 'story' is limited to providing clues toward detecting the disease that is hypothesized to be present.

The patient as a specific subject of inquiry—a person, a character or protagonist in a unique story—is lost in the typical process of medical history taking. Understanding the importance of the symptoms (e.g., pain, etc.) in causing distress to the patient, independent of the discovery of any underlying disease, is too often a foreign experience for physicians. How can the patient's medical history be transformed into a complete history—a story of a person's suffering? If we silently observe our patients, their body language, the inflection of their voices when they speak, their dress, their posture, the overall presence they create, what do we see? Through what lens do we see them; with interest, compassion, indifference, frustration, boredom? How might this affect the real history (narrative) that we acquire or encounter? How do we intersect with their story?

Individual life stories (including our own) are in need of healing. Alexander Solzhenitsyn's famous statement from the *Gulag Archipelago* may well apply in this setting. He said that the boundary between good and evil does not pass between countries or social classes or political parties, but through the heart of every human being.[65] This conflict plays itself out in human illness and suffering and often is the underlying force driving the patient's narrative and our own.

What is missing in a conventional medical history? Medical history taking usually does not make room for a full assessment of the four domains of Cicely Saunder's Total Pain[66]—the interplay between the physical, psychological, social, and spiritual manifestations of human

[65] A. Solzhenitsyn, *The Gulag Archipelago*, part 4 (New York: Harper & Row, 1975), 615.

[66] C. Saunders, and N. Sykes, *The Management of Terminal Malignant Disease*, 3rd ed. (London: Hodder and Stoughton, 1993), 1–14. Please also see page XX of this manuscript.

distress and suffering. To take a 'holistic' medical history would potentially create the opportunity to identify the link between physical
distress and hidden elements of the person: grief, fear, guilt, spiritual/
existential distress. Such an approach takes time, however, and often
cannot be accomplished at one encounter, especially in the busy, dis-
tracted environment of modern health care. It is also relational, predicated on the development of a relationship of trust between the patient
and the caregiver wherein their individual stories converge. This convergence must also occur with a full recognition by the caregiver of the
absolute necessity of maintaining professional and personal boundaries
while at the same time creating a point of real convergence between
two persons.[67] This can often be facilitated by the participation and
collaboration of members of an interdisciplinary team, in order to gain
the strength inherent in multiple perspectives while also protecting the
patient and caregiver by involvement of multiple persons.

Rita Charon defines narrative competence as, "the set of skills
required to recognize, absorb, interpret, and be moved by the stories
one hears or reads."[68] She emphasizes how critical these skills are to
the success of the would-be healer. "To enter a story is to make room
for its teller, and the doctor with narrative skills habitually confirms the
patient's worth in the process of attending seriously to what he or she
tells." Dr Charon emphasizes a very important element for understanding the relatiship between narrative and suffering in stating, "Only
in the telling is the suffering made evident."[69] It is this competence to
interact effectively with patients and the stories of their illnesses that
may be central to the effective acquisition of a truly holistic medical
history. Such competence "requires a combination of:

1. textual skills (identifying a story's structure, adopting its mul-
    tiple perspectives, recognizing metaphors and allusions);

[67]This will be a major focus of the discussion presented in Part 2 of this book:
"The Therapeutic Encounter."
    [68]R. Charon, "Narrative and Medicine," *New England Journal of Medicine* 350(9)
(2004): 862–4.
    [69]Ibid.

2. creative skills (imagining many interpretations, building curiosity, inventing multiple endings); and

3. affective skills (tolerating uncertainty as a story unfolds, entering the story's mood)."[70] The clinician who has acquired narrative competence "becomes a witness and not a judge, a companion and not an interrogator, an ally and not simply the bearer of bad news or inflictor of discomfort."[71]

Dr Charon has described a new approach to the practice of medicine, i.e., narrative medicine, which may represent in many respects the rediscovery of an older form of the healer's art. Narrative medicine is "medicine practiced with the narrative competence to recognize, interpret, and be moved by the predicaments of others."[72] By virtue of its approach, narrative medicine restores balance between the individual and statistics, "both the singular and the statistically significant must be comprehended in the study of disease or its treatment."[73] Training programs in narrative medicine:

1. "teach specific aspects of narrative competence;

2. "encourage health care professionals and students to write about their patients in nontechnical language, helping them to uncover and understand their implicit feelings toward and knowledge of their patients; and

3. "provide rigorous training in reading literary texts to supply health professionals with the equipment to interpret and make sense of the stories of others."[74]

[70]Ibid.

[71]R. Charon, "Narrative Medicine Creates Alliance with Patients," *Medscape from WebMD*, posted 19 January 2006, accessed 12 November, 2010.

[72]R. Charon, "Narrative Medicine: Form, Function, and Ethics," *Annals of Internal Medicine* 134(1) (2001): 83–87.

[73]Ibid.

[74]Ibid.

The approach to caring for the sick developed in narrative medicine in many respects represents the opportunity for the healer to engage in a very different form of the therapeutic encounter. It also represents a way to truly enhance the quality of the work done by the medical 'detective'. Essential clues that can emerge only from a more complete understanding of patients' stories can then further guide the effective diagnosis and management of not only their diseases but also their suffering. There is a recognition that in the convergence of the stories of both the patient and the healer, a critically necessary element of healing is taking place. In part 2 of this book, the nature of the therapeutic encounter will be examined in greater depth.

"All illness . . . has . . . two dimensions: a physical deficit and a spiritual violation. And when there is no cure, the one thing we can offer is to really understand the story that is playing out, to aid and abet its satisfactory conclusion."[75]

---

[75] A. Verghese, ibid.

PART 2

The Therapeutic Encounter

"The refusal of all forms of suffering and the suppression of pain as the highest value of civilization and the consummation of social development; the fear of biological death considered as the absolute end of human existence: all of this leads a great many of our contemporaries to expect that salvation comes from medicine and encourages them to make of the physician a new priest of modern times."[1]

[1]Jean-Claude Larchet, *The Theology of Illness*, trans. by John & Michael Breck (Crestwood, NY: St Vladimir's Seminary Press, Crestwood, 2002), 11–12.

CHAPTER 4

Defining the Encounter

A N ELDERLY WOMAN is walking down her narrow cobblestoned street, trying not to stumble, on her way to visit her friend, another woman of advanced years, who has been her longtime confidant and is also the godmother for her children. Although she is walking more slowly because of increasing fatigue and pain in her back that have been a growing problem, she feels happy and hopeful that she will see her friend soon. As she walks, she is comforted by the thought, "I know she will have some good advice for me."

What is a therapeutic encounter? What specifically makes an encounter therapeutic? Does the intent behind the encounter determine whether or not it is therapeutic? Is special expertise required on the part of one or more participants in the encounter? Can it only be called therapeutic based on outcomes? What kinds of outcomes qualify as 'therapeutic'? What elements make up a therapeutic encounter? Which are essential? Which are peripheral? Is the encounter always characterized by an unequal interaction, i.e., not an interaction between equals? What are the minimum and maximum numbers of participants necessary to the encounter? Does the therapeutic character of the encounter always flow in one direction?

Considering the vignette described above of the old woman who is visiting her friend: Does this constitute a therapeutic encounter? This chapter will explore the nature of the therapeutic encounter between physician (or other health professional) and patient but always with an awareness that the role of healer (and one in need of healing) may be assumed by anyone. For in some very real sense, every human person is called upon to be a healer in a multiplicity of 'therapeutic encounters' throughout one's life.

Different models of medicine have been described which attempt to define the therapeutic encounter. Among these models are:

+ The reductionist or biomedical model, i.e., medicine is applied biology (Donald Seldin);

+ The expansionist model where medicine is more than biology; it also includes psychology, sociology, and "the patient and his attributes as a person" (George Engel);

+ Medicine defined in terms of its end or purpose, e.g., 'Health' is the end of medicine (Leon Kass); and

+ The physician-patient relationship as viewed within a phenomenological approach—Medicine is defined within a negotiated agreement between the patient and physician.[1]

When one considers this last model, is the therapeutic encounter essentially a transaction? Certainly, the encounter between physician and patient often takes on aspects of such an exchange. The physician must help the sick person answer four questions:

1 What is wrong?

2 What will it do to me?

3 What can be done for me?

4 What should be done for me?[2]

Is there room in such a transaction for a relationship, and if so, what kind of relationship? It is not a relationship of equals. One becomes a patient when one turns to another (e.g., physician, caregiver, or healer) for specialized help or assistance. The special knowledge and skills of the physician or healer represent real or perceived power over the

[1]E.D. Pellegrino, "The Healing Relationship: The Architectonics of Clinical Medicine," in E.E. Shelp, ed., *The Clinical Encounter* (Dordrecht, The Netherlands: D. Reidel Publishing Co., 1983), 153–172.
    [2]Ibid.

patient. The relationship is often characterized by a sense of helplessness on the part of the patient—being at the mercy of the physician.

Modern medical dualism affects the relationship profoundly. The focus on disease discovery and treatment shifts priorities dramatically. For example, on an economic level, in general physicians are paid to treat disease, not to care for human suffering. The incentives drive the physician/healer away from forming relationships. Reimbursement comes from a proper diagnosis and disease-focused treatment plan, not time spent supporting another suffering person. With regard to physician-patient communication, the focus is entirely on determining the diagnosis of a treatable physical condition (i.e., disease). However, diseases don't suffer, persons suffer. The suffering of the patient, the concerns which brought the person to the physician in the first place, may not be addressed at all. Ultimately, with a therapeutic encounter reduced to the level of a transaction. there may be a lost sense of vocation on the part of the physician/healer. A pure biological reductionist approach in which the patient is reduced to being a repository of disease is antithetical to seeing the patient as a person, especially one whose suffering is an icon of the suffering of the Crucified One.

There are several important goals of effective physician-patient communication. The first is to build a real relationship of trust. Mutual trust must be based on complete honesty. However, being honest does not mean bludgeoning patients with the 'truth'. Informed consent applies as much to sharing potentially traumatic information as to performing an operation. This may mean establishing mutually acceptable ground rules for communication (e.g., direct to patient or indirect through family). One must be sensitive to cultural differences which will often define the acceptable pattern of communication. Essential to this process is acquiring the skill of giving one's full and undivided attention to the patient as a person.

In addition to creating a relationship of trust, there must be an actual exchange of information between the physician/healer and the patient. The patient has a need to know what the problem is and to understand it while also feeling known and understood by the physician (i.e., taken seriously). Patients who are allowed to tell their story (given more time to speak during an interview) are more likely to trust their physician. Unfortunately, physicians tend to underestimate their patients' need for information and often convey the information in confusing technical language or medical jargon.

Effective medical decision-making by both patients and physicians cannot occur without good communication. Two different models of this process have been used in medical practice:

1. Paternalistic (physician-centered) in which a physician uses an unequal relationship to direct decision making by the patient (with variations on the typical pattern); and

2. Shared decision making (patient-centered) in which the patient is given as much information as possible and is encouraged to make an 'informed' decision.

A balance of both is probably best, although the process is dependent on culture, age, and even gender.

Within the therapeutic encounter, most patients' concerns can be grouped into seven dimensions of care:

1. *Respect for patients' values, preferences, and expressed needs*— What are the patient's goals of care, both in the short and long term? What is the patient's desired role in the decision making process?

2. *Coordination and integration of care*—Does the patient receive consistent information, and is the care that is provided seamless, thoroughly integrated with all other aspects of the patient's care?

3. *Communication and education*—Does the patient have the information s/he needs to manage as independently as possible?

4. *Physical comfort*—Is pain relieved? Are basic needs (e.g., self-care, etc.) being met? Has the ability to function independently (functional status) been maximized?

5. *Emotional support and alleviation of fears and anxieties*—Have fears regarding the illness' impact on personal survival, functional status, financial and social security been addressed? Is there a supportive social network (e.g., friends, family, church, etc.)?

6. *Involvement of family and friends*—Are family and friends included in an appropriate way in the planning and provision of care?

7. *Continuity and transition*—Do the patient and family (friends) understand the plan of care (e.g., which medications to take, when, and follow up issues)?

The goal of including the patient's perspective should be to create an informed dialogue which promotes sharing of responsibility. This sense of shared responsibility or partnership in one's care has been shown to enhance clinical outcomes.[3]

As has been mentioned earlier in this book, there is a critical need for physicians to pay great attention to patients' stories of their illnesses, to step back from the role of being disease detectives for at least a brief moment. It is essential to fully absorb the patient's story, for the person is often hidden within the story and revealed by its telling. The process must transcend the standard history and physical and represent a combined effort of both patient and physician.[4] It is this combined effort built on trust that can be a solid foundation for a real therapeutic encounter. Important elements in the joint construction of narrative by patient and physician include:

+ Patients must be fully involved. There must be 'give-and-take' in the dialogue between physician and patient. Physicians must allow patients to find their voice and thus may need to subordinate their own need for control in the process.

[3]T.L. Delbanco, "Enriching the Doctor-Patient Relationship by Inviting the Patient's Perspective," *Annals of Internal Medicine* 116 (1999): 414–418.

[4]H. Brody, "My Story is Broken: Can You Help Me Fix It? Medical Ethics and the Joint Construction of Narrative," *Literature and Medicine* 13 (1994): 79–92.

+ The narrative or explanation of what is wrong must be meaningful from the perspective of the patient. The physician may have to respectfully address misplaced preconceptions the patient may have about the illness or even attempt to work to some extent within the 'flawed' framework of the patient's understanding where possible.

+ However, the story or explanation of the illness must be credible from a medical standpoint. Don't construct a story that is false or medically implausible to please the patient.

+ Ultimately, the narrative explaining the illness should facilitate a rapid recovery by the patient or help the patient adapt to new limitations imposed by the illness.

There is another often very challenging aspect to the therapeutic encounter, especially within large secular, pluralistic societies. In complex, diverse societies physicians and patients meet either as moral strangers or moral friends. Moral strangers often do not share the same set of beliefs or moral presuppositions (e.g., a Roman Catholic physician caring for a Muslim patient). Occasionally a patient and caregiver do share a common set of beliefs or world view as moral friends (e.g., a Buddhist physician caring for a Buddhist patient). Engelhardt has proposed the concept of a 'peaceable community' in which it is possible for 'moral strangers', physicians and patients to meet and negotiate with each other regarding care. Under these circumstances, the Golden Rule, "Do unto others what you would have them do unto you," becomes "Do not do unto others what they would not have done unto themselves, and do with them that which is mutually agreed," respecting autonomy; or "Do to others their good," with respect to the principle of beneficence.[5]

Physicians are no longer in authority but are authoritative 'travel guides' through the medical maze. "Physicians and patients must, then,

[5]H. Tristram Engelhardt, Jr., "The physician-patient relationship in a secular, pluralistic society," in *The Clinical Encounter*, 253–266.

live on two moral tiers, one, that of their particular moral community as well as that of the general secular society available to all individuals in a liberal individualistic nation-state: a state where respect for freedom is a constraint upon political actions, and authority is derived from the consent of those involved."[6] Where the relationship between moral strangers is unequal, this means that every effort must be made by the would-be healer to avoid the temptation to actively proselytize a vulnerable patient. The challenge is to remain faithful to one's convictions while protecting each patient's freedom.

Sometimes the therapeutic encounter is initiated in the context of a crisis—an emergency. Acute life-threatening illnesses or major operations can serve as life-transforming events by being "wake-up calls" for patients. It is important for physicians and surgeons to explore with their patients what an acute life-threatening illness or major operation means to them as individuals. Buried within their understanding (and fears) of what such major disruptions in their lives may mean to them are the seeds of much potential suffering as well as opportunities for growth as persons.[7]

In this chapter, a review of the medical literature has revealed that the therapeutic encounter has been described in many different ways, ranging from the perspective of a broadened biological worldview to a phenomenon of communication between individuals usually in an unequal relationship with all the opportunities for misunderstanding and potential moral ambiguity that implies. But is there something more? When the old woman described at the beginning of this chapter finally meets her friend, will a therapeutic encounter occur? It may be worthwhile to consider a very different model of the therapeutic encounter—medicine as mystery. A central element missing in all models of medicine is humility; humility of the physician/healer, humility of the approach—a recognition of the mystery inherent in each person. In Christianity, the therapeutic encounter, the healing relationship between patient and physician (or any healer) is redefined by the

[6]Ibid.
[7]T.J. Petry, "Surgery and Meaning," *Surgery* 127 (2000): 363–365.

incarnation. "As you did it to one of the least of these my brethren, you did it to me."[8] This is at the heart of the reciprocal character of healing, just witnessing the suffering of another, as did the repentant thief,[9] can be a transforming experience. A healing relationship defined within the reality of the incarnation may occur without words. All that may be necessary is to experience or witness (be present for) the suffering of another or for the suffering one to experience the compassion and love of the caregiver. Fundamentally, there can be a reciprocity of healing in the therapeutic encounter. The healer is the patient and the patient is the healer, because where a communion of love exists, the healing power of God is also fully present.

[8]Matthew 25.40.
[9]Luke 23.40ff.

CHAPTER 5

Total Pain and the Person

T HE SINE QUA NON of the therapeutic encounter is the person
(or in clinical language, the patient) whose distress or suffering
has been the catalyst to initiate the process. Returning to the concept of
Total Pain, individuals who suffer bring their distress to the therapeutic
encounter on at least four intersecting levels:

1. Physical—pain and other symptoms sufficiently distressing and
   persistent that they can no longer be ignored or are acutely dis-
   ruptive and may even be perceived as threatening to the individual's survival;

2. Psychological—changes in mood and anxiety (e.g., depression,
   grief, and panic), and/or altered cognition (e.g., confusion/delir-
   ium, dementia);

3. Social—altered relationships (e.g., interpersonal conflicts, loss
   of autonomy, loss of supports); and

4. Spiritual—threats to meaning, values, existence, and one's relationship to the Other.

Although discrete domains of pain are identified by the concept of
Total Pain, the lines separating the domains are cognitive boundaries, not necessarily real boundaries. Thus, physical pain is also experienced as psychological, social, and ultimately spiritual distress. The
converse is also true, that spiritual distress has physical aspects. In fact,
it may be primarily experienced by a majority of people on this level.
Of course, there are also 'pains' which have primarily a physical, psychological, social, or spiritual presentation; *but* always look for the other

domains—suffering affects the whole person and even transcends the individual. In this chapter, the many potential ways the intersecting elements of Total Pain can interact within the experience of suffering and how these must be recognized within the therapeutic encounter will be explored in greater detail.

For the would-be healer in the therapeutic encounter it is essential to recognize the suffering of the patient. As noted earlier, since suffering affects persons, the standard 'objective' measures used to diagnose physical ailments will not be helpful. Quite often suffering may be centered in a symptom or symptoms which threaten the integrity of the patient as a person. The meaning associated with a given symptom or symptoms may define the nature of the suffering experienced (e.g., if cancer-related pain is progressing, the fear of impending death can cause intense suffering). Failure to recognize and treat suffering is often a reflection of the inability of the caregiver to focus on the person rather than the disease. A 'blindness to persons'[1] often characterizes those (especially physicians) who have been trained to approach illness as a purely biological phenomenon. As discussed in the previous chapter, symptoms should no longer be mere clues to assist in making the diagnosis of a disease. More importantly, they are crucial elements of a story; the story of the patient's suffering. As health professionals and would-be healers engage with these central elements of the patient's suffering, they enter that story.

One should have a high index of suspicion that suffering is present when confronted with serious life-threatening illness accompanied by distressing symptoms. Be prepared to ask open-ended questions: "Are you suffering? What is the worst thing about all of this? . . . Are there things that are even worse than the physical pain? Are you frightened by all of this?"[2] Such an approach is relevant for all who would assume the role of healer and care for human suffering regardless of the type

---

[1] E.J. Cassell, "Diagnosing Suffering: A Perspective," *Annals of Internal Medicine* 131(7) (1999): 531–534.

[2] Ibid.

of professional training (i.e., clergy, as well as physicians and other caregivers).

It takes time, patience, and humility to diagnose and begin to understand the suffering of another. As you ask open-ended questions, be prepared to listen in the sense of the Greek word *akouo*, i.e., to understand, even with the potential for obedience/service (i.e., *hypakouo*).[3] Ask yourself who it is to whom you are listening in the suffering of the other. *Hypakouo* also implies a real inversion in the relationship between physician (healer) and patient—even a physical subordination. At times it may be essential to use a low chair or even kneel at the bedside of those who are suffering so that one can now look up to meet their gaze.

Additional questions/concerns persist regarding the diagnosis and recognition of suffering which relate to its fundamental nature. Do sources of individual suffering have different meanings for the same individual over time? The conscious perception of one's own suffering will be conditioned by the context in which it is experienced. For example, the same type and intensity of pain experienced in social isolation may be appreciated very differently when the person is no longer isolated and enjoys the support of others. The meaning associated with a particular symptom is not only determined by the individual directly experiencing the symptom but is also conditioned by the community or social network in which the person experiences distress. A common slogan that has been taught to young recruits in the U.S. Marine Corps is *Marines don't have pain*. Whereas this may be useful in the toughening of recruits for battle, when later those same individuals may be experiencing very real physical pain from a life-threatening illness or injury, the past training can be a source of intense suffering. Persons depend on their social networks to validate the reality of their distress. In some sense, we need permission from others to suffer (at least at the conscious level).

Can the same symptom/affliction cause different types of suffering on a communal level? Even if the symptom (or source of suffering) does

---

[3] Arndt and Gingrich, 31, 845.

not cause much apparent distress to the afflicted person, the symptom or affliction is also perceived by the wider community of the afflicted individual's social network and given various meanings by the persons within the network. It is possible that close contacts of the afflicted person may be conscious of even deeper suffering than that of the afflicted one. This underscores the communal aspect of suffering.

The role of consciousness in suffering is unclear. Do the cognitively impaired suffer? Do infants and children suffer? In other words, suffering may be a state of being, independent of self-perception. It may be possible that others, e.g., loved ones and caregivers, may *consciously* experience suffering or 'co-suffer' on behalf of those they love.

How does curative therapy relate to suffering? Not infrequently, a cure can come at the price of ongoing suffering, as a byproduct of treatment. The meaning and value of survival per se versus the quality of life that can be achieved after the cure may define the degree to which suffering is present. Suffering patients hoping for cure and their physicians must count the cost of treatment together, ideally before embarking on the therapeutic journey.

Answers to many of these questions may often be found through examination of the individual stories of patients' suffering. The stories presented here, starting with the physical domain, are intended to reflect real types of suffering encountered in the clinical setting and will highlight different facets of the intersecting elements of Total Pain.

Physical Pain

A 66-year-old man has received radiation to relieve intense difficulty swallowing caused by a locally advanced cancer at the junction between the esophagus and stomach. He now complains of progressive nausea and upper abdominal pain that interfere with his sleep. He is tearful when describing his symptoms. Before he became ill, he had a hearty appetite and always looked forward to meals with his wife. He is very much distressed by his inability to tolerate food even though his ability to swallow has improved significantly after the radiation. His wife is also upset by his apparent lack of appreciation for her cooking, which he had always enjoyed in the past.

At face value, this story appears to be primarily about severe physical distress. However, if one examines the context of this man's distress more closely, it is more like an onion than a solid sphere. As one layer is explored and stripped away, progressively deeper but related layers of distress are exposed. The following discussion illustrates some of the directions that a deeper exploration of his pain might take.

The very thing that used to be a consistent source of comfort and pleasure for him—eating, even though it is again a possibility for him after the radiation, is now accompanied by intense pain and nausea. There is no more 'comfort food' for him to anticipate with pleasure. Rather, this most basic pleasure has been transformed into a constant, palpably distressing reminder of his cancer, of his death!

Food, its acquisition, preparation, and consumption, is an activity, an experience central to human existence, to life itself. For those living in developed countries it may be mostly taken for granted, whereas for the many poor of the world it is the dominant concern driving one's daily struggle to survive. While the pursuit of food is a most basic force catalyzing human activity, the sharing of food in a common meal is perhaps the quintessential example of the shared experience of being human. Across all cultures, hospitality is most often demonstrated in the form of sharing one's sustenance, no matter how modest this may be.

Even though the relationship between this man and his wife may have begun with romantic infatuation when they were young, the old aphorism, "the way to a man's heart is through his stomach," is often truer than most would like to admit. Humans thrive on regularity and predictability. Their relationship has been cemented over many years by the common meals they have shared. His once ardent protestations of love for his wife may have degenerated into the more frequent, "That was a great meal!" Although that is not an adequate substitute for saying (and putting into practice), "I love you," his wife may have gradually accepted his appreciation for her cooking (and her unspoken love put into it) as the primary expression of their core relationship. Their extreme distress which has been initiated by the cancer through disruption of this central bond between them may appear to a casual observer as being out of proportion to such a seemingly 'trivial' loss.

There is also a deeper meaning associated with a shared meal, "breaking bread together." The union of believer with incarnate Savior takes place in the form of a meal. The metaphor is both mystery and reality. The mundane is transformed into the ineffable. "Take, eat; this is my body."[4] No earthly meal can be quite the same after these words were spoken. Whether or not the patient and his wife appreciate this deeper reality, the disruption of their shared meal by the cancer and all that it represents is connected mysteriously to that other meal. They are being challenged to rediscover and deepen their love for each other on a new level, stripped of former assumptions and laid bare in the face of death.

As in the story that was just examined, physical suffering typically demands priority in terms of treatment. It may isolate the one who suffers, may have tremendous symbolic meaning, and is rarely experienced without affecting the other domains of Total Pain, especially spiritual or existential pain. The existential distress created by physical suffering may in large part be due to the fact that it directly threatens one's denial of death.

During a home visit to follow up on her pain from progressive widely metastatic breast cancer, a 38-year-old mother of two children ages eight and ten tells her hospice nurse that she is a bad mother. When the nurse asks her why she thinks this, she responds, "I always used to enjoy preparing meals for my family and sitting with the children when they return from school to hear about their day. Now, I just feel too tired to fulfill my duties as a wife and mother. Frankly, I would rather take a nap. I feel so ashamed!"

Fatigue is often recognized as the most common and all-pervasive symptom of those with advanced illness. For active persons, fatigue represents an assault on a core element of their identity. The declining ability to perform one's normal duties, even the basic tasks of living,

[4]Matthew 26.26.

becomes an ever constricting band that progressively narrows one's existence and limits one's horizon. As associates at work or family members assume the responsibilities that the ill person can no longer fulfill, increasing social isolation follows. The mother's decreasing ability to provide for the basic needs of her children and perhaps especially her lack of energy to freely express her love for them in tangible ways, become tormenting reproaches to her, forcing her to question her fundamental identity as a mother and value as a person. Her world eventually becomes inverted. She is rapidly transitioning to one who is now dependent on those who only recently depended so heavily on her.

A 42-year-old woman seeks help for severe pain, numbness, and tingling in the right chest wall that has persisted seven months after a mastectomy for cancer. She is quite tearful during the clinic visit. "Everyone tells me I should not complain but be grateful, since my surgeon says I am cured of the cancer. The pain is so bad I don't want to get close to my husband. Besides, I don't feel like a complete woman anymore. I don't see how he could find me attractive now."

Not infrequently, those who survive, who are 'cured' of their life-threatening illnesses, bear the long-term effects of their treatment and struggle with the illness to their graves. Their suffering can take the form of a special and unique burden of living a distorted existence, cured but maimed, with chronic unremitting pain or other symptoms and disabilities as constant reminders of the limitations of medical treatment. The ideal outcome after curative treatment for a life-threatening illness should be not only conquest of the disease (e.g., cancer) threatening the person's existence, but also relief of the distress caused by the disease and restoration of function that may have been impaired by the presence of the disease. Unfortunately, the treatment often leaves its permanent mark on the "cured" person. There may be a limited ability to function. The patient may even be unemployable. With the change or loss of function may come loss of one's identity, e.g., "I'm not the same person that I was before the operation." Relationships including intimacy may be dramatically altered following disfiguring operations, thus creating great social pain. Chronic pain after curative treatment can be especially challenging, as it is often invisible to others. The label "cure" implies that everything is fixed, there are no more problems. Any complaints after a "cure" almost suggest ingratitude. "Why, you should be all better by now!" This reverberates in the mind of the "cured" patient as survivor guilt. "Why did I survive, when so many others have not? Why am I complaining when I have been cured?" Diseases may be cured but persons need to be healed.

Psychological Pain

A 75-year-old man with a history of chronic depression is told by his physician of his new diagnosis of advanced pancreatic cancer. He expresses a sense of resignation when he hears the bad news: "I expected something bad. My whole life has been a painful struggle. It only seems fitting that I should also die in agony."

Although the incidence of depression is known to be increased in patients with pancreatic cancer, the tone of irony in this patient's voice should alert his physician to the possibility that there may be more involved in his patient's response to the bad news. Here is a life story crying out to be told. The critical questions are, Who will listen? and What will be the quality of the listening? The cumulative psychological suffering of a lifetime is now culminating in this man's terminal illness. His only frame of reference is his past suffering, which has now become the lens magnifying and defining his distress. It is highly likely that even if his cancer produces significant physical pain as it progresses, its major expression in this man's experience may be to further exacerbate his deep depression and despair. Clinicians may need to 'adjust' their skills as listeners according to the nature of the story unfolding before them. They must seek to understand and to identify the lenses through which their patients perceive their distress. In the psychological wounds and scars of a lifetime may be hidden the key to unlocking the prison of a patient's present suffering. "Please tell me about your struggle. I am here to listen," might be a good start, especially if the clinician sits down with the patient and fully attends. In all humility, it may be essential to recognize one's limits and draw on the expertise of colleagues with advanced training in psychology and psychiatry to collaboratively address such deep and complex distress, without abandoning the patient.

On morning rounds at a residential hospice, the nurse from the night shift reports that one of the patients, a 53-year-old woman with widely metastatic melanoma, was up several times during the night asking for medication to 'relax' even though she reported better pain control than upon admission. The nurse also comments that she was anxious when left alone. The patient seems calmer this morning but appears tired. She was admitted for inpatient hospice care yesterday because of uncontrolled pain from new subcutaneous nodules on her left chest wall. The melanoma originally presented on her right leg.

Visible, palpable signs of disease progression in cancer are as powerful in their psychological impact as any vision of the 'Grim Reaper'. Night is meant for sleep but sleep is also a metaphor for death. Even the metaphor can evoke terror in one facing the imminence of death, thus preventing sleep. Intense anxiety is generated by the thing that must not be named (for naming it would make it real). Even though there may be a desire to talk more directly about one's fears of death, the use of euphemisms (e.g., passing away, etc.) and avoidance of saying the 'D' word in many cultures, including modern Western society, reinforce the taboo against speaking about it directly. The increasing psychic tension of avoidance with the need to confront the issue may frequently erupt as intense anxiety. Medications should never be used as an alternative to allowing persons in distress to express and discuss their fears. However, if patients are so anxious that they cannot calm down sufficiently to acquire much needed rest prior to facing the fearful word, medications as well as other interventions (to be discussed later) to address the anxiety may be essential.

An 83-year-old woman with multiple myeloma is admitted to inpatient hospice care for worsening confusion and agitation. Her daughter who lives with her has been giving her increasing doses of lorazepam (an anti-anxiety medication) to calm the increasing agitation. When asked about the agitation, the daughter indicated that her mother was complaining of pain and sleeplessness, so she gave her the lorazepam because of her fears of giving "too much morphine."

Sometimes, through ignorance or misunderstanding, good intentions can exacerbate suffering. Paradoxically, but especially in the elderly, in the context of uncontrolled pain the use of anti-anxiety medications may result in worsening agitation and confusion (delirium). Here two anxieties have collided to cause greater suffering. The escalating anxiety of the mother due to increasing, poorly controlled pain interacts with the well-meaning but ill-founded fears and anxiety of the daughter regarding the potential dangers of morphine. Although the mother's descent into delirium may represent some form of physiological defense against severe uncontrolled pain, it has not lessened her fundamental need for pain relief, only made it much more difficult for her to clearly express her pain and for her daughter to recognize it. There is an 'infectious' character to psychological distress, especially with regard to anxiety, and this character can catalyze the extension of psychological pain to a shared social pain.

A 38-year-old mother of two children (ages 12 and 15) has advanced metastatic cervical cancer. She is extremely cachectic (i.e., severe weight loss and muscle wasting), has been bedfast in a residential hospice for the last five days, and is having trouble swallowing her medications. Her husband and children are present much of the time at her bedside keeping vigil. She is alert and appears calm when her family is present. Her nurse reports, however, that she has been extremely anxious and tearful during the times her family has been away.

Grief is not just an experience of the bereaved. The dying also grieve their losses and the impending separation from loved ones (i.e., they experience anticipatory grief). It may be very difficult for this mother to process her anticipatory grief as her family keeps nearly constant vigil at her bedside, especially if they prevent any discussion or acknowledgement of what is coming. A verbal denial of her impending death by her husband or children may impel her to be complicit in the denial to spare them further distress, while at the same time she has so much she needs to share with them about their future without her. The tradition described so movingly in the scriptural accounts of the Old Testament patriarchs giving their last blessings to their children is being denied to her. If she does try to discuss these larger issues and either her husband or one of her children emphatically state, "You must not say that. We couldn't go on without you," her suffering will be intensified ten-fold. Her family must in some way give her permission to die as she needs in a similar manner to give them her parting 'blessing'. Caregivers should be sensitive to these dynamics and gently aid the process of this family dialogue. Medication to sedate a dying person who is experiencing this form of anxiety will only thwart the process.

A 48-year-old schizophrenic man is a common sight on the streets of his city near the main square. One day he is brought to the emergency department of the city hospital after he coughs up a cupful of blood. X-rays reveal a large mass in his right upper lung. On examination he is very thin with labored breathing at rest and moves slowly getting out of bed. He denies pain, shortness of breath, or other symptoms. He is anxious to get back out on to the streets, mumbling something about the important work he is doing in collaboration with the pigeons on the square.

Even though individuals with schizophrenia who have advanced illnesses may often deny or minimize physical distress, it is not at all clear whether their disordered thinking (i.e., psychotic symptoms) actually protects them from suffering. He may not be able to perceive or understand the illness as a threat to his integrity as a person in the same way a person without serious mental illness would perceive it. However, the ability to comprehend a threat to one's integrity as a person should not be the sole criterion for identifying the presence of suffering. After all, who among us fully understands the nature of the threats that confront us as persons? It is worth remembering at this point that the ancient Greek meaning of the word *pascho* from which we derive suffering originally meant, "have something done to one."[5] The notion of its

[5]Liddell and Scott, 1285, 1347.

being primarily a bad thing that happened to one developed over time and began to approximate suffering by the early Christian era. Its full meaning in the Christian context came only with the development of the Church's understanding of Christ's suffering. It is very important to emphasize the sense in which the passive nature of this experience may be central to the whole concept of suffering. Bad things happen to human persons, not necessarily by their choice, and yet this reality is the foundation upon which we build our lives. Indeed, none of us chooses to exist. Nonetheless, we come into existence, sometimes good but quite often bad things happen to us (we suffer), and we eventually die. For the mentally ill, this tragic aspect of being human is frequently a life-long struggle with bad things happening to them. Moreover, the daily, even moment-by-moment struggle for a schizophrenic to differentiate 'real' from 'unreal' is a special form of suffering in which the real person is continually in process of emerging but only incompletely and with a distorted image.

Mental illness is often a barrier to good care and is already a source of social isolation. When the mentally ill are able to make decisions, they are often reticent to execute advance directives (i.e., documents stating preferences about their care at the end of life) in spite of being competent. They may be less willing to consider *Do Not Resuscitate* orders and/or withdrawal of life-sustaining therapies.[6] Even though their whole life may have been filled with suffering on a daily basis, they often seem to value that less-than-perfect life as something very precious. Mental health providers are often surrogate family for the mentally ill. When death is approaching, it is crucial to strengthen the connections to their 'family', and doing so may even require unconventional strategies to provide care for their increasing distress. As much as possible, this may mean bringing the support and care they need to them in an environment that is familiar, supportive, and non-threatening,

[6]M.E. Foti, "Massachusetts State Mental Health Program," accessed on 6 June, 2012 at: http://www.promotingexcellence.org/mentalillness/3303.html. This is an excellent resource that addresses the special needs of those with serious mental illness at the end of life.

which in the case of this gentleman might be outside a hospital setting, at least initially.

The way in which the seriously mentally ill experience the often severe pain and other distressing physical symptoms which accompany advanced illnesses like cancer is a powerful example of how tightly integrated the different domains of Total Pain are. Symptom assessment is more complex and difficult. They often have distorted pain perception and may be poor historians. Worsening psychotic symptoms may be the only signs of increasing physical distress.

Fundamentally, psychological distress affects the way one perceives one's suffering. Altered mood, high anxiety, reduced or distorted cognitive function, or an intense grief reaction all become filters through which the 'reality' of one's affliction is perceived, and they often intensify the suffering and paralyze one's response to it. At the same time, the assessment and relief of suffering in this context can be very challenging and difficult. To the degree to which psychological 'pain' inhibits the ability for self-reflection, real growth and healing at the end of life may be compromised.

When physical pain is controlled, depression and anxiety are not a threat, and one is able to reflect clearly, are there still specifically psychological or emotional forms of suffering? I propose that there are at least five distinct forms of psychological pain that contribute to the Total Pain of those who are struggling with advanced life-threatening illnesses:

1. Uncertainty/Fear;
2. Denial/Procrastination;
3. Sense of isolation/Abandonment;
4. Shame/Guilt; and
5. Grief/Yearning.

The following case studies will illustrate how these different forms of psychological distress can contribute to Total Pain.

A 75-year-old woman with chronic lymphocytic leukemia is quite anxious and agitated when she comes to her physician's office for a follow up appointment. She has been reading on the internet about her disease and reports that she discovered from her research that the course of the disease can be quite variable with the potential for rapid progression and death. She states that she had the impression from prior consultations that the disease is not immediately life-threatening. She then declares that she cannot live with such uncertainty.

Uncertainty, especially uncertainty about what the future holds regarding a life-threatening illness, is very difficult for most human beings to endure. Oddly enough, it is not infrequently the ally of denial. Thus, denial and uncertainty may co-exist simultaneously in the same individual. Uncertainty is an inherent part of the practice of medicine. Biological systems are less predictable because of complexity and individual variation. Uncertainty is a great source of anxiety and psychological suffering not only for patients but also for their physicians. It is particularly intolerable for the sick because of the apparent or real threat of the illness to their existence. Urgent decisions are demanded by the threat imposed by the illness and the need to act/treat. When certainty is most needed, its lack greatly complicates the lives of the seriously ill and can paralyze the decision-making process. Death is a certainty. The timing of death is not so certain. Prognostication is notoriously difficult. "Does it have to be a certainty for me, right now? Can't we make it a theoretical consideration, a potential adverse outcome of treatment, for a bit longer?"

Uncertainty, denial, and fear are inextricably linked to each other. Fear and uncertainty can act as the enemies of denial. Uncertainty is a sword that cuts both ways. Uncertainty that one's most optimistic hopes and predictions for the future are not realistic erodes one's denial. Fear and uncertainty about death, an event ultimately beyond human control, threatens the illusion of control that so many humans depend upon to function each day and to plan for the future. "Trust in others is one of the central human solutions to the paralysis of unbearable uncertainty. For these reasons the sick put their trust in doctors.

The requirement for trust adds to the relationship between doctor and patient. Sick persons, then, are people who are forced to trust. The better the doctor, the more trustworthy and the stronger the relationship. But doctors are also faced with uncertainties and are also threatened."[7] For some patients, the 'bad' news of a new diagnosis of a life-threatening illness, or of learning about the progression of their disease (e.g., advanced cancer) can be easier to bear than continued uncertainty. Sometimes, patients will even express a real sense of relief just to know what they are facing.

A 64-year-old woman with progressive pancreatic cancer with liver metastases, three years after a 'curative' pancreatic resection, has been referred for pain and symptom management. She is complaining of severe pain at multiple sites but is very reticent to take strong opioid pain medication, saying, "I shouldn't need that yet." After several attempts to control her pain with weaker analgesics, she reluctantly agrees to trial morphine but then insists on taking a lower than effective dose and is still uncomfortable.

Persons struggling with serious life-threatening illnesses manifest their denial in many ways that are often linked to their interpretation of particular symptoms. A conscious recognition that one's cancer-related pain is getting worse would be a tacit recognition that the disease is progressing and is therefore rejected. Denial regarding a terminal diagnosis may ultimately increase anxiety and not be an effective coping strategy. In the multisite longitudinal *Coping with Cancer Study*, patients with advanced cancer who were able to identify themselves as "terminally ill" and "at peace" were defined as having "peaceful awareness" of their prognosis.[8] "Peacefully aware" patients had less psychological distress, were more likely to have advance care discussions with their physicians, and had the highest overall quality of death as reported by their caregivers after their death. Caregivers of peacefully aware patients were in better

[7]E.J. Cassell, *The Nature of Suffering and the Goals of Medicine*, 2nd ed. (Oxford University Press, 2004), 71. By permission of Oxford University Press, USA.

[8]A. Ray, S.D. Block, R.J. Friedlander, B. Zhang, P.K. Maciejewski, and H.G. Prigerson, "Peaceful Awareness in Patients with Advanced Cancer," *Journal of Palliative Medicine* 9(6) (2006): 1359–1368.

physical and mental health six months after the loss than the caregivers of those who were aware but not peaceful. The majority of patients who were aware that they were terminally ill were also able to be at peace. The challenge is to gently assist patients in confronting their denial. This usually requires a relationship of trust between the patient and health professional which may evolve only slowly over considerable time and multiple encounters.

A 73-year-old woman with advanced colon cancer that has spread to her liver and lungs is losing weight and struggling with increasing fatigue but is still relatively pain free. She understands that her illness is incurable. In conversations with the hospice social worker she has expressed regret that she quarreled with her sister 10 years ago but is still not speaking with her. When the social worker offers to help her make contact with her sister, she says, "Oh, I'm not ready for that yet."

There is often a powerful emotional inertia or even an apparent 'paralysis' of the will that seems to inhibit acts of reconciliation at the end of life. Procrastination is a variant form of denial. It can completely interrupt any effort at addressing the 'unfinished business' of the dying. In Christian terms it is closely linked to repentance or the lack thereof. She may be afraid of the powerful emotions that are often involved in the process of reconciliation. There may be other factors involved inhibiting action on her part. Pride or persistent malice may be preventing her from addressing this urgent issue. Perhaps on a deeper level, she may even be afraid that if she is reconciled with her sister, there would be no more compelling issues keeping her alive. Unfortunately, she may be comfortable with the way things are. Change, especially when it may involve personal humiliation, can be very painful. Healing rarely comes without a cost. These issues need to be explored with her in a non-threatening manner. Gentle but persistent reminders, encouragement based on positive memories of the subject, may be the most helpful in overcoming this form of denial. Helping her find a common ground for empathy with her sister may go much further than fear of judgment in the next life.

A hospice physician is asked to see a 69-year-old woman with advanced colon cancer that has grown through her abdominal wall and replaced it with a large foul smelling cauliflower-like mass of necrotic tumor. The nurses and other visitors are unwilling to enter her room because the odor makes them quite nauseated. As a result, this normally very sociable lady has become quite isolated and has been left alone in her room most of the time.

This unfortunate woman is not likely to find much refuge from her distress in denial. It is very difficult for denial to overcome the very powerful witness of one's senses. Psychological suffering is also a sensual experience. Because persons are not disembodied spirits, suffering, especially psychological suffering, can be enhanced through the senses. Foul smells, horrible visual spectacles, cacophonous sounds, and even strong tastes may all contribute to intensify the psychological distress of the suffering one as well as that of the witnesses to the suffering. These may form the substrate upon which very painful life-long memories are formed. Such intense assaults on the senses can also paralyze or substantially weaken the most resolute commitment to be compassionate. This wavering in the face of such strong sensual challenges can threaten the core identity of those who by vocation or choice have wanted to be with those who suffer. Here is manifest a form of deep psychological suffering shared on a social or communal level, but often not recognized as such, thus serving to isolate the sufferers, one from another. The terminally ill are the 'lepers' of today. Death is not a socially acceptable companion. The smell of rotting, decaying flesh is too powerful a reminder for most of us of our own mortality, let alone the appearance of a loved one becoming progressively weaker and debilitated. The dying feel their isolation acutely. It is a very powerful force that can overcome even the greatest denial. Unfortunately, it often can be interpreted as a message, saying, "You have tarried in this world too long and have now become an embarrassment and scandal to your neighbors and to those whom you love," rather than a helpful corrective to unrealistic denial.

A 64-year-old man with multiple myeloma is admitted to the hospital because of a pain crisis. Previous pain flares have responded well to adjustments in his chemotherapeutic regimen. He is now requiring high doses of morphine to achieve partial control of his intense rib and sternal pain and is still unable to get out of bed due to severe pain with movement. He is distressed that his pain hasn't responded during this admission to the chemotherapy as it has in the past and becomes very angry when his hematologist tells him that there are no more treatment options available. "When I first came to you, you said there were plenty of treatment options!"

Physicians are not adequately taught how to prepare their patients (or themselves) for the potential of bad outcomes. For physicians who are sworn enemies of death, every death is a personal failure. A physician's denial is linked to a unique medical form of 'denial' in which there is 'no more treatment available' with the implication that the patient has failed the treatment, rather than an inadequate treatment has failed the patient. The frustration of the physician who would otherwise continue to treat, and the anguish of the patient who is 'abandoned', combine to form a unique collaborative form of psychological suffering. This is compounded by misconceptions on the part of both the patient who desperately wants help and the physician who wants to help. If not resolved, it may leave the remaining life experience of the patient somewhat embittered, and puts the physician at risk for burnout and, over time, even despair.

A 54-year-old man with a past history of intravenous drug use, chronic hepatitis C, and the recent diagnosis of advanced hepatocellular carcinoma (liver cancer) is an inpatient in a hospice. Although he is experiencing considerable pain in his abdomen and spine from his extensive disease burden, he is resisting taking strong opioid pain medications. "I deserve this pain. It is my punishment, my penance, for the sins of my youth."

Suffering that is consciously experienced does not exist in a psychological vacuum. Some of those who are aware of their suffering and are able to engage in personal reflection may identify a 'logical' cause-effect relationship between their past behaviors and their current suffering.

One's life history and its personal interpretation can form the substrate or foundation for future suffering.

A 36-year-old woman is an inpatient in hospice with far advanced cervical cancer. On rounds, the hospice physician asks her if the pain at multiple sites from her extensive cancer burden is adequately controlled. She initially nods yes, but then begins to sob uncontrollably. As her physician tries to console her, between sobs she points to her heart, saying, "Here, it is not controlled." She then goes on to describe the incredible devotion her husband has shown her throughout their marriage and especially during this illness. She then says, "I am not worthy of such love. I was unfaithful to him several years ago. I cannot bear the thought of him knowing about it. I am so ashamed!"

These two stories illustrate different aspects of how shame and guilt as forms of psychological pain interact in contributing to Total Pain. By their very nature, shame and guilt are forms of psychological suffering that extend outside the self, outside one's ego, connecting one to the suffering of others. Secret sins/wounds to relationships are a hidden but very real form of suffering, a shared suffering that may not be fully, consciously appreciated by all of those affected, at least not in this life. The fear of exposure is a special form of psychological torment. It threatens our core self-image and attacks our pride.

There is sometimes a strong desire to suffer as an act of contrition for past wrongs or sins. When the opportunity to suffer is directly linked to the apparent outcome of the past evil for which one feels contrition, it almost seems like a gift. For hospice providers, pain is always an enemy. For hospice patients, it may sometimes be considered a friend. Can there be a balance of walking beside our patients who have accepted their unique crosses, offering to support them when they stumble under the weight of their burden while not completely removing their burden which may have become for them a source of healing, even though we suffer in witnessing their distress?

A busy surgeon is unable to be present for much of the gradual decline and death of his elderly mother in a distant city secondary to multiple debilitating chronic illnesses. Although he is present for her funeral and the brief family

gathering afterward, he plunges back into the intense clinical routine of his
work immediately after returning home. A month later, he is informed by
an inpatient hospice of the death from recurrent disease of one of his patients
whom he had followed closely for three years after performing an operation
for pancreatic cancer. At this moment he is struck with an overwhelming
wave of grief for both this patient and his mother.

It is interesting how seemingly unrelated events (e.g., the two deaths) can make connections that trigger powerful emotions. The phenomenon of delayed grief represents the paradox of apparently better coping with grief (repressed emotions) at the time of loss with a later breakdown, versus intense emotions at the time of loss with better coping later (getting on with the "work of grieving"). The surgeon had the opportunity to provide the kind of detailed attention to caring for his patient with progressive pancreatic cancer that he desired to provide his mother during her decline but was denied by limited time and distance. Apparently, because of the close proximity in time between these two parallel events in his life, a mysterious emotional link between this patient's care and fate and that of his mother had formed in his psyche. Although grief is a highly personal experience, it is also a reflection, a mirror, of the relationships that form consciously and unconsciously between caregivers and dying persons. Preparatory grief is defined as the mourning of the terminally ill for the losses implicit in death. These include anticipated separation from loved ones, loss of position, independence, role in family, even the simple pleasures of life, as well as missed opportunities and regrets.[9] Individuals close to the patient, loved ones and even unrelated caregivers, also experience preparatory grief in a reciprocal manner with the patient, anticipating the imminent separation of death. Each human being through suffering, death, and the grief engendered by one's loss in some sense becomes an icon of the "Man of Sorrows" in whom the suffering and grief of the whole of humanity and the cosmos throughout time were concentrated. Our

[9]V.S. Periyakoil, and J. Hallenbeck, "Identifying and managing preparatory grief and depression at the end of life," *American Family Physician* 65 (2002): 883–90.

individual griefs are thus connected mysteriously with each other through the incarnation.

An 82-year-old widower has been steadily declining in his health from a slowly progressive renal carcinoma (kidney cancer) which has metastasized (spread) to several bones and both lungs. His daughter complains that he keeps asking her, "How much longer will I live? I miss your mother so much!" He is admitted to an inpatient hospice a few weeks later, after he becomes too weak to stand. The next morning on rounds, he tells you with great joy, "I saw her, I saw her!" When you ask, "Who did you see?" He replies, "I saw my wife. She came and told me that it is time for me to come and join her."

Grief, desire, and yearning form a bittersweet mixture that affects the dying and their relationships. After formal grieving ends, a persistent desire for the missing one by the bereaved in the form of a deep yearning may remain. In the elderly especially, such yearning may serve as a counterpoint to the process of preparatory grieving, sweetening the suffering. The desire for reunion with the beloved may be a positive force in overcoming denial. It may also play an important role in the healing of memories and reconciliation. Preparatory grief, on the other hand, can represent an opportunity for stripping away all pretense, the hypocrisy of one's existence. "I have no regrets," equals an unexamined life. Should not one grieve for one's mistakes, for the evil committed, the wounding of others?

Social Suffering—The Communal Aspect

"The harmonious ... family, their well-adjusted way of life ... in the space of a few days all this had been cut off from him. It was now on the *other* side of his tumor. They were alive and would go on living, whatever happened to their father. However much they might worry, fuss or weep, the tumor was growing like a wall behind him, and on his side of it he was alone."[10]

[10]A. Solzhenitsyn, *Cancer Ward*, trans. by N. Bethell and D. Burg (New York: Farrar, Straus, and Giroux, 1974), 16.

Social suffering is rooted in relationships. For each person who suffers, there exists the possibility of an ever expanding circle, social network, or community of those who are presented with the opportunity to serve as witnesses of this person's unique suffering, to suffer along with and provide support to the one who is suffering (or sometimes add to their suffering). This community might be ranked in order of proximity of relationships to the suffering one in this way:

1. Spouse/significant other—the other self, in some instances the "better half";

2. Parents—unique perspective, reciprocal of the children's;

3. Children—unique perspective, reciprocal of the parents';

4. Siblings—may be very close but may also be ambivalent;

5. Friends—freely given/shared love and co-suffering;

6. Acquaintances—boundaries with friendship blur; and

7. Strangers—Suffering has a cosmic aspect which in the Christian context is reflected in the Communion of the Saints as well as the well-known quote from John Donne that "no man is an island."[11] The health professional walks a fine line among all these relationships depending on the circumstances, but always must respect professional boundaries.

The communal or relational aspect of social suffering is manifested in various ways. It may find expression paradoxically in a deep sense of shared isolation experienced by both the suffering patient and also by those who encounter the barrier presented by the illness, as described so well in the example from Alexander Solzhenitsyn's novel *Cancer Ward* quoted above. Indeed, many of the psychological expressions of Total Pain discussed above also may have a communal aspect extending beyond each individual within the close relationships that exist between

[11]John Donne, from "Meditation XVII," accessed on 20 April, 2012 at: http://www.online-literature.com/donne/409/.

persons. Conflict between close relations/intimates may be the dominant or most visible form of social suffering that develops. It may be a reflection of the sometimes unpredictable and even cataclysmic interaction between the psychological distress of suffering patients and the interconnected psychological distress of their close contacts. For example, passionate, angry, or selfish people, when confronted with the crisis imposed by a life-threatening illness, whether it is their illness or that of a loved one, may face a real test of their commitment to relationships. Not infrequently, they may not pass the initial test but rather lash out in anger or frustration toward loved ones in their distress, only making their suffering worse by adding a strong social element to it. Health professionals may need to recognize that often the key to the effective relief of the suffering of their patients may be found in addressing the communal suffering that is present in their distressed relationships. Sometimes, this type of suffering may be present only in latent form, awaiting a thoughtless comment or harsh glance, the match that will ignite the blaze. A careful social history, assessing for potential causes of conflict between important social contacts and a suffering patient may be very helpful in identifying latent sources of social suffering. Other forms of distress experienced as social suffering in the context of relationships may also include the pain of anticipated separation, loss of trust/dishonesty, intimate shared suffering between caregiver and patient, the unique distress within the bond between child and parent in suffering, and suffering including persons but also extending beyond persons to embrace the cosmos. The following examples will illustrate these different aspects of social suffering.

A 69-year-old widower has an aggressive form of lung cancer (small cell carcinoma) that was complicated by a stroke that has left him weak on the right side and unable to speak. His disease has progressed in spite of treatment. He has been admitted to the hospital for symptom management to help relieve his shortness of breath and pain from a site of cancer spread (metastasis) to his right shoulder. After several days his symptoms are much improved. As plans for discharge to home with hospice support are being discussed in a family meeting with his two sisters, the younger sister accuses the elder sister of neglecting her brother when she cared for him prior to the hospital admission and insists that she be allowed to care for him in her home. Complicating the situation is the fact that the patient can only give one word or yes/no answers that are not entirely consistent as to what his actual wishes are. Also of importance is the fact that he has a large disability pension that may be of interest to both sisters in the conflict.

The conflict between the sisters is likely adding directly to the suffering of this unfortunate man who cannot express his own wishes clearly. Rather than seeing his family drawn together through his suffering he must witness the re-emergence of old animosities and sibling jealousy in the form of a competition to demonstrate who has more compassion. The fact that there may be another factor (i.e., access to and control of his pension) influencing the intense interest of both sisters in providing his care further complicates the picture. It may become difficult for his medical team to determine the safest disposition for him, if their confidence in the motives of the sisters is shaken. This crisis in one person's life may be the ultimate test of the quality of old, seemingly well established relationships within an entire family. What might have been a tremendous opportunity for the two sisters to develop a closer bond with each other if they could have cooperated together in the care of their dying brother has unfortunately degenerated into a demonstration of some of their worst qualities as human beings. Healing of the sisters' relationship would have helped him achieve a greater level of peace as he approached his death. Social isolation as a major contributor to the collective suffering experienced by this family has been intensified by the patient's disability as well as by the selfishness of the sisters. The three siblings are effectively isolated from one another. The relational nature of suffering is underscored by examples like this in which suffering transcends individual experience and is manifest most fully and even magnified in the context of relationships. When relationships are healthy, they may often be a potential means of limiting suffering as well as for promoting healing in general.

To bring healing and relief of suffering through relationships may be one of the most challenging endeavors for health professionals to attempt as healers. The older the pathology in a relationship, the more difficult it will be to effect a positive change. Since more than one person is involved, ideally there must be a voluntary movement on the part of all parties toward reconciliation or to at least some level of mutual recognition and understanding. It may require considerable time to reverse and undo a long standing history of suspicion and hostility. The crisis that may bring out the worst in a troubled relationship may also be the best opportunity for rapid healing of that same relationship. A loved one's terminal illness can act as a powerful catalyst for change. Because of the pressure exerted by the awareness of the imminence of death, sometimes relationships that appear likely never to heal may yet undergo reconciliation. Skilled members of the interdisciplinary team (e.g., social workers, psychologists, and chaplains) can make a great difference in helping to facilitate this crucial process of reconciliation within families when the opportunity presents. Unfortunately, it is so much easier to cause great suffering quickly, almost effortlessly, through neglect or disruption of relationships—and so difficult to mitigate once initiated.

A 56-year-old divorced mother of three daughters ages 29, 25, and 23 is referred to hospice for home care services. She was recently diagnosed with an aggressive malignant brain tumor (glioblastoma multiforme) affecting the right side of her brain (frontotemporal area) after she developed left sided weakness. Her eldest daughter told her physicians at the hospital to tell her mother that she had a "stroke". When the hospice physician arrives at the patient's flat she is met by all three daughters who want to meet with her before allowing her access to their mother. The eldest daughter again insists that the hospice physician must not share any information about diagnosis or prognosis with her mother. The middle daughter is ambivalent and the youngest daughter insists that her mother needs to know. An argument develops among the daughters.

Here is a situation in which the different personalities and roles of siblings within a family can have a dramatic impact on the development of social suffering. Birth order may have some impact on defining the different and conflicting approaches of the three sisters. The eldest daughter may have always exerted to some degree a protective or controlling role in the family, and that may translate into her need to control the flow of information during the visit by the hospice team. For many people, naming a problem makes it real. Her desire to protect her mother from bad news may be motivated at such a basic level. The youngest daughter may be expressing a challenge to the oldest sister's assumed leadership role in the family by her advocacy for full disclosure as much as making a plea out of respect for her mother's autonomy. The middle sister may be functioning in a well-worn role of peacemaker in yet another conflict between the oldest and youngest sister. These types of family dynamics may be more predictive of the conflict among the sisters than any well-defined rational process. The depth of fear that each of the sisters may feel about their mother's future may drive the intensity and vehemence of their argument. The mother's suffering is further intensified by seeing her daughters fight on her behalf. Is there any way to resolve this without increasing the conflict in the family? The hospice team may be able to circumvent and to some extent preempt further debate among the daughters by asking their mother what her understanding of her illness is without telling the diagnosis. Quite frequently by their responses it will become evident that patients have a clearer understanding of their diagnosis and prognosis than is appreciated by their protective loved ones.

Powerful ways to intensify social suffering are to insist on keeping secrets or withholding the truth. Such behavior is often rationalized by insisting that it is the only compassionate thing to do under the circumstances. While the truth, which indeed may be very painful, should never be forced on the suffering one, there are gentle ways to offer what eventually must be revealed, otherwise what might have been an honest relationship based on trust will be shattered. Anyway, the patient's imagination can conjure up sufficiently frightening visions to replace the truth.

Many aspects of social suffering may only be fully manifested during interactions between close intimates within relationships. The roles taken within conversations, the tone of voice used and even the body language of the participants may be very revealing. A patient's reactions to close social contacts during discussions of priorities and goals of care—to spouse/significant other, family members, and friends—may highlight many broken elements in relationships that will influence the intensity of the patient's distress and also identify hidden sources of social suffering. The impact of the patient's suffering on the suffering of caregivers may become evident in the context of a family meeting or a home visit. With the rapid changes affecting traditional relationships in modern western culture, it may be helpful to explore briefly what is meant by 'family'. The duration, depth, and intensity of relationships with the patient may be better indicators of the level of suffering produced in witnesses to the patient's suffering than the specific formal relationship. Thus, some of the closest relationships between persons (e.g., significant other/partner) may not have formal legal recognition as in marriage, and such a situation can lead to difficult and sometimes painful conflict when a patient loses capacity for decision making and the legal next-of-kin is asked to become the surrogate decision maker.

Family meetings represent critical opportunities for caregivers to explore and navigate the sometimes turbulent and even treacherous waters that define the various relationships that are so critical in the lives of those who suffer. During a family meeting, the nature and extent of relationships that connect the suffering one to other persons can be defined not only in order to identify sources of basic support in the home, but also to clarify the larger universe of social connections enjoyed by the suffering person. One's history of social contacts, one's social connectedness is highly correlated to having a history of chronic pain. Those who experience chronic pain typically have constricted social networks and are more isolated from their fellow human beings.[12] Misery begets misery. Social isolation (pain) is connected to

[12] A.M. Mitchinson, H.M. Kim, M.E. Geisser, J.M. Rosenberg, and D.B. Hinshaw, "Social Connectedness and Patient Recovery after Major Operations," *Journal of the American College of Surgeons* 206(2) (2008): 292–300.

physical pain and this negative interaction predicts more and worse distress when a new physical challenge is experienced.

It is important to note that unrelated caregivers (including members of the health care team) may sometimes become surrogate family for the suffering one. The intensity of suffering intensifies relationships in both positive and negative ways. It may stimulate close bonds between health professionals and dying patients to whom they provide care, while at the same time it may expose rifts in old relationships between family members. The challenge for the professional caregiver is to provide the intimate support and care to the person who is suffering, while at the same time maintaining professional boundaries in order to avoid aggravating conflicts within families. For the caregiver who sees those who suffer (and their loved ones) as icons of Christ in his suffering, this challenge can be even more poignant.

A hospitalized, elderly man who is declining rapidly from advanced congestive heart failure has impaired capacity for making decisions. A meeting has been arranged to discuss his goals of care with his wife and three adult children. One daughter brings a recording device to the meeting. When her mother sees it, she becomes quite angry and throws her cane at it, hitting the device from across the large table. She then says to the daughter, "I'm in charge here and you won't be making decisions for your father!"

The recording device is a powerful symbol of the broken relationships that exist in this family. Another form of social suffering develops when there is a loss of trust between individual members of a family or other close-knit group. Trust is the glue that holds families and other types of relationships together. Without trust, a relationship is essentially worthless. Even with strong blood ties, a relationship without trust will not function well, if at all, and will be a source of great social suffering. Trust, to remain viable, may also require the willingness to forgive.

A physician is about to sit down with a 24-year-old patient who has acute lymphocytic leukemia (an aggressive form of cancer the affects white blood cells) that is now refractory to treatment, to discuss his condition and prognosis. His father who is also present interrupts the physician at the beginning of the interview and declares that his son needs rest and insists that the physician should discuss any treatment-related issues with him and spare his son further distress.

Parents are committed from the beginning of their relationship with their children to nurture and protect them. When small children or infants are completely dependent on others for the most basic of needs this is an essential aspect of the parental role. It is very difficult to avoid reverting to this same approach when parents see the life of a child threatened, regardless of the child's age. Although the father's intervention is understandable under the circumstances, it may produce conflict with his son who is a competent adult. The son's physician can intervene gently by encouraging the son to set the ground rules for communication regarding his medical condition and thus acknowledge the father's concerns and need to protect the son, while also respecting the son's autonomy.

A 38-year-old single mother of two children, ages 12 and 14, has just been told by her physician that her breast cancer is refractory to further treatment. She then asks the physician, "Does that mean that I will die from the cancer?" When the physician does not reply for a few seconds, she says, "I can't die yet. My children will be orphans," and then bursts into hysterical sobbing.

A particularly poignant form of social suffering is the anticipatory grief of a dying parent who will leave surviving but still dependent children to an uncertain future. Her suffering as a parent is especially challenging because of her perceived inability to help her children after she dies. Intensive support from the social worker and other members of the interdisciplinary team (especially the chaplain) will be critical to relieving, at least to some degree, the intense anxiety and grief she feels on behalf of her children and their fate, as well as the intense fear and grief of the children. Not only will it be important for the social worker to identify a new support system and home for the children, but it will also be essential to assist and support meaningful communication between this mother and her children as they prepare for the coming separation due to her death.

An 8-year-old boy, his mother, and other family members are in the intensive care unit at the bedside of a 41-year-old man who is dying of leukemia that is now refractory to treatment. A decision by consensus among the patient's wife, family and medical team has been reached to allow the unconscious, dying patient to be weaned from life support. The palliative care team has made recommendations to relieve any distress the patient may experience during the process. The palliative care consultant has encouraged the primary medical team to keep vigil with the family during the remaining minutes of the patient's life. All of the 8-year-old boy's memories of his father are in the context of the illness and hospitals. A quilted blanket has been brought to his father by volunteers as a keepsake for the family. As his father is weaned off the ventilator, the boy alternates between fidgeting at the bedside and looking up with tears at the ceiling of the room. When his father breathes his last, suddenly, the boy takes up the blanket in his arms and with sobs, says, "This is mine!" No physician from the primary medical team was present to witness their patient's death and the unique expression of this son's grief.

Two very special and interrelated aspects of social suffering are present in this story: a young son's intense grief for his dead father and the response of professional caregivers to the death of their patient. When the young physicians caring for this dying patient were encouraged to keep brief vigil in solidarity with this family and patient in his last moments, they rapidly identified multiple tasks that could not wait and scattered in all directions to avoid the scene of this tragedy that was reaching its denouement. They had banished themselves from one of the most tender displays of love ever expressed by a child for its parent. The remarkable fact for this little boy was that his love and feeling for his father were able to completely transcend the sterility and coldness of the hospital environment, so that this man truly died in the bosom of his family. Perhaps, since he had primarily known his father in the context of his leukemia and hospitals, this was not so difficult for the boy. The sad irony was the lost opportunity for the physician members of the medical team to become part of the extended family at their patient's death bed. Professional as well as family caregivers are frequently offered the gift of deep and intimate fellowship with those with whom they are connected through suffering. These young physicians unwittingly denied themselves the opportunity to place the suffering of their patient in a larger, primarily non-medical context in which they could finally say good-bye as compassionate human beings to another human person departing this life. They also were unable to witness the transformation of an inanimate object, the quilted blanket, by the boy's intense emotion into a powerful expression and memorial of love. Unfortunately, it seems that modern medical education has been quite successful in training physicians to fear and deny the emotional connections they form with their patients and families.

A 63-year-old woman is delirious and dependent on a ventilator after developing failure of multiple organs following an abdominal operation complicated by intestinal leakage and severe infection. After several weeks without improvement in her condition, her family is asking that the life support be stopped and that she be allowed to die. A son who hasn't seen her in several years arrives from a distant town and states that "stopping care now would be equivalent to killing her!"

The opportunities created by modern medical technology to extend the dying process, especially in an apparently ambiguous context where recovery has been the expected or usual outcome, promote confusion and can exacerbate social suffering among the family and loved ones of very ill patients. From the perspective of members of the health care team, sometimes when such situations develop in the context of large family units it can become very challenging to maintain a therapeutic partnership with all parties. It is critical in such situations to provide frequent and consistent communication (including lots of listening). Identifying through consensus with family members a spokesperson or family representative through whom communication flows can be particularly helpful. Even after taking great pains to communicate regularly with the family representative(s), the sudden arrival of a distant family member can inject a whole new layer of chaos into the relationship with a large family. The son may have been distant not only in location—he may also have been distant in terms of both his communication and relationship with his mother and other family members. His statement may be an externalization of his own sudden recognition of his lost opportunities in the relationship with his mother that he has 'killed' through neglect. His overreaction and advocacy on behalf of his mother are not in synchrony with his siblings' responses to the situation, exacerbate their suffering, and may become a recipe for further conflict within the family as well as complicated grief for the distant son. In some circumstances a delay in fulfilling the wishes of the patient as defined by the surrogate decision maker to allow for all members of the family to gather to say farewell may be an important, if not essential aspect of extending the therapeutic encounter to address the suffering in the social domain. Clearly, if a family member must make the decision for an incapacitated loved one in the context of conflict within the family, the social suffering will be intensified.

Some aspects of social suffering experienced by bereaved survivors represent a special burden. Grief is an evolving process which includes various forms of regret. There are regrets that "it wasn't me." There are regrets about issues not addressed in the relationship at the time of death. The so-called "unfinished business" of the dying is often a two-way street. The bereaved survivors may also be left with "unfinished business" (e.g., wounds needing healing or forgiveness not received) that was not resolved with the deceased prior to death, and that may perpetuate their social suffering indefinitely. Somehow, there must be a reconfiguring of life without the loved one. The hole in one's existence as defined by the nature of the relationship with the deceased (i.e., spouse/significant other, child, parent, sibling, friend, etc.) must be filled in some way. As this eventually occurs, there may be a sense of guilt in the recognition that life has somehow gone on without the loved one.

There may even be an aspect to social suffering that extends beyond the relationships between persons to include in some mysterious way the environment, i.e., suffering on a cosmic scale. Joshua Lawrence Chamberlain, who had commanded the twentieth Maine regiment in defense of Little Round Top on July 2, 1863 during the battle of Gettysburg, returned many years later for a reunion with old comrades on the site of their struggle that was so crucial to Union victory. His reflections hint at this larger aspect to social suffering in which nature itself participates as more than a passive witness.

> They did not know it themselves—those boys of ours whose remembered faces in every home should be cherished symbols of the true, for life or death—what were their lofty deeds . . . on that tremendous day. Unknown—but kept! The earth itself shall be its treasurer. It holds something of ours besides graves. These strange influences of material nature, its mountains and seas, its sunset skies and nights of stars, its colors and tones and odors, carry something of the mutual, reciprocal. It is a sympathy. On that other side it is represented to us as suffering. The whole creation travailing in pain together . . .[13]

"The whole creation travailing in pain together." Large-scale shared suffering, as in war, genocide, major natural disasters (e.g., tsunamis, hurricanes, earthquakes, volcanic eruptions) seems to engage the entire cosmos in the suffering. Even the suffering experienced in one small corner of the cosmos became fully integrated with that occurring elsewhere, when earth was united to heaven in the incarnation.

Spiritual Pain

The experience of spiritual pain, in essence, represents the point of intersection between the other domains of Total Pain. Suffering within

[13]Joshua Lawrence Chamberlain, reflecting on the suffering and deaths of his comrades in defense of Little Round Top, Battle of Gettysburg, July 2, 1863, in *"Bayonet! Forward" My Civil War Reminiscences* (Gettysburg, PA: Stan Clark Military Books, 1994), 37.

the spiritual domain has been described as involving at least three major themes: meaning, value, and relationship.[14] Meaning in one's life is directly challenged by the threat imposed by unremitting pain, altered social roles, and uncertainty and anxiety about one's future—one's very survival. The existential questions can no longer be ignored. "Why am I suffering?" becomes an insistent taunt within one's soul which may be very difficult to rebut. Likewise, basic assumptions of daily existence about one's value as a person may be upended. If an illness has destroyed one's ability to perform one's duties, to fulfill one's role in the family or on a larger scale, in one's profession or in society, it may be very difficult to retain a sense of personal value. Those stressors that may induce deep social pain may in turn attack this bulwark of the self, one's sense of value. The third theme of spiritual pain, relationship, underscores for the suffering one how all aspects of one's existence have been altered by the physical, psychological and social pain. It may be impossible to maintain the same approach to relationships when the windows through which one perceives and encounters the world have been shattered by intense pain or other physical distress, severe anxiety or depression, and the consequent social isolation. The following scenarios or stories will illustrate how the intersection of the different domains of Total Pain within the spiritual domain may occur.

A 26-year-old woman has a very large tumor (retroperitoneal sarcoma) that occupies most of her pelvis and surrounds the major blood vessels (i.e., distal aorta and iliac vessels). An extension of the tumor compresses the blood vessels and nerve to her right leg. She is bedfast because of the compromised function of her right leg and the intense complex pain which is only partially responsive to medications (e.g., morphine and amitriptyline). She refuses higher doses of morphine which cause sedation, stating that they interfere with her ability to pray. She is unmarried and childless but has enjoyed visits from her young niece and nephew. As her weakness progresses, she becomes quite despondent, crying at times, complaining that it is difficult to pray.

[14]D.P. Sulmasy, "Spiritual Issues in the Care of Dying Patients," *Journal of the American Medical Association* 296 (2006):1385–1392.

For this young woman in distress, her poorly controlled physical pain is at war with her spiritual life. Achieving better control of her physical pain compromises her ability to pray due to the sedation she experiences as a side effect of higher doses of pain medication; and yet poorly controlled pain also affects the quality of her prayer life. She is caught in an apparently insoluble dilemma in which her most powerful source of meaning, prayer, is being diminished by her struggle with the tumor. The physical distress and debility produced by the growth of the tumor directly challenge her in the spiritual domain. In addition, the fact that the tumor is growing within her pelvis, depriving her not only of her future but also of any possibility of motherhood and a family of her own has a particularly cruel symbolism for her. To the extent that sedation from the pain medication, or increasing confusion and anxiety that may develop later in the course of her illness interfere with her ability to pray, it may be very difficult to differentiate between her psychological and spiritual suffering. Interventions in the social domain of Total Pain may be critical in helping her as she struggles to hold on to meaning. If she is willing, visits from fellow Christians and clergy who help her keep her spiritual vigil and pray with her, as well as access to the sacraments of the Church, can transcend any perceived inadequacy in her attentiveness to prayer.

A 49-year-old physician with a very busy clinical practice develops increasing fatigue, weight loss, and vague abdominal discomfort. She is eventually diagnosed with advanced, widely metastatic gastric (stomach) cancer. She is no longer able to practice medicine. With her reduced level of activity she becomes increasingly irritable and at times tearful and states: "My life no longer has any meaning."

"Physician heal yourself!"[15] Her identity and status as a healer are directly threatened by the cancer. Healers aren't supposed to get sick. It hardly seems just that one who has dedicated her life to healing others would now have to face a terminal illness, especially at such a young age, when she still has so much healing to do! Perhaps these are some of the

---

[15]Luke 4.23.

bitter thoughts tormenting this woman. The seeming omnipotence of the physician in the face of serious illness has been stripped away from her, leaving her as naked and vulnerable as any other soul in the face of death. Her especial torment is her acute awareness and understanding of the meaning and harsh reality attached to the subtle changes in her evolving symptom burden as her cancer progresses.

A 61-year-old devout man with newly diagnosed advanced pancreatic cancer that has spread to his liver is complaining of increasing difficulty sleeping, fatigue, poor appetite, low mood, and an inability to enjoy activities that previously gave him pleasure. Upon further questioning, he also expresses a profound sense of guilt and hopelessness.

The constellation of symptoms and physical changes experienced by this unfortunate man are seen not only with cancer progression, but they can also be features of clinical depression. His reported sense of hopelessness, feelings of guilt, and inability to experience pleasure (anhedonia) are highly suggestive that clinical depression is present. Any physical distress (e.g., pain) should be addressed as quickly as possible, while medical treatment for depression should also be initiated. Depression will color the lens through which he sees and interprets his world. For this devout man, untreated depression may overwhelm his spiritual resources as he struggles to find meaning in his illness and impending death. Thus, although his psychological suffering in the form of depression may be differentiated from spiritual suffering, it can clearly add to his suffering in the spiritual domain and exacerbate it.

A 64-year-old man with advanced lung cancer has been a religious skeptic most of his adult life. As the debility associated with his cancer progresses, he becomes desperate for any option that might provide a cure. He makes his confession and is formally reconciled to the faith of his youth, receiving the sacraments of holy unction and communion. When it becomes evident that he is still getting weaker and will die soon, he becomes angry and despondent saying: "I did my part. Why didn't God do his part?"

Fear of death appears to be the main force driving this man's actions. The great psychological fear and anxiety that he is experiencing are directly connected to a spiritual crisis. The religious faith of his youth he had abandoned as a sham. Now, having nothing better to replace it, he has turned to it again in desperation to fix his problem. Unfortunately, his problem, death, won't go away even after appealing to bad theology. Real theology must be tested "in the trenches" and his has not passed the test. Traditional Christian theology has never endorsed bargaining with God: "Not as I will, but as thou wilt."[16] Christ was still crucified and all Christians must take up their crosses and follow him (and that includes dying!). This man may benefit greatly from a gentle exploration of his understanding of the religious faith of his youth with correction of this misunderstanding (if he is open to it), so that he can begin to reframe his whole concept of healing in the light of his impending death.

A 38-year-old woman with advanced ovarian cancer is now bedfast and extremely cachectic (emaciated). Her husband has taken extended leave from work to remain at her bedside day and night. He continually encourages her to "get better because your children and I will not be able to go on living without you." Her abdominal pain that was previously well controlled is now no longer responsive to strong opioid pain medications.

Unresolved and especially seemingly unresolvable spiritual pain may often be expressed as escalating physical distress that no longer responds to normally very effective analgesic medications. This poor dying woman is effectively being asked by her husband to bear all the social suffering of her family in her body by attempting to honor his plea to get better in spite of the reality facing the family. By his statement he has shut the door, preventing her from saying her goodbyes, no matter how painful but nonetheless essential this act is for her and the family. To remedy the situation, her husband must ultimately give her permission to die. She must be able to consciously acknowledge and share her grief of the pending separation with her children and husband.

---

[16]Matthew 26.39.

A 53-year-old divorced man with pancreatic cancer that has spread to his liver has had progressive upper abdominal pain radiating to his back for several weeks, and it has been responsive to escalating doses of morphine. He has been increasingly isolated socially since his divorce 5 years ago and has not seen his three children since that time. He now presents with excruciating pain no longer responsive to morphine.

As has been noted above, lower levels of social connectedness are associated with chronic pain.[17] Social isolation is likely contributing to this man's experience of increasing physical distress associated with the progression of his cancer. This may further exacerbate his social isolation as he withdraws from social interactions with the increased pain eventually forming a vicious circle. As he becomes more aware of his imminent death, any opportunity to reconnect with his children or seek forgiveness from his ex-wife is gradually slipping away. This increasing social pain can only add to his total burden of suffering and interfere with any potential for healing of relationships before his death.

An 82-year-old widowed grandmother with advanced heart disease is experiencing increasing levels of breathlessness despite maximal medical management of her congestive heart failure. This situation has kept her from attending services at her church, which has been her greatest source of meaning and comfort. In despair, she expresses her wish, "If only the Lord would take me!"

A single physical symptom, breathlessness, for this elderly woman has embraced a whole universe of suffering. Her breathlessness is no longer just a very unpleasant sensation, at its worst something akin to suffocation. It now embodies the destruction of a whole world of meaning and relationships for this woman. It is her prison. It is the demon tormenting and preventing her from finding solace in her community of faith. It is no wonder that she seeks respite from her tormentor in death, but only when "the Lord would take me." Her physical, psychological, and social distress have fully merged into titanic spiritual suffering. There are probably many isolated elderly individuals who suffer

[17] A.M. Mitchinson, et al., ibid.

not unlike this woman, frequently alone in their anguish. Medication may help her breathlessness but intervention on a social level is needed to address spiritual suffering that is deeply rooted in social pain.

Pain in the spiritual domain of Total Pain is often a hidden aspect of a person's suffering. It may, in effect, be the leitmotif, the theme defining the totality of an individual's experience of suffering. It is the key to understanding not only the unique character of a person's suffering but also the person. Spiritual qualities that are foundational to personhood—meaning, value, and relationship—are put to the test in suffering. Spiritual pain may manifest itself, in an oblique manner, through the medium or context most common to an individual's existence. For example, if one lives primarily on a physical level, the spiritual distress will manifest itself there. Probe a physical symptom a little, and under the surface, deep, deep suffering may emerge. The same applies to what may appear to be minor changes in social roles or relationships—social pain may be tinged with profound spiritual significance. Psychological pain, in that it can color so strongly our perceptions of reality, is perhaps the most difficult to distinguish from spiritual pain. However, spiritual pain, like social pain, is shared among persons in a mysterious way. It is not necessarily dependent on the level of perception or understanding of those who are suffering. Thus, the innocent young child who uncomprehendingly experiences great physical pain and terrible emotional hurt through social isolation or deprivation as a result of illness, trauma, or natural disaster, still experiences in a very real sense spiritual pain; perhaps even more so, because like the Crucified One, its suffering is that of an innocent victim.

CHAPTER 6

The Healer

BEFORE EXPLORING in greater depth the characteristics that define a healer, it may be helpful to examine the rationale or motivation for being a healer in the first place. Since the Enlightenment most advocates for the health and welfare of their fellow human beings have appealed to natural rights expressed in the American Declaration of Independence[1] and the French Rights of Man[2] as providing the universal mandate to address the collective needs of citizens through the laws and political institutions of individual nation-states. Indeed, Rudolph Virchow, the great nineteenth-century physician and founder of modern pathology, has been quoted as describing the relationship this way, "Medicine is a social science, and politics nothing but medicine on a grand scale."[3] More recently, especially in light of the appalling abuses of human rights and mass suffering of the nineteenth and twentieth centuries, there has been a growing recognition that these ideals of the Enlightenment have not come close to being achieved for most members of the human race. Nonetheless, similar appeals to natural rights continue to be made on behalf of millions of humans, most recently in the realm of pain and suffering. Human Rights Watch has recently presented a very eloquent argument for a fundamental human right to pain relief in which the sheer number of suffering individuals

[1]"United States Declaration of Independence," accessed on 12 December 2010 at: http://www.earlyamerica.com/earlyamerica/freedom/doi/text.html.
[2]"Declaration of the Rights of Man and the Citizen," approved by the National Assembly of France, August 26, 1789. Summary of articles accessed at: http://www.constitution.org/fr/fr_drm.htm, 14 January, 2012.
[3]Rudolph Virchow, quoted in T.E. Novotny and V. Adams, "Global Health Diplomacy: A Call for a New Field of Teaching and Research," *San Francisco Medicine* (March 2007): 22, 23.

speaks for itself: "In September 2008, the World Health Organization (WHO) estimated that approximately 80 percent of the world population has either no or insufficient access to treatment for moderate to severe pain and that every year tens of millions of people around the world, including around four million cancer patients and 0.8 million HIV/AIDS patients at the end of their lives suffer from such pain without treatment."[4] And yet for Christians, this represents only a limited perspective of the problem.

For Christians, the question begins with anthropology. Christ's question to his disciples, "Who do you say that I am?"[5] is the fundamental starting point from which all questions of human rights *and duties* find their answers. The incarnation of Christ transformed anthropology. When the Divine Logos of God assumed human nature and entered his own creation as a vulnerable human infant, he embraced all aspects of our frailty as human beings, except for sin. By this supreme act of condescension, God has united his very nature to the human condition. He has made common cause with us in our distress. It is from this ineffably gracious act that any human dignity or rights flow. It is because he suffered that we can appeal to a right of all those who bear his image also to receive relief of their suffering. However, whereas the focus in the secular western mind is on human autonomy and individual rights, in Christian anthropology the focus shifts from self to the other. The other, the second person—the 'you' or more intimate 'thou', not the autonomous, omnipotent 'I'— ultimately becomes for Christians the One who said, "As you did it to one of the least of these my brethren, you did it to me."[6]

There is another aspect of Christian anthropology that also is relevant to this discussion. In the Biblical story of the Creation, the progressive ascent of the created order culminates in the creation of human

[4]From "Please, do not make us suffer any more ..." *Access to Pain Treatment as a Human Right*, Human Rights Watch, accessed at http://www.hrw.org/en/reports/2009/03/02/please-do-not-make-us-suffer-any-more-0 on March 22, 2010.

[5]Mark 8.29.

[6]Matthew 25.40.

beings in God's own image.[7] God, however, is not satisfied, "It is not good that the man should be alone . . . So the Lord God caused a deep sleep to fall upon the man, and while he slept took one of his ribs and closed up its place with flesh; and the rib which the Lord God had taken from the man he made into a woman and brought her to the man. Then the man said, 'This at last is bone of my bones and flesh of my flesh; she shall be called Woman, because she was taken out of Man.'"[8] Just as God, the Holy Trinity is a communion of love, we are not fully human unless we also are in communion or fellowship with others. A unique aspect of the human capacity for this communion is the complementarity of the genders. There are masculine and feminine traits that are essential features of whole persons regardless of the individual's actual gender. St Ephrem the Syrian (c. fourth century) had this to say about the relationship between the masculine and feminine, "Then Moses said, 'Male and female he created them,' to make known that Eve was already inside Adam, in the rib that was drawn out from him. Although she was not in his mind she was in his body, and she was not only in his body with him but also in soul and spirit with him, for God added nothing to that rib that he took out except the structure and the adornment. If everything that was suitable for Eve, who came to be from the rib, was complete in and from that rib, it is rightly said that 'male and female he created them.'"[9] Eve was *already inside* Adam. How often do male members of the healing professions flee from the Eve within them? Is tenderness truly foreign to the male of the species? Likewise, is the 'manly' fortitude to bear scenes of horrible suffering with a steady gaze uniquely a male virtue? If anything, the female of the species is probably in many ways better reconciled to a wedding of both these aspects of the human person than her male counterparts. Unfortunately, with the great emphasis placed in recent times on the

[7]Genesis 1.26ff.

[8]Genesis 2.18, 21–23.

[9]St Ephrem the Syrian, quoted from his "Commentary on Genesis," 1.29.2, in *Ancient Christian Commentary on Genesis 1–11*, ed. Andrew Louth (Downers Grove, IL: InterVarsity Press, 2001), 36.

physical and sensual character of gender differences, this other perspective of the masculine and feminine aspects of the human person has been to some major degree lost. Perhaps, rather than being a peripheral issue, this confluence of the masculine and the feminine aspects of the human person may be an element central to being an effective healer. A healthy tension between the two aspects may also provide much of the motive force driving the will to engage as a healer in the therapeutic encounter. As evidence of this wedding of the feminine with the masculine in the human person, especially in the context of deeply felt compassion, Christ himself did not hesitate to use a feminine metaphor in expressing his deep love and concern for his people: "O Jerusalem, Jerusalem, killing the prophets and stoning those who are sent to you! How often would I have gathered your children together as a hen gathers her brood under her wings."[10] In recording an encounter with the wounded during one of the last great battles leading up to the surrender of Lee to Grant at Appomattox in the American Civil War, Brevet Major General Joshua Lawrence Chamberlain relates how he

> walked out alone over the field [of battle] to see how it was faring for the "unreturning brave" . . . Burials were even now begun; searchings, questionings, reliefs, recognitions, greetings, and farewells; last messages tenderly taken from manly lips for breaking hearts; insuppressible human moan; flickerings of heart-held song; vanishing prayer heavenward. But what could mortal do for mortal or human skill or sympathy avail for such deep need? I leaned over one and spoke to another as I passed, feeling how little now I could command. At length I knelt above the sweet body of McEuen, where God's thought had folded its wing; and nearby, where wrecks were thickly strewn, I came upon old brave Sickel lying calm and cheerful, with a shattered limb, and weakened by loss of blood while "fighting it through," but refusing to have more attention than came in his turn. Still pictured on my mind his splendid action where I had left him rallying his men, I sat down by him to give him such

---

[10]Matthew 23.37.

cheer as I could. He seemed to think I needed the comforting. The heroic flush was still on his face. "General," he whispers, smiling up, "you have the soul of the lion and the heart of the woman." "Take the benediction to yourself," was the reply; "you could not have thought that, if you had not been it." And that was our thought at parting for other trial, and through after years. For so it is: might and love,—they are the all;—fatherhood and motherhood of God himself, and of every godlike man.[11]

Let us now go on to explore how health care professionals attempt to fulfill their roles as healers in the therapeutic encounter. In the modern health care environment, an essential requirement to serve those who are ill is the acquisition of specialized knowledge or skills. The formal training can range from an intensive six week course for nursing assistants to many years for physicians trained in subspecialty areas of medicine. It is the skills acquired that form the usual entrée for the health care professional to engage in the therapeutic encounter. Although much of what will follow in this discussion is based on the physician as a type of healer, it cannot be emphasized enough that the amount of training of the individual caregiver may have relatively little to do with the role of healer compared to the relationship that develops between the caregiver and the ill person. Thus, it may be possible that the nursing assistant will form a more effective therapeutic relationship with a given patient than the subspecialist physician with many years of formal training. Let us consider an example from the clinical setting that illustrates this problem.

A highly competent surgeon, well regarded for his technical skills by his colleagues, is making rounds in the hospital's surgical ward. He comes to the door of an unfortunate woman whose exploratory abdominal operation he performed the preceding day. He hesitates in the doorway to her room as she looks directly into his eyes with an imploring expression, as if to say, "You do have good news for me, don't you?" He then quickly blurts out, "You had

[11]J.L. Chamberlain, *The Passing of the Armies* (Gettysburg, PA: Stan Clark Military Books, 1915, reprinted 1994), 56–57.

cancer everywhere in your abdomen. We could do nothing . . . Uh; I need to go now to see my next patient."

This does not appear to be the act of a compassionate physician. However, it may not be absolute evidence of cold indifference; rather it may represent a lack of competent skills in communication in a person who truly does care about his patient. Technical excellence in the operating room or with medications is not enough. By his inept communication this surgeon may have created deeper wounds than with his knife. Compassion is not necessarily a natural attribute or skill of health care professionals. For many, if not most clinicians, it may be necessary to learn how to practice and demonstrate compassion. The following section will explore this in detail in the context of the healer as an actor.

The Healer as Actor

> "All the world's a stage,
> And all the men and women merely players.
> They have their exits and their entrances;
> And one man in his time plays many parts . . ."[12]

There is much that can be learned from the world's great literature about the healing professions. It is not an entirely flattering picture which emerges, however. Are physicians and other health professionals merely actors as suggested by Shakespeare's famous observation? Since the dawn of the scientific era of medicine in the nineteenth century with the cellular pathology of Rudolph Virchow, a distant or cold professionalism when encountering the sick has been viewed almost as a virtue for physicians to emulate. Indeed, a good bedside manner was inherently suspect not only among other medical colleagues but also with the public in general. A short piece in the British magazine *Punch* from the late nineteenth century highlights this in a humorous way:

---

[12]William Shakespeare, *As You Like It*, Act II, Scene vii, lines 139–142, in *Shakespeare: Major Plays and the Sonnets*, ed. G.B. Harrison, (New York: Harcourt, Brace, and World, Inc., 1948), 509.

Lady visitor: "Oh that's your doctor, is it? What sort of a doctor is he?" Lady patient: "I don't know much about his ability but he's got a very good bedside manner."[13]

This general perception has persisted to some extent into the current era "Despite the obvious need for the effective transmission of messages, there is a widespread perception that the doctor's conduct towards his patients serves as a substitute for clinical competence and that 'the worse the . . . physician, the better the bedside manner.'"[14]

The physician may actually employ many of the tools or props of the actor's trade. What are the white coat, use of complex technical jargon, careful modulation of voice, facial expressions, and body language, if not props? "'What can I do for you, Mr. Marlowe?' He had a rich soft voice to soothe the pain and comfort the anxious heart. Doctor is here, there is nothing to worry about; everything will be fine. He had that bedside manner, thick honeyed layers of it."[15] The character, Dr Amos Varley, in Raymond Chandler's novel, *The Long Good-Bye*, assumes this voice in his initial encounter with the lead character in this story but abruptly drops the pretense (and all the charm) once Marlowe makes it clear that he is not visiting him as a potential patient.

Many students embarking on their careers in medicine have been given a copy of William Osler's classic, *Aequanimitas*, in which the foremost physician of the early twentieth century extols the virtue of imperturbability: "The physician who . . . shows in his face the slightest alteration expressive of anxiety or fear . . . is liable to disaster at any moment."[16] This seems like a fairly strong endorsement of some level of acting on the part of the physician. This same quality of the physician prized so emphatically by Osler has also been described by another

[13]*Punch* (15 March 1884): 121.

[14]S. Posen, *The Doctor in Literature: Satisfaction or Resentment?* (Oxford: Radcliffe Publishing, 2005), 71.

[15]Dr. Amos Varley in *The Long Good-Bye*, by Raymond Chandler (London: Pan, 1979) 102–3.

[16]W. Osler, *Aequanimitas* (first printed 1889, reprinted London: HK Lewis, 1920), 5.

more recent physician author. "It is part of the mystique of the doctor that nothing surprises him."[17] Where does imperturbability end and unfeeling aloofness begin? There may be some real dangers associated with having no 'bedside manner'. It may actually be a reflection of boorish insensitivity and an aggressive, authoritarian approach for the purpose of intimidating and controlling patients. Ultimately, it may result in dehumanizing and devaluing the patient as a person. The American novelist Louisa May Alcott briefly served as a nurse for wounded and dying soldiers at a military hospital during the Civil War. She observed the apparent disconnect that may occur between the imperturbable physician and the suffering patient while assisting a surgeon who was examining a wounded soldier. "Though a capital surgeon and a kindly man, Dr P., through long acquaintance with many of the ills flesh is heir to, had acquired a somewhat trying habit of regarding a man and his wound as separate institutions . . . He had a way of twitching off a bandage, and giving a limb a comprehensive sort of clutch, which, though no doubt entirely scientific, was rather startling than soothing . . ."[18]

Sometimes the doctor gets it right. "He seemed to regard . . . [her problem] as the one case that had ever aroused his professional interest; but as it unfolded itself in all its difficulty and urgency, so he seemed, in his mind, to be discovering wondrous ways of dealing with it; these mysterious discoveries seemed to give him confidence and his confidence was communicated to the patient by faint sallies of humor. He was a very skilled doctor. This fact, however, had no share in his popularity, which was due solely to his rare gift of taking a case very seriously while remaining cheerful."[19] In this example, some important observations are made about the reasons for this physician's success with patients. He was able to create the impression that the person before him and her problem had absorbed all of his attention. As he was thinking about the problem in the patient's presence he was also able to provide

[17]W. Crichton, *A Case of Need* (New York: Signet, 1969), 51.

[18]L.M. Alcott, *Hospital Sketches* (first printed 1863, reprinted Cambridge, MA: Applewood Books, 1986), 91–92.

[19]A. Bennett, *The Old Wives' Tale* (London: Hodder & Stoughton, 1964), 461–3.

reassurance through the use of gentle humor, being cheerful in the face of adversity while still respecting the seriousness of the situation. The use of humor can be very serious business, indeed, if used properly. It can sometimes be the essential prescription to lessen the palpable tension that may be present as well as be the seed for a cautious hope. In other words, it may be a part of the foundation of trust that must be formed between the patient and her physician as they face a difficult and uncertain future together. How does this all relate to the issue of the physician as an actor? It is not made clear in this fragment of a story whether the physician also entertained major doubts about his ability to help resolve this woman's problem. He had to *act* in the most effective way he could to move in a direction of healing. A major portion of this *acting* was in his manner of communicating with her.

If one examines the particularly challenging phenomenon of communicating bad news to patients,[20] it becomes evident that this is *acting* par excellence. The actor's props are very important here. The 'theatrical' setting is critical, i.e., find a quiet, private place where the drama can unfold in the least traumatic fashion possible. Make sure that there are the necessary supporting actors present, i.e., a supportive family member or friend as well as the patient's nurse, if an inpatient. Maximize the effective use of body language, i.e., sit close to the patient, lean forward making good eye contact and if appropriate touch the patient (e.g., on the shoulder or hand). Receive direction from the director of your drama, the patient, by clarifying what the patient's understanding of the problem is. Depending on the patient's response, e.g., "I don't know why I am here," a warning shot may be necessary, e.g., "I am afraid I have bad news." Pausing after giving the warning shot or communicating the bad news can be very powerful and necessary. It is also high drama. The choreography develops in real time, always following the cues of the director (the patient). As much information is conveyed as desired and tolerated by the patient. Just like the fictional doctor, giving one's full attention to the patient is critical in this real *drama*. A judicious

[20]J.T. Ptacek, and T.L. Eberhardt, "Breaking Bad News: A Review of the Literature," *Journal of the American Medical Association* 276 (1996): 496–502.

combination of appropriate body language, attentiveness, and the clear willingness to repeat the performance as many times as necessary over the course of the illness to help the patient understand, can build trust and even hope. This can be done without telling lies but may require the incremental presentation of the full truth. In communicating bad news there is also a transfer of anxiety and stress from the physician, who is often quite anxious about giving the bad news, to the patient, who now absorbs this enormous load of stress. In some ways this initial angst of the physician about having to give the bad news is like stage fright experienced by an actor. Unfortunately, rather than giving essential information that a suffering patient needs to know, in a compassionate and supportive context, sometimes physicians may primarily transfer their anxiety (their psychological suffering) and the full burden of the bad news they bear to the patient. It is no wonder that there is a saying, "Don't shoot the messenger!" One can assault patients as much with words as with a physical instrument of torture.

Ethics and the Healer as Actor

If the physician or other health professional must at times be an actor to be an effective healer is this ethically acceptable? Can support be found from the four major principles of ethics (Non-Maleficence—do no harm; Beneficence—do a positive good; Autonomy—respect individual rights of self-determination; and Justice—the equitable distribution of resources) for role playing by health professionals? Perhaps a more useful approach may be to consider another branch of ethics called virtue ethics. In this context, the questions are more comprehensible. Here the focus is on the character of the healer, the kind of person a physician should be. Can or should a virtuous practitioner of the healing art act? Indeed, acting may be an essential aspect of being a virtuous physician, even though the notion of virtuous acting may seem oxymoronic. If physicians must act in their roles as healers, how must they act? Asking patients about their perceptions and expectations of physicians might be helpful.

In a study of women with breast cancer, the following characteristics were identified by the patients as important attitudes and behaviors of their physicians:

1) Communication based on active listening; Awareness of and respect for the woman's depth of knowledge about her illness;

2) Honesty;

3) Partnership;

4) Interest in the patient as a person; and

5) Use of appropriate touch to communicate.[21]

It is interesting to note that all of these characteristics identified by patients relate to necessary elements in the development and maintenance of a healthy relationship of respect between persons. They are all linked by the process of communication, but communication that is bi-directional. Is the physician hearing the patient, listening to the patient, and in what manner?

It may be helpful to examine again the definitions of hearing and listening to draw out an important distinction regarding the bidirectional communication that patients seek in their encounters with physicians. To hear is to "perceive by the ear" or "listen to; give or pay attention to" (often in a favorable light). To listen is "to give attention with the ear; attend closely for the purpose of hearing; give ear" with a secondary meaning of "pay attention; heed; obey" but also "*wait attentively* for a sound."[22] Clearly, the meanings of these words in English overlap, but there is a useful distinction to be made, especially in the case of the secondary meaning of *listen*. One may often hear incidental sounds (e.g., a dog barking in the distance, the noise of automobiles outside one's window) or be aware of them. Unfortunately, conversations with

[21]S.R. Harris and E. Templeton, "Who's Listening? Experiences of Women with Breast Cancer in Communicating with Physicians," *Breast Journal* 7(6) (2001): 444–449.

[22]Webster's New Universal Unabridged Dictionary (New York: Barnes & Noble Publishing, Inc., 2003).

patients may take on this character in which the busy physician has an agenda to communicate or speak *to* the patient and hears the patient's questions only as incidental 'noise'. On the other hand, the secondary meaning of *listen* implies much more taking place on the part of the one hearing. Here the physician is now not only seriously paying attention to the patient but also waiting attentively on the patient. Such listening can even be done with other senses. One can *listen* with one's eyes, sense of smell, in effect one's whole being. If one is inclined to prayer, such *listening* can become a form of prayer or deep, unconditional and complete openness to the suffering patient.

There is a major obstacle, however. How can one truly listen with all the noise, the distractions that are constantly present during the daily routine? Is there a way to find a place of stillness or silence in the therapeutic encounter? The noise is not just audible distractions. It is the whole host of obligations that multiply exponentially as the media age continues to progress, in their ever more efficient delivery via email and every other conceivable means to demand our attention. Worse even than these outside challenges are the distracting thoughts (Greek—*logismoi*) that are always present and ready to intrude, even when one consciously makes a real effort to shut out the external distractions. How then is one to find or cultivate real silence or stillness (Greek—*hesychia*) in the therapeutic encounter? It appears that only truly dramatic life-changing events are capable of really focusing one's attention for more than just a few moments. A life-threatening or terminal illness can focus one's attention like nothing else. In effect, a terminal illness and the process of dying are each person's kenosis. The kenosis of the dying (and of course we are all dying!) is a stripping or draining away of the 'noise' so that real silence or stillness (*hesychia*) can be experienced. This kenosis is the foundation for true hearing and listening. Stillness is a necessary precursor for real hearing and listening, as much for the caregiver as for the patient. Thus, it becomes quite clear why the ancient Christian precepts, "Remember your death! Think daily on your death!" are foundational not only to the spiritual life of monastics but to any person who wishes to really live, be fully aware, and open to the reality of other persons.

How does this relate to the phenomenon of compassion? If one can begin to listen out of silence, out of stillness to the story of another's suffering one can potentially begin to experience compassion and perhaps something even deeper and more profound, empathy. Compassion is defined as "A feeling of deep sympathy and sorrow for another who is stricken by misfortune, accompanied by a strong desire to alleviate the suffering."[23] Empathy is defined as "The intellectual identification with or vicarious experiencing of the feelings, thoughts, or attitudes of another."[24] The Greek root for these words is *pascho*—suffer. The compassionate one suffers *with* the other person. The one who has empathy *enters into and vicariously experiences* the suffering of another person.

The Jewish philosopher, convert to Roman Catholicism, and nun martyred in Auschwitz, Edith Stein, made a particular study of the phenomenon of empathy. She described it as a process involving three stages or levels:

1) The first level is *active listening*: experiencing the other person as an object (trying to put oneself in the other's place);

2) The second level is *identification merging*: experiencing the other's state of mind as one's own; and

3) The third level is *sympathy*: having now recovered one's sense of self and standing side by side with the other.[25] There is an emphasis here on the transient nature of the process (something akin to a moment of grace or epiphany) but the effect on persons experiencing the process need not be transient but can be a lasting change in their relationships, if only from their perspective.

[23] Ibid.
[24] Ibid.
[25] S.M. Maatta, "Closeness and Distance in the Nurse-Patient Relation. The Relevance of Edith Stein's Concept of Empathy," *Nursing Philosophy* 7 (2006): 3–10.

Interestingly, there may even be a biological basis for empathy. It has been possible through the use of an imaging technique known as functional magnetic resonance imaging (fMRI) to identify various centers within the brain which become activated (demonstrate acute increases in blood flow) during the experience of a painful stimulus. Collectively, these anatomic areas have been designated as the Pain Matrix. The anatomic sites that make up the Pain Matrix include sites that are responsible for the sensory perception of pain intensity and others which are involved in the perception of pain unpleasantness (the affective or emotional component of the experience of pain). The affective components of the Pain Matrix are primarily activated when one experiences empathy. This relationship was highlighted in an fMRI study of couples,[26] one of whom volunteered for exposure to a painful stimulus while both were simultaneously monitored in separate fMRI imaging units. At the time of administration of the painful stimulus in the next room, a light signaled this event to the other member of the couple. While the entire Pain Matrix was activated in the subject experiencing the painful stimulus, the loved one in the adjacent room demonstrated activation in those sites of the Pain Matrix associated with the affective component of pain. In some real sense, humans are 'hard-wired' or biologically programmed to be able to experience a significant portion of the pain of another person. Edith Stein's phenomenological model of empathy may indeed have a biological corollary.

Unfortunately, there are many barriers to the experience of empathy. When physicians or other health care professionals are considered, many factors may serve as impediments to developing empathy. When clinicians are often burdened with responsibilities for the welfare of many patients, the limited time they may have available for deeper encounters with individual patients can serve as a major deterrent. Clinicians are also taught to focus on details and have limited experience or formal training in assessing and understanding patients as

[26]T. Singer, B. Seymour, J. O'Doherty, H. Kaube, R.J. Dolan, and C.D. Frith, "Empathy for Pain Involves the Affective but not Sensory Components of Pain," *Science* 303 (2004): 1157–1162.

persons. Medicine prides itself on being a scientifically oriented culture of detachment in which there is tremendous fear of losing emotional control. Beyond a culture of detachment, clinicians must also contend with their own emotional inertia. One risks being changed in a profound and sometimes unfamiliar, even frightening or painful way by experiencing empathy. Detached emotional inertia is often felt to be a safer psychological refuge for the person who wants to fulfill the basic, routine duties and requirements of the work place without 'complications'. Perhaps the biggest impediment to developing empathy is the ego of the clinician, which may be especially true for physicians. One must be willing to make room for the other person and that person's distress in one's consciousness. Because of the reciprocal nature of relationships, on occasion the barrier to empathy may reside primarily with the patient. Sometimes patients are not particularly likeable; indeed they may be adversarial, abusive, and even threatening to the caregiver. In such situations, it may be essential to find a common history or shared experience that can serve as a bridge in developing a relationship of caring for the "difficult" patient.[27] To have pain is *to have certainty*. The patient has this certainty—the caregiver does not. Caregivers must overcome their tendency to doubt the patient. Caregivers should listen to their patient's complaints of pain (their suffering) "not to explain but to understand, not to diagnose but to witness and help."[28] Ultimately, St Jerome, one of the fourth-century fathers of the Church and translator of the Scriptures into Latin, described a clear foundation and basis for all empathy. "He whom we look down upon, whom we cannot bear to see, the very sight of whom causes us to vomit, is the same as we, formed with us from the selfsame clay, compacted of the same elements. Wherever he suffers we also can suffer."[29] The ultimate test of

---

[27]J. Liaschenko, "Making a Bridge: The Moral Work with Patients We Do Not Like," *Journal of Palliative Care* 10(3) (1994): 83–89.

[28]H. Schweizer, "To Give Suffering a Language," *Literature and Medicine* 14 (1995): 210–221.

[29]Jerome, quoted in G.B. Risse, *Mending Bodies, Saving Souls: A History of Hospitals* (Oxford University Press, 1999), 87.

empathy may be when there is no apparent audience; and the greatest barrier to empathy may be the lack of a decision to be empathic. The way in which physicians and caregivers act in their roles may be the reflection of such a decision.

How does one transform the acting into reality? A good place from which to start may be with a self-conscious awareness of the Golden Rule. How would the caregiver want to be treated if the roles were reversed? Is it possible to teach caregivers to be empathic? An interesting educational experiment with medical students in New Zealand asked this question.[30] In an early educational experience required of all medical students, each student was assigned to follow a dying hospice patient who consented to the relationship. The hospice patients were followed by their students until death. The medical students kept a journal to record the journey they made with the hospice patients toward death. There were five major aspects to the experience from the students' perspective. It was very different from what they expected. They found it to be emotionally powerful and very difficult to remain detached. There was an unexpected confrontation with religious and spiritual issues. It became a strong impetus for the students to engage in personal reflection. Finally, the students acknowledged that they had been stimulated to make a commitment to approach patient care differently as a result of the experience.

What if one still does not feel empathic or only rarely has twinges of such an experience? Cicely Saunders has emphasized the critical need to be stripped of all pretense, to undergo a real kenosis, in order to really meet the patient in a place where empathy may develop. "You are missing something, as well as the patient missing something, unless you come not merely in a professional role but in a role of one human being meeting another."[31] The actor must at some point remove his makeup

[30]R.D. MacLeod, C. Parkin, S. Pullon, and G. Robertson, "Early Clinical Exposure to People who are Dying: Learning to Care at the End of Life," *Medical Education* 37(1) (2003): 51–58.

[31]Dame Cicely Saunders, as quoted in T.R. Egnew, "The Meaning of Healing: Transcending Suffering," *Annals of Family Medicine* 3 (2005): 255–262.

and costume. Is he the same person he was before assuming the role, or has he been transformed by it?

"Suit the action to the word, the word to the action, with this special observance, that you o'erstep not the modesty of nature: for anything so o'erdone is from the purpose of playing, whose end, both at the first and now, was and is, to hold as 'twere the mirror up to nature: to show virtue her feature, scorn her own image, and the very age and body of the time his form and pressure."[32] In Shakespeare's Hamlet, the melancholy prince stages a play within the play to expose his usurper uncle as the murderer of his father. Indeed, Shakespeare through his character Hamlet makes the bold assertion that it is precisely through acting, *'to hold as 'twere the mirror up to nature . . .'*, that the truth can be discovered. Can caregivers be so bold as 'to hold the mirror up to nature' by reflecting on their own acting in their roles as healers? Is it possible even to transcend acting within the therapeutic encounter wherein one may, for example, listen beyond listening? With a self-conscious and reflective practice of 'good acting' within the therapeutic encounter, it may indeed be possible to transform very effective listening into being fully present, becoming a healing presence. Becoming a healing presence may be characterized by the ability to give one's full attention to another person and truly begin to hear the soul's distress within the silence of the encounter. Subordinating one's own ego completely to be fully open to the other can make it possible to be fully present on all levels: physically, emotionally, intellectually, and *spiritually*. Under such extraordinary conditions, it is even possible to transcend the limits of the space/time continuum. A glimpse of the eternal now of God may be encountered in a few moments of real empathy born out of silence. "Silence is always beautiful, and a silent person is always more beautiful than one who talks."[33]

---

[32]W. Shakespeare, *Hamlet*, Act 3, scene 2, 17–24, in *Shakespeare: Major Plays and the Sonnets*, ed. G.B Harrison, (New York: Harcourt, Brace, and World, Inc., 1948), 628.

[33]F. Dostoevsky, *The Adolescent*, trans. by R. Pevear and L. Volokhonsky (New York: Vintage Books, 2003), 212.

Could acting be an essential beginning to the journey of health professionals toward empathy? "Some pretense is often required for an effective relationship between doctor and patient, whether during a trivial office consultation or at a deathbed. The pretense is resented only when it is recognized as such."[34] Physicians and other health professionals should act from such conviction that they become the one whom they would portray. But, who is being portrayed in the therapeutic encounter by the 'actor'?

Health professionals may relate to those who are suffering or dying on three levels: impersonal (e.g., "the cancer" in room three), interpersonal (e.g., an exchange between persons), and intrapersonal (e.g., intimate co-suffering with the dying person/blending of two stories).[35] The ability to proceed from the impersonal through the interpersonal to the intrapersonal and the full experience of empathy will likely require a consistent, long term commitment that at times will feel like "acting".

A physician who has been caring for several dying patients recently becomes increasingly irritable with staff at the hospital where he works, his prior excellent work is starting to slip, and his breath smells of alcohol one morning. During a meeting with a patient this otherwise kind and compassionate physician becomes quite angry in response to a question from the patient about treatment options and swears under his breath.

Physicians are not well prepared to recognize or deal with their own grief for patients they lose to death. Primary care providers often have a much longer relationship with their patients and may experience greater grief in proportion to the length of the relationship. Female physicians tend to experience more symptoms of grief than their male counterparts but often have more coping behaviors. Attending physicians are

[34]S. Posen, *The Doctor in Literature: Satisfaction or Resentment?* (Oxford: Radcliffe Publishing, 2005), 72.

[35]From B.G. Glaser, and A.L. Strauss, "Awareness of Dying," (Chicago: Aldine Publishing Co., 1965), referenced in J.A. O'Connor, "Good Stories from There Develop Good Care Here: A Therapeutic Perspective," ch. 15 in *Coping with the Final Tragedy: Cultural Variation in Dying and Grieving*, D.R. Counts, and D.A. Counts. eds. (Amityville, NY: Baywood Publishing Co., 1991).

rarely used as a resource for coping by physicians in training. Since these role models for younger physicians do not often acknowledge their own grief, this may perpetuate the problem, producing another generation of future attending physicians who also repress their grief. "A conspiracy of silence toward emotions can potentially cause trainees to develop maladaptive coping patterns that lead to burnout and other forms of emotional distress."[36] Can acting by the healer come at a price?

Burnout among physicians and other caregivers is a common problem in health care. It has been defined as a "syndrome of depersonalization, emotional exhaustion, and sense of low personal accomplishment that leads to decreased effectiveness at work."[37] It has been reported to occur in 25–60 percent of practicing physicians at some point in their careers. An even higher incidence of 76% has been noted for internal medicine residents during their training.[38] Burnout is characterized by fatigue, inability to concentrate, depression, anxiety, insomnia, irritability, and loss of interest in one's personal life or work. Some of the risk factors for burnout include: inadequate sleep, excessive stress, lack of emotional support, poor communication or conflict within the interdisciplinary team, professional disappointments, and a perception of a loss of control over one's practice environment. With the increasing dominance of multiple forms of technology in medical practice and the accompanying depersonalization, it is not surprising that burnout is so common. The fallout from burnout on a personal level can be quite devastating. Common sequelae of burnout for affected health professionals include increased risk of substance abuse, suicide (especially among females), and frequent negative effects on relationships. On a professional level, burnout may lead to suboptimal patient care,

[36]E.M. Redinbaugh, et al., "Doctors' emotional reactions to recent death of a patient: cross sectional study of hospital doctors," *British Medical Journal* 327 (2003): 185–191.

[37]T.D. Shanafelt, K.A. Bradley, J.E. Wipf, and A.L. Back, "Burnout and Self-Reported Patient Care in an Internal Medicine Residency Program," *Annals of Internal Medicine* 136(5) (2002): 358–367.

[38]Ibid.

absenteeism, medical errors with subsequent malpractice litigation, high job turnover, and adverse effects on trainees, patients, families, and co-workers. Burnout can exacerbate the very suffering that health care professionals are pledged to relieve. It may cause affected health professionals to question their vocation to care for the sick and even to abandon their professional commitment entirely. Is burnout the inevitable outcome of making a commitment to co-suffer with one's patients?

A number of strategies have been proposed to foster the 'healthy' physician to prevent burnout. They involve recognition that there are a number of dimensions in which health professionals can achieve a state of wholeness or wellness as persons. Like the domains of Cicely Saunders' Total Pain, physicians and other health professionals must develop strategies for achieving a state of wellness (for addressing their own Total Pain) in the physical, psychological, social, and spiritual dimensions. Recreation which crosses all these dimensions may be a particularly important strategy. Basic and what should be obvious issues for physicians need to be attended to on a consistent basis to achieve better physical health including, adequate sleep, a healthy diet, and regular exercise. One third of physicians do not themselves have physicians.[39]

To maintain a reasonable degree of psychological health, physicians and other health professionals should embrace a program of simplifying as much as possible their often chaotic routines. Organizational and professional expectations promote a culture of overcommitment as the unspoken ideal for professional development. The whole physician in responding to professional and organizational demands must be able to know one's limits, stay organized, prioritize, and be able to set limits—to say no. In relationships with patients and colleagues it is crucial for physicians and other health professionals to maintain healthy boundaries while also being fully open and available to the other person before them so that empathy may develop, but in context of all

[39]C.P. Gross, L.A. Mead, D.E. Ford, and M.J. Klag, "Physician, Heal Thyself? Regular Source of Care and Use of Preventive Health Services among Physicians," *Archives of Internal Medicine* 160 (2000): 3209–14.

their other commitments. To avoid falling prey to the cynicism so often prevalent in busy health care settings, they must be able to balance a real sense of hope with the sometimes discouraging reality confronting them.

One's individual emotional and psychological well-being is closely connected in the social dimension with that of one's colleagues, friends, and family. It is essential to preserve effective communication based in mutual respect with one's co-workers, to seek out meaningful and healthy personal relationships within and outside the health care setting, and to set aside or discover "protected time" so that a balance between self-care and one's commitment to others can be achieved.

Being able to find meaning in one's work or vocation is an important aspect of achieving spiritual health. Ideally, one should be able to draw strength, experience a renewal of energy, from caring for those who are sick and suffering. This requires an openness and sensitivity to the spiritual issues that are present within the healthcare environment. This will be much easier for physicians and other health professionals if they have 'come to terms with their Higher Power'. A humble recognition of one's finitude, that there is Another who can help, to Whom one can turn in prayer, creates an infinite range of opportunities that can extend and transform the frustrations and limitations of the daily routine into unimaginable hope.

Recreation is often thought by the more serious-minded as being often a frivolous and even self-indulgent activity. However, recreation, if it is planned and organized with a focus on strengthening and expanding health in all four of the dimensions described above, is not only necessary but can even be a deeply spiritual, holy activity *re-creating* the person: "That physician will hardly be thought very careful of the health of his patients if he neglects his own."[40]

It is not always easy to draw spiritual sustenance from caring for those who suffer. Why is it that this activity which should be one of

[40]Galen (130–200AD), "On Protecting the Health," quotation 2533 from *Medicine in Quotations: Views of Health and Disease through the Ages*, 2nd Edition, E.J. Huth, and T.J. Murray, eds. (Philadelphia: American College of Physicians, 2006).

the greatest sources of meaning for physicians and health professionals, can and frequently does lead to burnout? It is time to return to the
question of who is being portrayed in the therapeutic encounter by the
'actor'. Actors model their performances on someone they admire and
wish to emulate, perhaps one of their teachers or a famous actor whom
they eventually hope to exceed in the skill of their performance. So also
physicians or other health professionals consciously or unconsciously
model their 'acting' on others. Using as role models other colleagues or
teachers may eventually disappoint and frustrate the 'actor'. The role
model will inevitably fall short of expectations. But what is the source
of these expectations? There is often an appeal to a higher standard to
which the best 'actor' must adhere. As discussed earlier in this book,
since the emergence of Christianity as the dominant religious force
in the Roman Empire, the standard in the West by which all compassionate acts are to be judged, to which the ill appeal for greater compassion, is the One who became incarnate to heal the broken condition of
humanity. Even if one is aware of this historical connection between
Christianity and compassionate care of the sick, what is often forgotten
is how healing came through the incarnation. God became a human
person, suffered and died to destroy the power of death and transform
the nature of suffering. Suffering and mortality continue to be the experience of humanity but now it is a transcendent suffering with a hope
extending through and beyond human mortality. Christians must still
accept the invitation to take up one's cross and follow the Crucified
One. To expect suffering in the effort to care for and bring healing to
others, this is the Royal Way, the path following *Ho Philanthropos*, The
Lover of Man. It is the crucified Christ who is the model for all Christian healing and for all would-be Christian healers. Burnout comes for
Christian healers when they are cut off from the Source of healing,
when they no longer are connected through prayer and the mysteries of
the Church to the Presence who is the Model for their 'acting'.

CHAPTER 7

Healing Modalities

W HAT KINDS OF SKILLS and methods does the healer bring to
the therapeutic encounter? By his explicit and deliberate use
of physical means in many of his healing miracles (e.g., John 9), Christ
blessed matter as a medium through which the healing grace of God
can operate in addition to non-physical means of healing. This is only
reasonable and consistent with the reality of the incarnational axiom
of Gregory of Nazianzus, "For that which He has not assumed, He has
not healed; but that which is united to his Godhead is also saved."[1] By
fully assuming our human condition, including its physicality, Christ
blessed the material aspect of his creation making of it a means of salvation and healing. Every healing mystery (sacrament) of the Church
utilizes a physical element whether it is the water of baptism, the oil
of anointing for the sick, the touch of the priest's stole (Greek—*epitra-
chelion*) during absolution in confession, or most importantly, touching
the very Body and Blood of the Lord himself in the elements of consecrated bread and wine during the Eucharist. It is in this context that
healing modalities commonly used in the therapeutic encounter must
be examined.

The following are some of the major modalities employed in the
therapeutic encounter:

1) Medications—external and internal;

2) Touch—'simple' physical contact, massage, the surgeon's knife,
   etc.;

---

[1]St. Gregory of Nazianzus, "Epistle 101, To Cledonius the Priest against Apollinarius," in *Cyril of Jerusalem, Gregory Nazianzen*, ed. by Philip Schaff. and Henry
Wace, vol. 7 of *Nicene and Post-Nicene Fathers* (Peabody, MA: Hendrickson Publishers, Inc., 1994), 440.

3) Faith and Prayer;

4) Communication—verbal and non-verbal;

5) The interdisciplinary team; and

6) Presence

Before examining some of these types of healing modalities in more detail, it is also important to make the distinction between modalities used in the therapeutic encounter with 'curative' intent and those primarily used for comfort. Therapy provided with curative intent can be divided into 'conventional' and 'unconventional' approaches. Examples of conventional medical therapies with a primary focus on cure include:

1) Drugs—antibiotics for pneumonia;

2) Surgery—appendectomy for acute appendicitis; and

3) Intensive care nursing—after life-threatening blunt trauma or burns with the goal of full recovery and long-term survival.

Unconventional approaches to health care (e.g., Complementary and Alternative or Integrative Medicine) that are also offered frequently with 'curative' intent include:

1) Herbal medicines;

2) Food supplements;

3) Vitamins;

4) Mind-body medicine (e.g., hypnosis);

5) Acupuncture;

6) Chiropractic;

7) Therapeutic touch; and

8) Distant healing (healing by prayer and faith healing).

Essentially all the same modalities, both conventional and unconventional, used with curative intent may also be useful for comfort. What is different is the focus. The primary goal has shifted from eliminating a disease to the relief of suffering and to caring for the person who has a disease or diseases which it may or may not be possible to cure. Other factors are critical to this approach. Equal attention must be given within an integrated approach to the psychological, social, and spiritual aspects of the patient's suffering. Unfortunately, the better definition given to understanding the biological (physical) mechanism of a person's illness, the less likely these other critical perspectives will be addressed. Complementary and Alternative Medicine (CAM) approaches to disease and human suffering have often claimed to address these issues in an integrated holistic manner. Healing at a distance (prayer) and touch are examples that have been studied experimentally.

The success of the modalities that are offered in the therapeutic encounter often depends on rather mundane but critically important issues as the following example illustrates.

An 81-year-old man who has poor short term memory is being followed by a hospice team for advanced prostate cancer that is complicated by severe pain from widespread skeletal metastases. Although his hospice nurse is making frequent home visits each week, his pain is poorly controlled. His hospice nurse notes that he is apparently missing doses of his scheduled morphine. The patient's elderly wife is frightened about his medications and sometimes withholds them from him. He is now largely confined to bed or a chair because of intense incident pain with any movement. He expresses his frustration by saying, "This is no way to live! A dog is treated better than this!"

The best analgesic medications in the world will not relieve pain, if the patient does not receive them; and not only receive them, but at the appropriate dose and at the appropriate time. Something apparently as simple as medication compliance can dictate the difference between comfort and dignity versus severe unremitting suffering. An elderly patient with some cognitive impairment can suffer even more because of the loss of control over his or her own care along with increasing dependence. Although individual therapeutic modalities have varying degrees of efficacy, this patient's story highlights the great need for competent and responsible caregivers in palliative care to provide those modalities in an effective and safe manner. If the family caregiver is frightened, unwilling, or simply unable to provide the care and support needed, there will not only be greater suffering for the patient but also intense social suffering within the larger family unit. Hospice providers may also suffer when they see home situations they cannot effectively change because of limited resources and unwillingness or inability of primary caregivers to learn their tasks well or take them seriously. Situations like the one described above sound a cautionary note about the use of healing modalities in the therapeutic encounter. Effective education and communication with patients and caregivers, provided with patience and compassion, are essential to maximizing any potential benefit that may be received from a therapeutic modality. These require commitment of time and an empathic understanding of the patient and family caregivers, on the part of the health professionals providing care in the therapeutic encounter.

Touch in the Therapeutic Encounter

Two members of a palliative care team are called by a nurse to the bedside of an elderly man with advanced prostate cancer widely metastatic to bone. He is agitated and delirious, writhing in bed, apparently from uncontrolled pain. One of the team members, a physician, asks the patient's nurse to prepare morphine for subcutaneous injection. While the nurse is away obtaining the morphine, the two team members continue to observe the agitation and distress of the patient. He is not responsive to verbal communication. The palliative care team members are standing opposite one another at the patient's shoulders. Without conferring with each other, they begin to simultaneously massage his shoulders in a gentle, steady and persistent manner. By the time the nurse returns with the morphine (about ten minutes later), the patient has calmed down and is no longer agitated.

In a mysterious manner, the physical contact initiated simultaneously by the nurse and physician with this delirious patient transcended his acute confusion where words had been of no avail to communicate compassion and bring relief of his intense pain. The physical contact destroyed the isolation created by his pain and compounded by the delirium. The quality of the massage technique was not as critical to the effect as the collective concern and intent that initiated the spontaneous action from the two colleagues. Physical touch in the form of massage spoke directly to this person in distress, communicating palpable empathy while also producing pain relief even more rapidly than an externally administered analgesic medication. Where the morphine helps as a physical intervention through its binding to opioid receptors, massage transcends this effect to affect also the social (isolation), psychological (delirium), and likely spiritual distress that is often present, and so massage can provide a healing intervention for the whole person who is experiencing Total Pain. "The body does not only express the person; to a certain extent it *is* the person. The person does not merely *have* a body, it *is* a body, even though the person as such infinitely transcends bodily limits. This is why everything that involves the body involves the person as a whole."[2]

Massage (e.g., effleurage back massage, foot massage) is a therapeutic modality that has been demonstrated to be an effective adjuvant (supporting) treatment for the relief of pain and anxiety after major operations as well as in advanced illnesses.[3-5] Other forms of therapeutic touch exist which also involve actual physical contact between healer and patient. *Physical* healing touch can range from the 'laying on

[2]Jean-Claude Larchet, *The Theology of Illness*, trans. by John Breck and Michael Breck (Crestwood, NY: St Vladimir's Seminary Press, 2002), 14.

[3]M.M. Piotrowski, C. Paterson, A. Mitchinson, H.M. Kim, M. Kirsh, and D.B. Hinshaw, "Massage as Adjuvant Therapy in the Management of Acute Postoperative Pain: A Preliminary Study in Men," *Journal of the American College of Surgeons* 197 (2003): 1037–1046.

[4]A.M. Mitchinson, H.M. Kim, J.M. Rosenberg, M. Geisser, M. Kirsh, D. Cikrit, and D.B. Hinshaw, "Acute post-operative pain management using massage as adjuvant therapy: A randomized trial," *Archives of Surgery* 142(2) (2007): 1158–1167.

[5]J.S. Kutner, M.C. Smith, L. Corbin, L. Hemphill, K. Benton, K. Mellis, B. Beaty, S. Felton, T.E. Yamashita, L.L. Bryant, and D.L. Fairclough, "Massage Therapy versus Simple Touch to Improve Pain and Mood in Patients with Advanced Cancer. A Randomized Trial," *Annals of Internal Medicine* 149(6) (2008): 369–379.

of hands' of a 'faith healer' (or be a part of the process of ordination or of conferring other forms of sacramental healing) to massage performed by a physical or massage therapist, or the comforting touch of a nurse. Even the 'touch' of the surgeon's knife may qualify depending on the spirit in which it is applied.

All of the senses are enlisted when persons become connected to one another within an individual therapeutic encounter. Activation of memories that are embedded within the sensory experience of past encounters strengthens and modifies in subtle ways the current encounter. "It is a fact to me from frequent observation that the simple reality of being touched with gentle respect can sometimes unleash the most powerful emotional reactions. For even the skin itself possesses a memory, and a simple touch, if it feels good and reaffirming, can trigger the re-experiencing of the most deep-rooted deprivation and distress."[6] Sometimes the touch of the healer, in addition to curing the physical disease, can also undo years of emotional pain and isolation due to stigma. "There came a man full of leprosy; and when he saw Jesus, he fell on his face and besought him, 'Lord, if you will, you can make me clean.' And he stretched out his hand and *touched* him, saying, 'I will; be clean.' And immediately the leprosy left him."[7]

A 78-year-old male with slowly progressive prostate cancer becomes paraplegic from spinal cord compression due to metastatic disease in his spine. He is now receiving home hospice services and has developed several fluctuant areas over his lower back and an open ulcer over his left buttock with necrotic (i.e., dead), foul-smelling material present. The odor is very upsetting to the patient and his family. His hospice nurse is frustrated by the failure of expensive debridement solutions to control the problem.

Are there other options? The knife is quick and may even be kind! Necrotic, foul smelling tissue can be rapidly eliminated without the delay associated with use of enzyme solutions. When tissue is necrotic

---

[6]M. De Hennezel, *Intimate Death: How the Dying Teach Us How to Live*, trans. by C.B. Janeway (New York: Alfred A. Knopf, 1997), 141.

[7]Luke 5.12–13.

(and also when it is insensate due to spinal cord compression), it is also free of any pain sensation which makes it possible to remove this foul smelling source of distress easily with sharp dissection with a knife in the patient's home. If done gently with kind words and a respectful manner, the application of the knife during the home visit or at the bedside in the hospital can become another form of intimate healing contact with a patient. This is especially true, if the procedure is done in a spirit of humility with the surgeon's full attention being given to restoring the suffering person's comfort and dignity.

Faith and Healing in the Therapeutic Encounter

In a conversation between a 46-year-old patient and her palliative care physician, who is treating her severe pain related to progressive skeletal metastases from advanced breast cancer, she tells her physician, "I have faith that God will use my cancer doctor to heal me of the cancer." She also indicates in the conversation with her palliative care physician that she has found peace in relying on this belief. Later, the palliative care physician has a conversation with her colleague who is the patient's oncologist and mentions her statement regarding her faith in the oncologist's 'being an instrument of God' to heal her. He, however, expresses some frustration with her attitude, "I know she will die soon and I do not share her faith that I am God's instrument of healing in her life." A month later, the palliative care physician sees her patient with progressive breast cancer in follow-up of her cancer-related pain. At the prior visit, her pain was well controlled with the opioid regimen prescribed by the palliative care physician. She now complains of excruciating pain in the same areas of her spine that had responded well to the medications even as recently as a week ago. Tearfully, she also says, "My cancer doctor has abandoned me! He says I cannot have any more treatment."

Where is her faith now? What initially appeared to be an affirmation of religious faith may actually represent unlimited trust placed in a physician, born out of a desperate mingling of fear and hope. "No more treatment" for this woman has not only translated into a sense of abandonment not only by her oncologist but also by God. She has been presented with a real challenge to her religious faith. Her oncologist's brutally accurate assessment of her condition and his conscious recognition of his inability to alter her likely prognosis have become barriers preventing him from really hearing the concerns of his palliative care colleague about the patient's impending emotional and spiritual crisis. If he had been able to maintain a relationship of trust with her extending through and beyond the conversation about "no more treatment," the intense suffering she experienced might have been significantly mitigated.

That revered figure from late nineteenth- and early-twentieth-century medicine, William Osler, addressed the relationship of faith to healing in a way that has typified the attitude of many medical practitioners in the modern era: "Faith is indeed one of the miracles of human nature which science is as ready to accept as it is to study its marvelous effects . . . Literature is full of examples of remarkable cures through the influence of the imagination, which is only an active phase of faith."[8] In other words, faith is something akin to the placebo effect! There is almost an intense need on the part of many intellectuals trained in the western rationalist tradition to find a reason-based, materialistic explanation for the miraculous, even if they profess religious faith. In contrast to this is the apophatic tradition of the ancient Church, where there are mysteries (the ultimate example of which is communion with the Eucharistic Body and Blood of Christ) which can only be experienced and yet never fully understood by the faithful. Providing a naturalistic or biological explanation for a disease and its cure may shed some light on a mystery of human suffering, but like peeling back one layer of an onion, does not necessarily arrive at the heart of the matter. Scientific optimism that all "miracles" will ultimately be explained by the progress of science is even a part of the thinking of many Christians. In reference to the ancient Hippocratic roots of the drug aspirin, one of the participants at a symposium on health and faith stated: "The recognition, therefore, of what took more than 3000 years or so to

[8]W. Osler, "The Faith that Heals," *British Medical Journal* (June 18, 1910): 1470–1472.

understand should indicate that it may take another 3000 years before we understand processes we today call miracles."[9] But some miracles will never be subject to scientific inquiry, and mystery remains.

Distant Healing

The daughter of a 63-year-old patient with advanced ovarian cancer asks to speak privately with her mother's hospice nurse during a home visit. She is concerned that her mother has been going to a 'healer' who has promised to adjust the energy fields surrounding her body to restore her to health. She is upset because her mother is spending the family savings on the 'treatments.' Tearfully, her daughter admits that her mother has been more hopeful since she has been going to the 'healer' and she does not want to keep her mother from having a treatment that may be helpful.

A 59-year-old man with advanced lung cancer is receiving aggressive symptom management in a residential hospice. He is experiencing progressive debility and terrifying hemoptysis (coughing up as much as 30 milliliters of blood at a time). The hemoptysis worsens in spite of palliative radiation. Without explanation, his hemoptysis stops for several days. He tells the hospice team triumphantly that he has had several friends at his church praying for him and he is sure that his cancer is going away. The next day, his hospice physician is called to his bedside. He is now extremely anxious and short of breath after coughing up about 5 milliliters of blood. After giving him some subcutaneous morphine, his breathlessness improves but he then turns in bed toward the wall and will not speak with the team.

Distant healing has been defined in the medical literature as, "A conscious dedicated act of mentation attempting to benefit another person's physical or emotional well-being at a distance."[10] There are two main categories of 'distant healing' recognized by scientific investigators:

[9] T.C. Theoharides, "Miracles: A Medical Perspective," in J.T. Chirban, ed., *Health and Faith, Medical, Psychological and Religious Dimensions* (Lanham, MD: University Press of America, 1991), 120.

[10] F. Sicher, E. Targ, D. Moore, and H.S. Smith, "A randomized double-blind study of the effect of distant healing in a population with advanced AIDS—report of a small scale study," *Western Journal of Medicine* 169 (1998): 356–363.

1) Therapeutic touch (e.g., Reiki and external qigong) in which healing is thought to occur through an exchange of 'supra physical' energy and usually does *not* involve actual physical contact, in contrast to massage; and

2) Prayer which by most investigators' definitions includes intercessory prayer (for a person), supplication (for a specific outcome), and non-directed prayer (no specific outcome requested), e.g., "thy will be done."

A systematic review of randomized trials of distant healing cautiously suggested that since "approximately 57% of trials showed a positive treatment effect, the evidence thus far merits further study."[11] As noted above, some forms of therapeutic touch (e.g., Reiki, external qigong) do not involve actual physical contact with patients but are thought to relate to some form of 'energy' transfer and detection of an energy field around patients. In a highly publicized study,[12] practitioners of therapeutic touch were asked to identify under blinded conditions the experimenter's hand hovering over either their right or left hand. They were unable to predictably detect the experimenter's 'energy field'— thus 'debunking' Reiki on scientific grounds. It is important, however, to make a distinction between discrediting a hypothesis regarding the mechanism of action of a particular therapeutic modality, in this case Reiki, and the actual effect of the modality in the full context of a therapeutic encounter. What was not examined in the 'debunking' study was the role of the relationship between suffering persons seeking relief of their pain or other distress and practitioners of Reiki. For many, if not most therapeutic encounters the relationship that is formed between patient and healer may ultimately be more critical to determining the 'success' of the therapy than measurable biological effects alone. One

[11]J.A. Astin, E. Harkness, E. Ernst, "The Efficacy of 'Distant Healing': A Systematic Review of Randomized Trials," *Annals of Internal Medicine* 132 (2000): 903–910.

[12]L. Rosa, E. Rosa, L. Sarner, and S. Barrett, "A Close Look at Therapeutic Touch," *Journal of the American Medical Association* 279(13) (1998): 1005–1010.

should never discount the power inherent in a relationship of trust where one person comes to another for support and caring.

A distinction has been made between religiosity and spirituality in the medical literature investigating prayer and healing. In this literature, religiosity has been defined as personal adherence to the beliefs and practices of organized religion and spirituality has been defined as a personal search for meaning or for a personal relationship with a higher power. Studies have examined religiosity by measuring church attendance, etc. Spirituality has been more difficult to measure. The relative hazard of dying was 46% lower for those who regularly attended religious services (at least once per week) than for occasional attendees. Factors that may have been important determinants of survival (e.g., smoking, alcohol use, and social supports) typically have not been analyzed (controlled for) in many of these studies.[13] There are many perceived problems with such studies. There is no way to control for patients praying for themselves. Typically, most experimental designs in the effort to achieve 'blinding' of subjects and investigators regarding the random assignment of recipients of the intervention have required that there should be no direct contact with patients in the studies. Why would a benevolent God respond only to prayers for people in the treatment group? There is a recognition that many would consider such studies to be inherently blasphemous, although this has not prevented enthusiasts from pursuing such work as reflected in the following quote. "No experiment can prove or disprove the existence of God, but if in fact [mental] intentions can be shown to facilitate healing at a distance, this would clearly imply that human beings are more connected to each other and more responsible to each other than previously believed. That connection could be actuated through the agency of God, consciousness, love, electrons, or a combination. The answers to such questions await further research."[14]

[13]L. Gunderson, "Faith and Healing," *Annals of Internal Medicine* 132 (2000): 169–172.

[14]E. Tarq and K.S. Thomson, "Can prayer and intentionality be researched? Should they be?" *Alternative Therapies in Health and Medicine* 3 (1997): 92–96.

One approach to control for self-prayer and unsolicited prayers for the control group has been to "pray" for the outcome of simpler non-human biological experiments with cellular models or enzyme systems. Pray your way to better scientific outcomes! Whatever became of the null hypothesis? Fundamentally, the scientific method of being inherently skeptical of one's hypothesis, with the assumption that it will be disproven by the experiment (i.e., the null hypothesis) is upended in such research. In a controversial example of recent research of this type, the investigators tested the hypothesis that remote, intercessory prayer for hospitalized cardiac patients would reduce overall adverse events and length of stay.[15] Nine hundred ninety consecutive patients newly admitted to a coronary care unit (CCU) were randomized by the last digit of their hospital numbers so that even numbered subjects received intercessory prayer and odd received usual care. Outcomes were measured as a 'CCU course score.' The CCU course score was determined as events (and interventions) that ranged from 1 to 6; 1 = relatively simple interventions, i.e., simple monitoring, anti-anginal medications, etc.; 2 = more complicated medication interventions to control arrhythmias, maintain blood pressure, or prevent the development of pneumonia; 3 = advanced cardiology interventions; 4 = dangerous arrhythmias (e.g., ventricular tachycardia, ventricular fibrillation), major operations; 5 = cardiac arrest; 6 = death. Scored events were summed to obtain an overall score for the entire CCU stay. It was possible to have a score worse than 6 and survive; an obvious flaw in the scoring system. Patients and staff were both blinded regarding subject assignment to either the intervention or control groups. In an unusual departure from standard practice, the human studies committee allowed an exemption so that informed consent was not required, an exemption that had its own ethical implications. The decision to grant an exemption may have been a reflection of the skepticism of committee members regarding

[15]W.S. Harris, M. Gowda, J.W. Kolb, C.P. Strychacz, J.L. Vacek, P.G. Jones, A. Forber, J.H. O'Keefe, and B.D. McCallister, "A randomized, controlled trial of the effects of remote, intercessory prayer on outcomes in patients admitted to the coronary care unit," *Archives of Internal Medicine* 159 (1999): 2273–2278.

the efficacy of prayer in this context and their possible lack of concern regarding any potential harm associated with its use. A total of 75 intercessors organized as 15 teams of 5 members; each only knew the first name of the patients for whom they prayed. There was a random assignment of intercessors to teams. Intercessors had to agree with the following statements "I believe in God. I believe that He is personal and is concerned with individual lives. I further believe that He is responsive to prayers for healing made on behalf of the sick."[16] Intercessors came from different Christian backgrounds: 35% were nondenominational, 27% were Episcopalian, and the remainder was made up of other Protestants and Roman Catholics. Eighty seven percent were women with a mean age of 56 years. Intercessors were regular church goers (at least weekly attendance) and prayed on a daily basis before participation in the study. Prayer began within one to two days after CCU admission for those patients randomized to the experimental group. Intercessors were asked to pray for 28 days for the patients and to pray for "a speedy recovery."[17] The investigators reported an 11 percent reduction in CCU scores for the prayer group (p=0.04) compared to the usual care group. No differences in length of stay or in individual parameters used for the scoring between groups were identified.

As might be expected, the study elicited a storm of letters to the editors who published the article. The letters identified a number of problems with the study. There were methodological concerns about the CCU scoring technique. It was an unvalidated scoring system that appeared to be contrived. The possibility of accruing a total CCU score worse than 6, even though a score of 6 in their system was assigned for death as an outcome, was especially problematic. As noted above there were ethical concerns with the study. There was no informed consent, ostensibly to eliminate selection bias of only 'prayer receptive' subjects. Even though they showed a statistically significant difference between groups in the study, what was the actual biological significance? Did the prayer intervention actually make a real difference? Another concern

[16]Ibid.
[17]Ibid.

was that pure intercessory prayer was not possible in a blinded study in which the intercessors did not know the subjects of their prayers. The study also raised the question of whether Christian prayers are essentially more efficacious than those offered by adherents of other religious faiths. The most fundamental and basic criticism offered in the flurry of letters to the editor was that the study was blasphemous.

The need to subject God to the scientific method, as if his existence or his actions in the created order were so many hypotheses to be tested, is yet again a characteristic modern approach to great mysteries that cannot be known or understood this way. In reference to a similar perceived conflict between science and faith in regard to human origins, Jean-Claude Larchet states, "the existence of Adam in his primitive state is 'ante-historical,' just as human existence following the parousia [second coming of Christ] will be post-historical. Spiritual history, then, cannot be replaced by historical science ... we are dealing with two different modes of apprehension that cannot be reduced one to another. Each concerns different modes of being and of becoming. Faith and spiritual knowledge correspond to a domain in which the laws of nature are transcended and to a mode of existence that is, in the proper sense of the term, 'super-natural.'"[18] Like Simon Magus (Acts 8.9–24), many today want to have control over the 'magic' healing power of prayer but are not interested in a relationship with the real living Source of that power. Thus, there must be a way to study it sufficiently to understand its "mechanism" and then have the power for oneself, to be fully autonomous, a law unto oneself, a 'creator.' But, Christ heals persons not statistics. His way to healing is still via the cross. Prayers for healing must always be in the context of a relationship with the Healer: "Not my will, but thy will be done."[19] God is not a cosmic "bellhop" or "waiter" upon whom we can call at our whim, once we find the right "process" or formula.

[18]J.C. Larchet, 23.
[19]Luke 22. 42.

Communication as a Therapeutic Modality

A physician was making rounds in a residential hospice one morning and came to the bedside of a patient who had been non-responsive for the past 24–48 hours and who appeared to be actively dying from advanced cancer of the pancreas. His wife and elderly mother were keeping vigil at the bedside. He greeted them and began to examine the patient. The patient's mother then asked the physician, "Why didn't you greet my son?"

Bodies are ignored, persons are addressed. When did this dying man become a 'body' to be ignored and no longer a person to be addressed? His very perceptive (and sensitive) grieving mother noted a significant, if unconscious change in the physician's relationship to her dying son. The physician's treatment of the patient as an object is a reflection of the social death described in chapter 3 of this book. The physician had unconsciously and prematurely categorized the dying man as 'dead'. The varied understanding of what constitutes a person is also illustrated by this example. For the patient's mother her unresponsive, dying son was still very much a person. Would he lose his personhood immediately at the moment of cessation of vital functions? It is always safer and more appropriate to assume that a person is present, even if no apparent response is given to verbal communication. The reverent concern for the physical remains of the dead person shown by traditional Christianity is a strong reminder that the person is still very much connected to his or her body, whether dead or alive in the biological sense. When other family or friends are present at the bedside of the dying, their presence can be a manifestation of the interconnected nature of the social suffering of the patient and family. Acknowledging all of the persons present is also acknowledging all of the individual and collective suffering present in the room. Words are not the only way and may not even be the best way to communicate this acknowledgement. Sometimes gentle touch directed to the unresponsive person (e.g., a hand on the shoulder) while keeping silent vigil, even for only a few minutes at the bedside, is a much more effective form of communication. This is true whether others are present or not. "Silence is a mystery of the age to come, but words are instruments of this world."[20]

There are some secular cognates of confession that have been investigated as potential means of healing through which seriously ill individuals are able to communicate the stories of their suffering and sometimes gain relief in the process. Typically, in this type of narrative healing process the sick person would be asked to write an essay expressing his or her feelings and thoughts about a difficult or traumatic experience. Studies, particularly in the psychology literature, suggest that such exercises improve health outcomes. One study[21] tested the hypothesis that writing about a stressful experience would affect disease status in chronic illness in patients with asthma and rheumatoid arthritis. One hundred seven patients (58 with asthma and 49 with arthritis) completed the study and were randomized to write either about the most stressful event of their lives or (as controls) about topics which were emotionally neutral (e.g., describe their plans for the day as a time management exercise). The writing exercise occurred over 20 minutes on three consecutive days and was anonymous. Outcomes that were measured in the study included, for patients with asthma, an objective measure of pulmonary function, the forced expiratory volume in one second (FEV1), and for patients with rheumatoid arthritis, a structured interview by a rheumatologist. This interview followed a standardized approach utilized for clinical trials of new therapies for that condition, and it included 1) symptoms assessment with rating of their severity; 2) global assessment of disease activity; 3) identification of the distribution of pain and swelling; 4) the presence and severity of deformities; and 5) patient functional status. Analysis of the results demonstrated no difference

[20]St Isaac the Syrian, "Homily 65" in *The Ascetical Homilies of Saint Isaac the Syrian* (Boston: Holy Transfiguration Monastery, 1984), 321.

[21]J.M. Smyth, A.A. Stone, A. Hurewitz, and A. Kaell, "Effects of writing about stressful experiences on symptom reduction in patients with asthma or rheumatoid arthritis: a randomized trial," *Journal of the American Medical Association* 281(14) (1999): 1304–1309.

demographically or in terms of baseline disease status between the experimental and control groups. Statistically significant improvement was seen in both asthma and rheumatoid arthritis patients at 4 months. There was an approximate 10% increase in FEV_1 in asthma patients. Arthritis patients had predominantly mild overall disease activity compared to moderate overall disease activity at baseline. The results of the study raised some questions and concerns. Even though there were statistically significant differences demonstrated between the experimental and control groups, were the changes significant from a biological perspective or from the perspective of the person? The baseline burden of disease was not severe. It is unclear what the potential benefit of such therapy might be for more severe illness. The effects on asthma were seen as early as two weeks, whereas effects in rheumatoid arthritis were not seen until 4 months. Another concern about the methodology was that the writing experience was quite upsetting for members of the experimental group at the time of writing. There were even negative physiologic changes noted in heart rate and blood pressure as well as effects on immune function. Typical topics for the stressful experience described in the writing exercise of the experimental group included death of a loved one, major accidents, or significant problems with relationships. Of particular interest was the fact that about half of the patients in the experimental group responded to this intervention. Unfortunately, the differences between responders and non-responders were not clear, yet those differences might have helped to identify better candidates for what was an emotionally traumatic experience. Finally, the long-term durability of the response is unknown. The study does underscore the potential power of telling one's story as part of the experience of healing.

A major challenge for those who are suffering in the context of serious or life-threatening illness is to find meaning in their life and particularly meaning in their suffering. Creating a patient's biography can sometimes assist in the process of finding meaning. "Life review enables a person to identify what has been accomplished or created, and what will be left behind as a result ... a sense of meaning may be captured in the recognition of the uniqueness of the individual."[22] Volunteer 'biographers' first record an oral biography and then prepare a written transcript which is bound for the patient to pass on to loved ones. Usually positive memories are shared, although if a high level of trust develops between patients and 'biographers,' patients may 'unburden' and tell more intimate and negative details of their lives (more like the sacrament of confession). Patient biography is similar to confession in terms of the potential for self-revelation and finding meaning but is unlike confession in that repentance may not be the driving force or motivation behind the activity. "The subjects choose what they want to tell and what they want to ignore."[23] Thus, the 'biography' may avoid dealing with specific issues (i.e., sins) that interfere with healing of the dying one.

The Interdisciplinary Team as a Healing Modality

A 52-year-old man with advanced primary cancer of the liver is receiving palliative radiotherapy as an inpatient for painful metastases in his spine. He was receiving care at an inpatient hospice that is over 150 miles away prior to the referral for radiotherapy. During a conversation with a team member, he speaks with great emotion of his girlfriend about whom he is very much concerned because she also has 'advanced cancer.' As he is nearing the completion of his radiotherapy, he confirms his desire to be with her to help with her care rather than return to the inpatient hospice. The social worker on the team has great difficulty contacting the girlfriend, who seems to avoid answering calls. When finally she is contacted, she denies any interest in having the patient stay with her, although she has access to his bank account and freely spends his money. After he is told that his girlfriend is not able to have him stay with her after the radiotherapy is completed, the patient becomes quite sad, withdraws, cooperates less in his care, and his pain becomes much more difficult to control.

[22]I. Lichter, J. Mooney, and M. Boyd, "Biography as Therapy," *Palliative Medicine* 7 (1993): 133–137.
    [23]Ibid.

Without the careful and compassionate detective work of the social worker on the interdisciplinary team, this patient's social suffering might not have been uncovered until late in his care. The social worker's discovery early enough to intervene may have helped prevent his experiencing even greater pain, if he later learned of his abandonment by his girlfriend without the emotional support available from the team. No single profession can claim to address all aspects of the care of the sick. "It is axiomatic that what is needed is the delivery of health care via a seamless web of health professional services oriented to the patient's and the public's best interests rather than each profession's self-interest."[24] Such an approach would require the full integration of care developing out of real collaboration between the health professions. The processes underlying health care delivery would need to be rethought from the perspective of the patient, i.e., the patient would have to be included in the process. "The greatest challenge facing the academic health center community is to restore the marriage between humanistic concerns and scientific and technical excellence in health care delivery practices."[25] A healthy and collegial interaction among representatives of the different health professions in an interdisciplinary team, including those that are concerned with the social or pastoral (spiritual) aspects of patient care, can be a powerful corrective to the often heavy focus on the purely technical, 'medical' aspects of care.

To achieve such a transformation in the interaction of health professionals so that they can collectively become a force for healing beyond the sum of their individual contributions, it may be useful first to examine the organization and culture of the 'traditional' medical team. The 'traditional' medical team is hierarchical. Usually, the physician is the unchallenged leader of the team. Subordinate members receive and execute physician orders, in a manner not unlike a military chain of command. There is very little opportunity for dialogue or reciprocal communication. This type of team organization can create unrealistic

[24]R.J. Bulger, "The Quest for the Therapeutic Organization," *Journal of the American Medical Association* 283 (2000): 2431–2433.
[25]Ibid.

expectations for the physician leader who may often be the least experienced team member. Potentially, it can lead to autocratic and incorrect decisions made in haste without consultation. It can be a recipe for resentment and conflict within the team, with real potential for patient harm as a consequence. The traditional hierarchical team is predicated on the notion that all illnesses are or will ultimately be treatable and thus curable by Medicine (of which physicians are the ruling elite).

What are the fundamental characteristics of the interdisciplinary team in palliative care? At a minimum it consists of representatives from the following disciplines: nursing, medicine, social work, and pastoral care. Ideally, it could also embrace and benefit from the involvement of other health professionals, including psychologists, pharmacists, complementary therapists, lay volunteers, etc. A recognition that the omnipotence of Medicine does not extend to the "cure" of suffering and death is the starting point for palliative care. In such a context, all available skills and perspectives that might alleviate the suffering must be integrated and offered for the benefit of the patient. Although individual members of the team have their own sphere of professional expertise, ideally they attempt to create a symphony of common effort toward one goal, care for the suffering one that must extend beyond their individual egos. Implicit in such an approach is the possibility that empirical experience, in fact any life experience, may often be more useful when confronting a mystery than formal knowledge alone. Humility is an essential ingredient in the dynamics of interdisciplinary team work. Solutions to problems can come from unexpected quarters and apparently unlikely sources, if team members are able to break free of the prejudices and mindsets inherent in their original discipline. Listening (in all its facets) must be cultivated as the first and most critical tool of the healer, listening not only to other members of the interdisciplinary team, but especially to the patient. Ultimately, in some sense, the suffering patient must be the central member of the interdisciplinary team. Patients often hold within themselves the solutions to their suffering. It is the task of the interdisciplinary team to support patients on their journeys of suffering, never abandoning them, and offering them tools from their collective expertise to ease the way. If the interdisciplinary team functions well, not only can it extend its function beyond the sum of the individual types of professional expertise of its members, but also it can create a therapeutic environment. A therapeutic environment is more than the particular architecture of a hospital ward or clinic. How do *all* the caregivers interact with one another and with the patient? One hopes that there is a consistent expression of loving compassion for the patient from the entire team. Ideally, the compassion of team members also extends beyond the patient to each other. A therapeutic environment exists to the extent that a therapeutic organization (team) is present. In addition to the interdisciplinary team, the family can also be a therapeutic environment, but unfortunately is not always.

> Can the team be organized so that two people always come when it's a question of a procedure that may be painful? One simply to offer her presence, her warmth, and attention, while the other, just as attentively, does what has to be done with all possible competence. When three people get together like this, each wishing to draw on the presence of the other two in order to face a difficult moment, a composite being with truly miraculous powers is brought into existence.[26]

When the team—including the patient—achieves this level of transcendent mutual concern and compassion, it becomes a small image of the love that flows between members of the Holy Trinity. This is the model for the ideal team. But what if the team is dysfunctional?

A hospice home-care nurse has been closely following an elderly man with advanced prostate cancer and widespread skeletal metastases. He has been essentially living a bed-to-chair existence for the last two weeks. After much encouragement from the hospice nurse, he has agreed to try a small dose of morphine. He claims to be comfortable and expresses appreciation for her efforts. He has been primarily taking the morphine at bed time. The nurse asks the hospice physician to see the patient, "I think he is minimizing his

[26]Hennezel, *Intimate Death*, 50.

pain." *The hospice physician sees him quickly on a home visit and assesses him as being comfortable and says, "We can't force him to take pain medication." The nurse continues to believe that he is in much greater pain than he reports but now feels powerless to address the problem.*

Palliative care health professionals have a moral/ethical duty to advocate for the relief of their patients' suffering. Conflicts may arise when there is disagreement between palliative care consultants and referring clinicians who are unwilling to act on recommendations from the palliative care consultants (typically about issues of futility or symptom control). Such conflicts, without adequate resolution, may lead to moral distress in members of the palliative care team, a sense of hopelessness or impotence, and eventually burnout.[27] Moral distress has more often been described in the nursing literature where nurses may identify issues of uncontrolled pain, suffering, or futility that are perceived to be ignored or inadequately addressed by physicians, as in the example above. Nurses may then feel powerless to advocate adequately for their patients, and this feeling of powerlessness can lead to moral distress. Without being grounded in some greater moral framework (e.g., religious faith), without the realization and acceptance that we are not actually in control, moral distress may be an inevitable consequence of advocating for human suffering. "Patience, patience, patience!"[28] We must remain faithful to our vocation and not abandon the patient but remain present. If one is a person of prayer, it is essential to pray even more.

[27]D.E. Weissman, "Moral Distress in Palliative Care," *Journal of Palliative Medicine* 12(10) (2009): 865–866.

[28]I. Balan, *Elder Cleopa of Sihastria: In the Tradition of St. Paisius Velichkovsky*, trans. by Mother Cassiana (Lake George, CO: New Varatec Publishing, Protection of the Holy Virgin Orthodox Monastery, 2001), 94.

CHAPTER 8

The Patient

W HO IS THE PATIENT in the therapeutic encounter? To help answer this question, let us examine a story of St Antony the Great (+356 AD) from fourth-century Christian Egypt recorded in the early fifth-century Lausiac History of Palladius.[1] In the story Eulogius was walking in the market place struggling with inner thoughts regarding his salvation and a desire to make his life count for something.

> Eulogius . . . found a man lying in the market-place, a cripple, with neither hands nor feet. His tongue was the only part of his body that was undamaged, and was used to appeal to the passer-by. . . . So Eulogius stood and gazed at him and prayed to God and made a covenant with God (saying): "Lord, in Thy name I take this cripple and comfort him until death, that I also may be saved through him. Grant me patience to serve him!"
>
> Well, the cripple lasted on for fifteen years and was nursed by him, being washed and tended by the hands of Eulogius, and fed in a way suitable to his malady. But after the fifteen years a demon attacked him, and he rebelled against Eulogius. And he began to dress the man down with great abuse and reviling, adding: "Assassin, deserter, you stole other folk's property, and you want to be saved through me..." So Eulogius went off to the neighboring ascetics and said to them: "What shall I do, because this cripple has brought me to despair? ... I pledged myself to God and I am afraid.... I do not know what to do ..." But they said to him: "While the great one is still alive"—for so they called Antony—"put the cripple in a boat

[1]Palladius, *The Lausiac History of Palladius*, trans. by W.K. Lowther Clarke, Translations of Christian Literature, Series 1: Greek Texts (London: The Society for Promoting Christian Knowledge, and New York: Macmillan, 1918) 92–95.

. . . and take him to the monastery and wait till Antony comes out from the cave and refer the case to him."

[Antony replied:] "Cast him out? But He Who made him does not cast him out. Will you cast him out? God will raise up a man better than you, and he will succour him." Eulogius, who had been calm up till now, trembled. And Antony leaving Eulogius began to castigate the cripple with his tongue and cry: "You crippled and maimed man, deserving neither earth nor heaven, will you not cease fighting against God? Do you not know that it is Christ Who is serving you?" . . . So having reprimanded him, he left him alone too. . . . [He] returned to Eulogius and the cripple and said to them: "Do not wander about any more, go away. Do not be separated from one another, except in your cell in which you have dwelt so long. For already God is sending for you. For this temptation has come upon you because you are both near your end and are about to be counted worthy of crowns. Do nothing else therefore, and may the angel when he comes not find you here." So they journeyed in haste and came to their cell, and within forty days Eulogius died, and in three days more the cripple died too.

Do you not realize that it is Christ who is your servant? These words of St Antony are at the heart of the therapeutic encounter. For the Christian tradition of caring for human suffering, one question must be answered: "But who do you say that I am?"[2] Everything flows from the answer to this question.

What should be our attitude to the suffering of others? The Elder (Russian: *Starets*) Zosima in Dostoevksy's novel, *The Brothers Karamazov*, makes a bold assertion in answer to this fundamental question for Christians: "Make yourself responsible for all the sins of men. For indeed it is so, my friend, and the moment you make yourself sincerely responsible for everything and everyone, you will see at once that it is really so, that it is you who are guilty on behalf of all and for all."[3]

[2]Mark 8.29.
[3]The Elder Zosima, in Fyodor Dostoevsky, *The Brothers Karamazov*, trans. by R. Pevear and L. Volokhonsky, (New York: Farrar, Strauss, Giroux, 1990), 320.

In essence he is saying that the one who would follow Christ in His ministry of healing must become a little "Christ" even unto the bearing of others' burdens of sin and suffering. This willingness to bear the distress of others should be central to the role of healer in the therapeutic encounter. The more that is borne willingly, the more one can bear. The late Mother Teresa of Calcutta, founder of the Catholic order of Missionaries of Charity, modeled this in her life and work. "We all long for heaven where God is, but we have it in our power to be in heaven with him right now—to be happy with him at this very moment. But being happy with him now means:

> Loving as he loves,
> Helping as he helps,
> Giving as he gives,
> Serving as he serves,
> Rescuing as he rescues,
> Being with him twenty-four hours,
> Touching him in his distressing disguise."[4]

A number of virtues are operative in an effective therapeutic encounter.[5] First, listening in the sense of *hypakouo* (i.e., understand with a heart obedient to the call to serve the other) is an essential foundation for a real encounter to begin or continue. Second, another key virtue is to attend fully in the encounter. Being able to give one's full attention (as in prayer) to the patient, even for a short time, can give an enormous sense of value (real compassion) to the one who is suffering. Inattention, of course, can do just the opposite. Third, there must be a real dialogue conducive to healing. There are two components to dialogue: expressive and receptive. Physicians and caregivers need to be expressive and *not* impressive (domineering) in the encounter. Physicians and caregivers also need to be receptive almost as much as they

[4]Mother Teresa of Calcutta, quoted in M. Muggeridge, *Something Beautiful for God: Mother Teresa of Calcutta* (Garden City, NY: Image Books, 1977), 50.

[5]M. A. Adson, "An Endangered Ethic—the Capacity for Caring" *Mayo Clinic Proceedings* 70 (1995): 495–500.

are expressive—dialogue is about a relationship. Acknowledgement is the fourth virtue that is operative in an effective therapeutic encounter. Acknowledgement is recognition of another person's (the patient's) identity and unique value. It is also recognition of the reality of the illness which this patient and physician/caregiver must face together. Anything less on the part of the physician or caregiver represents a form of abandonment. Ideally, a healing intimacy is born out of this recognition. In a very real sense, the patient is the healer and the healer is the patient. For Christians, Christ is both the suffering patient and also the healer, just as in the Eucharist he is both Priest and Sacrifice who offers and is offered for the healing of the entire world. This reciprocity of healing in the therapeutic encounter even transcends time, just as the Liturgy of the Church also occurs continually in the eternal now of God. Acts of mercy and healing here are leaving their footprints in eternity. "The works we do now will be the healing we experience there, in Paradise:'Whoever has washed the feet of the saints will himself be cleansed in that dew; to the hand that had stretched out to give to the poor will the fruits of the trees themselves stretch out; the very footsteps of him who visited the sick in their affliction do the flowers make haste to crown with blooms, jostling to see which can be the first to kiss his steps.'"[6]

It is essential then to remember to whom one is listening in witnessing the suffering of another. Empathic listening is critical to recognizing (diagnosing) suffering. Stay silent inside and out ... practice *hesychia* (i.e., silence or stillness) so that you can encounter the"still, small voice" within the suffering that is present before you. Hear everything: what is said and what is left unsaid."Let it all come in without interpreting or judging."[7] Approach each encounter remembering this admonition of

[6]St. Ephrem the Syrian, quoted by Susan Ashbrook Harvey, "Embodiment in Time and Eternity: A Syriac Perspective" *St Vladimir's Theological Quarterly* 43 (1999): 105–130. See also: *St Ephrem the Syrian: Hymns on Paradise*, trans. by Sebastian P. Brock (Crestwood, NY: St Vladimir's Seminary Press, 1990).

[7]E.J. Cassel, "Diagnosing Suffering: A Perspective," *Annals of Internal Medicine* 131(7) (1999): 531–534.

Christ: "Judge not, that you be not judged."[8] Be simply open to mystery in the presence of the suffering one. If one sees the other as an icon of Christ, being open to his presence in the other is to become prayer, in which all things are possible.

Because humans have the precious gift of freedom, how individuals may respond to the offer and opportunity of healing within any given therapeutic encounter is never a foregone conclusion. This was even true in a unique therapeutic encounter involving three persons. "One of the criminals who were hanged railed at him, saying, 'Are you not the Christ? Save yourself and us!' But the other rebuked him, saying, 'Do you not fear God, since you are under the same sentence of condemnation? And we indeed justly; for we are receiving the due reward of our deeds; but this man has done nothing wrong.' And he said, 'Jesus, remember me when you come into your kingdom.' And he said to him, 'Truly, I say to you, today you will be with me in Paradise.'"[9] Christ is healing from the Cross, the ultimate therapeutic encounter. One rejects the healing and the other steals Paradise. He, who on a human level appeared to need rescuing from death, heals in the very act of dying—and his first cure is a thief!

[8]Matthew 7.1.
[9]Luke 23.39–43.

PART 3

Healing in Death

'In my end is my beginning.'[1]

"With this last sentence of the second of his Four Quartets (East Coker), TS Eliot expresses all the potential for renewal of hope and discovery of meaning that the terminally ill seek as they face death. The word *end* has two meanings that are expressed in ancient Greek with two different words directly relevant to the spiritual struggle of the dying; end as a 'state of completion or maturity' (Greek—*telos*) and end as 'last' (in time, e.g., end of life) (Greek— *eschatos*).[2] It is the discovery and experience of these two qualities of the end, balancing a full awareness of having arrived at the last stage of one's life with a sense of the opportunity for completion and full maturation, that can transform one's end into a beginning."[3]

---

[1] T.S. Eliot, *Four Quartets*, (New York and London: Harcourt Brace Jovanovich, 1971), 32.

[2] Liddell and Scott, 699, 1773.

[3] D.B. Hinshaw, "The Spiritual Needs of the Dying Patient," *Journal of the American College of Surgeons* 195(4) (2002): 565–568.

CHAPTER 9

Spirituality at the End of Life—
The Secular Perspective

"He who has a *why* to live for can bear with almost any *how*."[1]

W<small>HY WOULD A BOOK</small> focused on presenting a traditional Christian understanding of healing be concerned with the secular perspective of healing? A fundamental aspect of the traditional worldview of Christians is that the Holy Spirit blows where it wills so that truth is not limited by labels, although the fullness of the faith and truth resides within the Church. Persons of good will from any background are real participants in the search for truth. Thus, insights from other sources can sometimes be 'baptized' into the Christian understanding, if they are fundamentally consistent with the Church's tradition, even if they did not emerge within a specifically Christian context. Another consideration is the need to clarify real differences and deficiencies in the secular understanding compared to that of the Church's teaching and tradition where they exist. This is especially true when the issue under consideration is the relationship between spirituality and healing. This chapter will present an overview of the current secular understanding of spirituality as it relates to health care, and in particular to care of the dying. Differences or concepts and approaches consistent with as well as inconsistent with traditional Christian teaching will be highlighted. Finally, the limitations of imposing a specifically secular approach to spirituality in health care will also be examined.

The National Consensus Project for Quality Palliative Care—which originally represented a collaboration between three professional organizations in the United States, the Hospice and Palliative Nurses Asso-

---

[1] F. Nietzsche. "Maxims and Arrows," *Twilight of the Idols* (1888), 12.

ciation, the American Academy of Hospice and Palliative Medicine, and the National Hospice and Palliative Care Organization—has identified eight major domains of clinical practice in palliative care.[2] One of these eight domains is Spiritual, Religious and Existential Aspects of Care, in recognition of the great importance of these elements in the experience of persons suffering with advanced illnesses.

Spirituality has been defined as "that which allows a person to experience transcendent meaning in life. This is often expressed as a relationship with God, but it can also be about nature, art, music, family, or community—whatever beliefs and values give a person a sense of meaning and purpose in life."[3] This nice working definition by Dr Puchalski was recently modified as the product of a consensus conference on spirituality in palliative care that met in 2009. "Spirituality is the aspect of humanity that refers to the way individuals seek and express meaning and purpose and the way they experience their connectedness to the moment, to self, to others, and to the significant or sacred."[4] Note the absence of any direct reference to God or a higher power in the new consensus definition. The goal of the conference was "to identify points of agreement about spirituality as it applies to health care and to make recommendations to advance the delivery of quality spiritual care in palliative care."[5] The attendees of the conference also endeavored to create a working definition of healing. "Healing is distinguished from cure . . . it refers to the ability of a person to find solace, comfort, connection, meaning, and purpose in the midst of suffering, disarray, and pain. The care is rooted in spirituality using compassion, hopefulness,

[2]National Consensus Guidelines for Quality Palliative Care can be accessed at: http://www.nationalconsensusproject.org/guideline.pdf.

[3]C.M. Puchalski and A.L. Romer, "Taking a Spiritual History Allows Clinicians to Understand Patients More Fully," *Journal of Palliative Medicine* 3 (2000):129–137.

[4]C. Puchalski, B. Ferrell, R. Virani, S. Otis-Green, P. Baird, J. Bull, H. Chochinov, G. Handzo, H. Nelson-Becker, M. Prince-Paul, K. Pugliese, and D. Sulmasy, "Improving the Quality of Spiritual Care as a Dimension of Palliative Care: The Report of the Consensus Conference," *Journal of Palliative Medicine* 12(10) (2009): 885–904.

[5]Ibid.

and the recognition that, although a person's life may be limited or no longer socially productive, it remains full of possibility."[6] When achieving consensus is the driving force, such efforts seem to be focused on finding the lowest common denominator. Unfortunately, they often become normative in practice since they have the imprimatur of being published in the peer-reviewed medical literature. With this approach, spirituality can become yet another tool of the health care professional available to address the complex distress of patients with life-threatening illnesses. In practice, because of the limited comfort of many health professionals with the whole topic, it is typically invoked and offered when everything else fails.

There has been a growing awareness of a divide in American culture and society between those who profess to be religious and those who identify themselves as being spiritual persons but not particularly religious. A Gallup poll in January, 2002 asked the question, "Are you religious or spiritual?"[7] Fifty percent of Americans described themselves as religious, 33% said they were spiritual but not religious, 11% indicated they were neither religious nor spiritual, 4% were both religious and spiritual, and 2% were uncertain.

As noted earlier in this book, investigators have tried to understand what patients consider to be a 'good death'. In one of the studies,[8] the importance of forty-four attributes of quality at the end of life were evaluated in a random survey of patients, bereaved family members, physicians, nurses, social workers, chaplains, and hospice volunteers. A disturbing finding of the study was the marked difference between physicians' attitudes and priorities regarding death compared to those of all other respondents to the survey. Again, issues that were important to patients (and other respondents) but not so important to physicians

[6] Ibid.

[7] G.H. Gallup, Jr, "Americans' Spiritual Searches Turn Inward—Gallup Poll Tuesday Briefing," www.gallup.com, accessed February 11, 2003.

[8] K.E. Steinhauser, N.A. Christakis, E.C. Clipp, M. McNeilly, L. McIntyre, and J.A. Tulsky, "Factors Considered Important at the End of Life by Patients, Family, Physicians and Other Care Providers," *Journal of the American Medical Association* 284(19) (2000): 2476–2482.

were primarily spiritual in nature. Unfortunately, as the medical profession and the modern health care system have increasingly assumed greater responsibility for care of the dying, death has been progressively medicalized, with the result that other aspects of dying (especially spiritual aspects) have been either ignored or forgotten. "Death is the edge of a mystery, and turning our faces toward the problematic, through the persistent use of technology, at the hour of death keeps us from having to face mystery. Death is no problem to be solved; it resists any such formulation ... by keeping our attention on end-of-life problems, we ignore the mystery of the end of life."[9]

Recognizing Spiritual Distress

At the heart of the spiritual distress of the dying is suffering. As was explored in detail in the second part of this book, spiritual distress or pain permeates all other domains (physical, psychological, and social) of Cicely Saunders' Total Pain. How can clinicians identify spiritual distress in their patients? A good first step is to take a 'spiritual history'. By taking a spiritual history, the physician acknowledges the importance of spirituality and gives the dying patient permission to discuss spiritual issues. One popular tool[10] for guiding the process is structured using the following acronym:

F: Faith—Do you consider yourself religious or spiritual? Do you have a faith? If you do not have a faith, what are major sources of meaning in your life?

I: Importance—Is it important in your life?

C: Community—Are you part of a spiritual (or faith) community?

[9]M. Bevins and T. Cole, "Ethics and Spirituality: Strangers at the End of Life?" in *Annual Review of Gerontology and Geriatrics*, ed. M.P. Lawton (New York: Springer, 2000), 16–38.

[10]Puchalski and Romer, ibid..

A: Address—How can your healthcare providers address (and respect) these issues in your care?

In promoting use of this tool, Dr Puchalski emphasizes that spirituality is an important, if not the central component of each patient's overall well-being, and this is particularly true for the dying.[11] Spirituality is an ongoing issue—readdress it over time. In fact, one cannot address it fully without forming a relationship with the patient as a person. This takes time and often many separate encounters. Once the subject of spirituality has been raised, it is essential to not impose one's beliefs on others—respect each patient's autonomy and vulnerability. Taking a spiritual history may also help identify situations where referral to chaplains, spiritual directors, and others, may be appropriate and necessary. However, the one whom the suffering patient trusts the most will likely be the one with whom deeper spiritual concerns will be shared. Thus, all members of the interdisciplinary team must be prepared to assist with spiritual care. Self-awareness is critical to the successful use of the spiritual history during the therapeutic encounter. Know thyself. "You can't address a patient's spirituality until you address your own."[12] Other investigators have tried to find a 'shorthand' means of taking a spiritual history, e.g., a phrase or single question that gets to the heart of the spiritual history.[13] There was a strong correlation of peacefulness expressed as a positive response to the question, "Are you at peace?" with measures of emotional and spiritual well-being but also to a lesser extent with measures of physical, functional, and social well-being. Use of this simple question is a non-threatening and nonsectarian means of opening a conversation about emotional and spiritual concerns. The patient's response will guide further inquiry. The following stories from clinical care are examples of the importance of taking a spiritual history.

[11]Ibid.
[12]Ibid.
[13]K.E. Steinhauser, C.I. Voils, E.C. Clipp, H.B. Bosworth, N.A. Christakis, and J.A. Tulsky, "Are You at Peace? One Item to Probe Spiritual Concerns at the End of Life," *Archives of Internal Medicine* 166 (2006): 101–105.

A 52-year-old man with rapidly progressive and symptomatic pancreatic cancer is being evaluated in the palliative care clinic. When asked about a religious preference, he denies any interest in formalized religion. When he is asked what gives him a sense of meaning and purpose in life, he readily indicates that the fellowship he experiences in his motorcycle club is his source of purpose and meaning. When he was later hospitalized in a pain crisis, the members of his motorcycle club kept faithful vigil with him at his bedside providing emotional and spiritual support during his struggle with the pain. They were his spiritual community.

A 62-year-old man underwent a complex operation for cancer in his head and neck region with reconstruction 8 years ago. He now presents after an indolent course with extensive metastatic disease in the neck and chest. He is a retired lay preacher. He currently denies pain or other distress and states that he will be raptured before he develops any distress. He then asks his palliative care physician if he also believes in the Rapture.

Taking a spiritual history should not degenerate into a debate about religious beliefs, especially regarding the beliefs of the health professional who is proposing to care for the suffering person. Ideally, the physician should always turn the focus back to the patient and his needs. It might be helpful to ask the patient to explain more about his belief and hope in the Rapture without answering his question directly. Challenging his belief will likely cause him great distress or change the focus of the relationship to a desire on his part to convert the physician to his belief, instead of a focus on the common ground of mutual respect which should be the safe ground for their therapeutic encounter.

A 67-year-old man presents simultaneously with two non-obstructing cancers of the colon. After he elects to not have an operation, or further cancer treatment, he is referred for inpatient palliative care. When he is asked: "What gives you a sense of purpose and meaning in life?" he responds without hesitation and with a big laugh, "Smoking and drinking. I like the taste!"

What may seem to be a flippant response like the one given by this man is often evidence of a person who may be quite shy and uncomfortable to share his innermost anxieties and fears. Humor is quite an effective defense mechanism for one in distress. It is also a way of more firmly establishing boundaries when one is not yet prepared to bare one's soul. This gentleman required a long period of building relationships of trust with members of the palliative care team on the initial foundation of superficial encounters before he felt safe enough to share his inner self. The spiritual history identified the challenge facing the palliative care team in developing a relationship of trust with this patient.

A physician is seated alone at the bedside of a very debilitated and cachectic, 60-year-old hospice patient in his home. He has steadily resisted taking morphine for his severe pain due to multiple bone metastases from advanced renal carcinoma (kidney cancer). In an attempt to convince him to take the medicine, the physician says, "It is very hard to be able to focus on the important things in your life when you are in pain." He then becomes tearful and responds, "But, you don't know me. During my military service I killed innocent civilians, including women and children. Should I accept relief of my pain, when I caused so much suffering and death?"

It is very difficult to be prepared for unexpected revelations like that shared by this desperate soul. The hospice physician would not begin to be able to address this man's intense physical distress without having obtained this crucial spiritual history. Indeed, addressing this patient's spiritual pain as the first priority will be the key to relieving his physical as well as Total Pain. For the patient's hospice team, addressing their own ambivalence about the patient as a person may also be a critical and necessary aspect of the care they provide him. Such revelations may test the limits of empathy. An open acknowledgement of this possibility in the discussions of the interdisciplinary team may be a crucial first step in helping team members overcome the shock and potential hostility they may feel toward the patient.

The three major categories of spiritual needs of the dying that were noted above are meaning, value, and relationship.[14] They are

[14]D.P. Sulmasy, "Spiritual Issues in the Care of Dying Patients," *Journal of the American Medical Association* 196 (2006):1385–1392.

interconnected in the experience of the dying and represent important themes to explore more fully as a relationship of trust develops between the members of the interdisciplinary team and the suffering person. This interconnection among the three major categories of spiritual needs of the dying can be demonstrated when one considers the loss of meaning. Meaninglessness is often a consequence of a perceived loss of one's future, autonomy, and relationships. Thus, persons who experience meaninglessness have lost any sense of grounding in the two other major categories of spiritual needs, since loss of one's future and autonomy are tied closely to one's sense of value as well as one's relationships.

Individual autonomy has become an increasingly important, if not dominant, value of western societies since the Enlightenment. The illusion of control over one's world that is so closely associated with the autonomous westerner's creed is sorely tested by the confrontation with one's own mortality. "It is not uncommon that for much of one's life the need for control is the operative force. Spiritual issues lie dormant until the situation becomes desperate—beyond one's apparent control."[15] Denial becomes a powerful mechanism to maintain control, and it then results in avoidance of discussions about diagnosis and prognosis. The need to be in control can effectively block or limit the great opportunity for spiritual growth that is inherent in the process of facing the great existential questions on a very real and personal level. The denial within the autonomous western mind may even be reflected in the relatively low numbers of positive responses to surveys regarding spiritual concerns about death. In a national survey by the Gallup Foundation,[16] the following spiritual concerns about death were examined with the percentage of positive responses in parentheses:

+ Not being forgiven by God (56%);

[15]M-L Friedemann, J. Mouch, and T. Racey, "Nursing the Spirit: the Framework of Systemic Organization," *Journal of Advanced Nursing* 39 (2002): 325–332.
[16]The George H. Gallup International Institute, "Spiritual Beliefs and the Dying Process," *A Report of a National Survey Conducted for the Nathan Cummings Foundation and Fetzer Institute* (October, 1997), 34–35.

+ Not reconciling with others (56%);

+ Dying when you are removed or cut off from God or a higher power (51%);

+ Not being forgiven by someone for something you did (49%);

+ Not having a blessing from a family member or clergy member (39%); and

+ What it will be like for you after you die (39%).

For most spiritual issues in the survey only half of respondents registered concern. An even lower percentage of respondents were concerned about whether they would receive a blessing/support from a member of the clergy as well as having questions about the nature of the afterlife. These responses may be further evidence of the increasing secularization of American culture.

There are several potential signs of spiritual distress: physical distress (e.g., pain) either unresponsive or no longer responsive to standard therapies; acting out or refusal to cooperate—the so called "bad" hospice patient; emotional and social withdrawal; and fears of loss of control, which can be manifested as abruptly wanting to change the plan of care to more aggressive treatment or, alternatively, demonstrating increasing dependence. Many of these signs can be manifestations of a threatened or collapsing denial system. Some palliative care specialists have expressed concern about challenging patients' denial during critical moments in their illness. "Clinicians agree that denial generally should not be challenged when a patient is in the midst of a crisis because doing so risks undermining the patient's psychological equilibrium."[17] How often have clinicians missed an opportunity to uncover and address spiritual distress when they follow this precept too rigidly? Clearly, discernment based in a good relationship between the

[17]S.D. Block, "Psychological Considerations, Growth, and Transcendence at the End of Life. The Art of the Possible," *Journal of the American Medical Association* (285) (2001):2898–2905.

individual patient and health professional must guide any challenge to or exploration of the patient's denial. In general, one should probably use a cautious, thoughtful, and compassionate approach when dealing with denial, recognizing the opportunities for spiritual growth as well as the risks of spiritual harm when it is challenged. The following case history illustrates how challenging and complex a spiritual problem denial can become.

A 59-year-old man with advanced lung cancer is admitted for progressive debility and hemoptysis (i.e., coughing up blood). The hemoptysis worsens in spite of palliative radiotherapy. As his death approaches, he insists that all aggressive resuscitative measures be taken, because he states that a pastor told him that God would heal him, if he quit smoking.

It would be so helpful for this suffering man if he could be open to the old aphorism: 'Hope for the best but prepare for the worst.' A frontal assault based on the 'facts' of the futility of aggressive resuscitative measures in this context will rarely, if ever, be successful with a patient whose decisions are coming from deep denial. This may be especially challenging if the denial is expressed as religious faith. A more fruitful approach might be to explore in greater depth his faith history. Is his recent experience a return to the faith of his childhood or is it without precedent in his life? What kind of religious experiences did he have earlier in life? Were they confirmed in his present experience or had he fallen away from faith? Who does he understand God to be? How do these religious questions relate to the actual source or sources of greatest meaning in his life? Is he willing to discuss his fears? What has been his experience of loss and death among persons close to him? By engaging him in a respectful discourse with the goal of eliciting his self-revelation through asking open-ended questions, it may be possible to approach the inner man and at the same time gradually challenge his primitive, magical thinking about manipulating God.

Where do culture and spirituality intersect in care at the end of life? The emphasis in western medicine on individual autonomy can create conflicts in the care of patients with cultural and religious traditions that view illness, suffering and death differently.[18] Decision-making and communication in many cultures may be more family-based or even delegated to another family member (e.g., Mediterranean cultures). Perceived and real inequities in healthcare access or historical quality of care may influence a whole subculture's approach to various issues (e.g., African Americans' hesitance sometimes to trust white physicians). Some cultures are quite uncomfortable discussing death directly (e.g., Japanese, Native Americans). The autonomous westerner's "right to know" can be in direct conflict with the perceived power of the spoken word. *What is not explicitly said may not become reality.* Seeking support for dying loved ones from agencies outside of the family (e.g., hospice) may be viewed in some cultures (e.g., Hispanic culture) as a failure to fulfill one's filial responsibility. When there is a lack of appreciation of even subtle cultural issues affecting the therapeutic encounter, the most compassionate health professionals may inadvertently produce substantial spiritual distress for patients and families. A humble recognition by health professionals of their likely ignorance of many cultural issues can be acknowledged openly with patients and families by asking for their clarification of the cultural and religious practices that are important in their care.

Because of the increasing 'medicalization' of death, physicians have often mistaken intense spiritual experiences that may occur near death with signs of delirium. Unfortunately, such confusion by the caregiver may even lead to unnecessary use of sedating medications which could interfere significantly with the quality of patients' dying. Frequently, in the last days of life, a patient's dream life may change. Patients in the last hours to days of life may experience vivid and often symbolic dreams (e.g., taking a journey, finishing a building project). The dying patient may be uncertain if it occurred while asleep or awake. This phenomenon has been well known across time and cultures. It is certainly part of the traditional Christian experience of death. Besides vivid dreams, not infrequently the dying person will be found speaking to unseen

[18]N.D. Thomas, "The Importance of Culture throughout All of Life and Beyond," *Holistic Nursing Practice* 15 (2001):40–46.

presences who are often deceased relatives. More often than not, the experiences are comforting for the dying person (although they may be perplexing to loved ones and caregivers). The Russian writer Turgenev who was quoted at the beginning of this book has a beautiful description of just such a dream encounter related by Lukeria prior to her death in his story, *The Living Relic*.

> And I had another dream, too ... but maybe it was a vision. I really don't know. It seemed to me I was lying in this very shanty, and my dead parents, father and mother, come to me and bow low to me, but say nothing. And I asked them, "Why do you bow down to me, father and mother?" "Because," they said, "you suffer much in this world, so that you have not only set free your own soul, but have taken a great burden from off us too. And for us in the other world it is much easier. You have made an end of your own sins; now you are expiating our sins." And having said this, my parents bowed down to me again, and I could not see them...[19]

Before considering different approaches to providing spiritual care that have been described in the medical literature, it may be helpful to differentiate between spiritual and religious pain.[20] Religious pain has been defined as "a condition in which a patient is feeling guilty over the violation of the moral codes and values of his or her religious tradition ... Patients in spiritual pain are those who have concluded, through their own self-judgments, that there is something wrong with them at their core."[21] This distinction made between religious and spiritual pain is recognition, at least by some scholars, that consideration of the spiritual needs of patients, even within the secular medical context, should include awareness that there may be distinctly religious aspects to the spiritual distress that is present. What is not made clear by the above definitions is that the 'religious' and 'spiritual' pain can be one and the

[19]Ivan Turgenev, "A Living Relic," chapter 18 in *A Sportsman's Sketches*, vol.2, trans. by Constance Garrett (New York: Macmillan, 1916) 243–244.
[20]L. Satterly, "Guilt, Shame, and Religious and Spiritual Pain," *Holistic Nursing Practice* 15 (2001):30–39.
[21]Ibid.

same for many persons of faith. In other words, violation of the values of one's religious faith may lead to precisely the kind of self-judgment in which one's spiritual core is very much in question.

Spiritual Care

Addressing the spiritual needs of persons with serious illness should not be isolated from the rest of the care provided, but rather should be integrated within all aspects of the care. "It is important to view spiritual care not as a compartmentalized feature of treatment but as an attitude that infuses the overall approach to whole-person care regardless of one's defined role in the care of a dying person."[22] This is where the work of the interdisciplinary team as more than the sum of its individual members' expertise becomes of crucial importance. Unfortunately, it is rare in actual practice that such full integration of holistic spiritual care comes to fruition. There are likely many reasons for this, but some major ones include a lack of time for individual and joint reflection among team members, disparate religious backgrounds or levels of grounding in spirituality within the team, and competing priorities largely driven by a medical model that has little or no time for spirituality.

The major types of interventions offered as forms of spiritual care in the secular health care setting include: psychotherapeutic approaches, pastoral care (e.g., chaplains), religious or sacramental ministry, complementary therapies, specifically 'medical' or pharmacological approaches to spiritual distress, and 'basic' spiritual assistance potentially provided by any caregiver.

Psychotherapeutic techniques that have been developed to help suffering persons find meaning in their distress owe a primary debt to Victor Frankl, the twentieth-century Viennese psychiatrist who was able to put his own theory to the test in the harsh crucible of the Jewish Holocaust. The core elements of his therapeutic approach were

[22]K.P. Kaut, "Religion, Spirituality, and Existentialism near the End of Life: Implications for Assessment and Application," *American Behavioral Scientist* 46(2) (2002): 220–234.

described in a remarkable volume written largely from memory in the weeks after his release from Auschwitz concentration camp entitled, "Man's Search for Meaning".[23] He named his therapeutic approach, Logotherapy or meaning-based therapy. Logotherapy is focused on the meaning of human existence as well as on man's search for such a meaning. It helps individuals in spiritual distress discover who they are, how they wish to interpret their present situation, and what they want to become. Frankl's major principles of Logotherapy are:

1) Life has meaning and never ceases to have meaning up to the last moment of life;

2) The desire to find meaning is a primary instinct and motivator of human behavior; and

3) Humans have the freedom to find meaning in existence and to choose their attitude toward suffering.

In addition he identified three main sources of meaning in life:

Creativity—one's work, deeds, dedication to causes; *Experience*—art, nature, humor, role, relationships, love; and *Attitude*—the attitude one takes in response to unavoidable suffering.

Two major psychotherapeutic approaches that have been developed to address the spiritual distress of persons with advanced life-threatening illnesses are greatly indebted to Frankl's work. Dignity therapy represents in many ways an extension of biography therapy.[24] It is a brief individualized psychotherapeutic intervention for those experiencing existential distress, particularly a loss of meaning. The goal of the intervention is to engender a sense of meaning and purpose in order to reduce suffering in the dying. The intervention consists of a thirty-to-sixty-minute taped interview (usually one) at the hospitalized patient's

[23]V. Frankl, *Man's Search for Meaning*, trans. by I. Lasch (Boston: Beacon Press, 2006).

[24]H.M. Chochinov, T. Hack, T. Hassard, L.J. Kristjanson, S. McClement, and M. Harlos, "Dignity Therapy: A Novel Psychotherapeutic Intervention for Patients near the End of Life," *Journal of Clinical Oncology* 23 (2005):5520–5525.

bedside or in the patient's home, an interview that is then reshaped (edited) into a narrative. The narrative is read to the patient in another session and the patient is allowed to edit it. Engaging in the structured process of creating the narrative by exploring meaning in one's life is believed to be a source of hope and healing. On another level it can be a means of creating a legacy that can be shared or given to surviving loved ones. Some sample questions from the protocol give a feeling for the experience. "Tell me a little about your life history; particularly the parts that you either remember most or think are the most important. Are there specific things for your family to know or remember? What roles have you played? What are your most important accomplishments? Are there particular things that you feel still need to be said to your loved ones? What have you learned from life? What advice do you have for those left behind?"[25]

Another approach that is quite similar to Dignity Therapy has been developed for groups. Meaning-Centered Group Psychotherapy for patients with advanced cancer is a group psychotherapeutic application of Logotherapy as compared with the individual orientation of Dignity Therapy.[26] It consists of an eight-week intervention with weekly ninety-minute sessions incorporating a mixture of didactics, discussion, experiential exercises focused around themes related to meaning and advanced cancer. Patients are given assigned readings and homework related to the themes for each session. The themes developed in each session include:

1) Concepts of meaning and sources of meaning;

2) Cancer and meaning;

3) Meaning and historical context of life;

4) Storytelling, life project;

[25]Ibid.

[26]W. Breitbart, "Spirituality and Meaning in Supportive Care: Spirituality- and Meaning-Centered Group Psychotherapy Interventions in Advanced Cancer," *Support Care Cancer* 10(4) (2002): 272–280.

5) Limitations and finiteness of life;

6) Responsibility, creativity, deeds;

7) Experience, nature, art, humor; and

8) Termination, goodbyes, hopes for the future.[27]

In its present form Meaning-Centered Group Psychotherapy is time-intensive and expensive, and unfortunately this fact has limited its development and further use outside a large cancer-center-type setting.

Although seeking meaning may well be a basic instinct or drive within the human person, is it always a potential path to healing? Is the search for meaning, per se, inherently healthy or morally good? What if one's greatest source of meaning is to do evil? Unfortunately, some of Frankl's tormentors in Auschwitz may well have been able to agree with him about the basic premise, but would likely have then insisted that their 'work' in Auschwitz was a tremendous source of meaning for them!

The chaplain's role in the spiritual care of persons suffering with advanced illnesses has been largely defined in the context of western (especially British) models of hospice care.[28] A major task of the chaplain is to understand and clarify the spiritual meaning of all that is experienced by those involved within palliative care in the context of the chaplain's own relationship and understanding of God. This, of course, presupposes that chaplains are well grounded in their own faith and relationship with God. Chaplains discern and help other members of the interdisciplinary team discern the spiritual needs of dying patients as well as anticipate the spiritual needs of a patient's caregivers. They can offer a ministry of word and sacrament (if appropriate) or pastoral counseling to patients, family caregivers, and to health professionals caring for the patient. Most critically, they can be present to and

---

[27] Ibid.

[28] Adapted from P. Speck, *Oxford Textbook of Palliative Medicine*, Second Edition, eds. D. Doyle, G. Hanks, and N. MacDonald (New York: Oxford University Press, 1998), 812.

remain alongside those facing death or grief, while (it is to be hoped) transcending traditional religious boundaries. "Listening is one of the greatest spiritual gifts a chaplain can give a suffering patient."[29] This opportunity to participate in a ministry of listening is potentially available to all who care for the suffering.

How do religion and spiritual care interface? An individual's spirituality is often grounded in a specific religious faith. Religion is a source of meaning and framework in which to understand the great existential questions of suffering and death. Religious rituals 'actualize' belief/doctrine and provide tangible comfort and meaning. Chaplains and other health professionals often are intermediaries in assisting patients to find appropriate religious support. It is extremely important for members of the interdisciplinary team to ask about the potential need for specific religious support earlier rather than later.

Complementary therapies are treatment modalities that have typically fallen outside mainstream medicine, primarily because they have often not fit the standard disease model. Precisely because of this fact, some of the complementary approaches may be addressing the person rather than the disease. There is increasing evidence of their potential value in the therapeutic encounter, as was noted with regard to massage therapy in Part 2 of this book. Another example of a powerful complementary therapy which may work at the level of the person is music therapy.[30] Music therapy can provide a comforting and calming presence. Knowing the patient's musical "history" is very important. A person who loves classical music, for example, might not respond well to country western style music and vice versa. Music can sometimes serve as the catalyst for release on emotional, spiritual, and even social levels at the end of life. Other forms of complementary therapy that are often used in the spiritual care of those near the end of life include:

---

[29]S. Burns, "The Spirituality of Dying. Pastoral Care's Holistic Approach Is Crucial in Hospice," *Health Progress* 72 (1991): 48–54.

[30]R.E. Krout, "Music Therapy with Imminently Dying Hospice Patients and their Families: Facilitating Release near the Time of Death," *American Journal of Hospice Palliative Care* 20 (2003):129–134.

touch (e.g., massage), art therapy, poetry, and animal companions (e.g., pet therapy). Common to all of these approaches is an effort to reduce the isolation of the dying person while at the same time reawakening the dying person's connection to the living. It is always important to realize that cultural values will influence the use and acceptability of these kinds of therapies (e.g., massage may be perceived in some cultures as being too intimate a form of contact).

Are there situations where uncontrolled physical distress essentially becomes uncontrolled spiritual distress or vice versa? "No man can be rendered pain free whilst he still wrestles with his faith. No man can come to terms with his God when every waking moment is taken up with pain or vomiting."[31] When a person is in a crisis of distress, whether it is predominantly physical or is a combination across the entire spectrum of Total Pain, the potential use of heavy sedation, so-called palliative sedation, has been advocated.[32] It can serve as a means of either briefly breaking the cycle of escalating uncontrolled distress (i.e., giving the patient a respite with sleep) or of providing control of unremitting distress in the last hours and days of life. Although there is relatively little disagreement among palliative care physicians about using pharmacologically-induced sedation in those rare instances of severe, poorly controlled physical distress that are not responsive to medical approaches, the appropriateness of using palliative sedation to treat severe existential/spiritual distress is not so clear. When used for a brief period (e.g., 24–48 hours), it may give the suffering person a chance to rest while also giving the patient's palliative care team an opportunity to do the necessary detective work to identify potential causes of the crisis of Total Pain so that a holistic solution might be trialed as the person emerges from the sedation. When palliative sedation has been used in bedbound patients who appear to be in the last

---

[31]Quoted from the introduction, *Oxford Textbook of Palliative Medicine*, p. 6.

[32]R.L. Fainsinger, A. Waller, M. Bercovici, K. Bengtson, W. Landman, M. Hosking, J.M. Nunez-Olarte, and D. deMoissac, "A multicentre international study of sedation for uncontrolled symptoms in terminally ill patients," *Journal of Palliative Medicine* 14 (2000): 257–265.

hours to days of life, it has generally been felt to not shorten the life of the patient. However, heavy sedation will eliminate any ability of suffering persons to interact cognitively with their environment and other persons. It will also inhibit prayer. When it is used to treat spiritual distress, the question inevitably arises, whose spiritual distress, that of the patient, the family, or the medical team? It can at times appear to be motivated by the same rationale underlying physician-assisted death. If suffering is perceived to be the ultimate enemy and the physician cannot bear to co-suffer further with the patient, palliative sedation, like euthanasia, can be used to interrupt the suffering. This approach can effectively interfere with the work of the dying, and may ultimately represent another form of abandonment of the suffering person by the health care team.

Every caregiver may at some point be called upon to address the spiritual needs of a suffering person. Basic interventions that all caregivers can make to help address the spiritual needs of dying patients include: consistently express empathic concern; demonstrate respect for patients' ultimate concerns and values; be present for them, affirming their value as persons by non-abandonment; and listen to what they have to say about life and its meaning.[33] More complex concerns and issues should be referred to hospice/hospital chaplains or patients' spiritual advisors.

It is recognized that healing cannot occur in a vacuum. It requires a form of partnership between patients and their caregivers. "Partnership implies that the journey is one of shared experience where two people work together toward a resolution rather than one in which the expert doles out advice, leaving the patient to sort through the problems alone."[34] Conversations with the dying are difficult to contain within a short clinic visit or single ward encounter in the hospital.

[33]D.P. Sulmasy, "Spiritual Issues in the Care of Dying Patients," *Journal of the American Medical Association* 296 (2006):1385–1392

[34]C.M. Puchalski, "Listening to Stories of Pain and Joy: Physicians and Other Caregivers Can Help Patients Find Comfort and Meaning at the End of Life," *Health Progress* 85(4) (July–August, 2004): 20–22.

The content and quality of such conversations will depend on the level of trust that has developed between patients and health professionals. Trust depends on a relationship which usually forms over time. The conversations may often involve questions that do not have easy answers; rather the relationships that are formed may be more critical than the answers, per se.[35]

It has been recognized in the palliative care literature that there is potential for healing in death. This potential for healing may extend beyond dying persons to their bereaved loved ones and even their caregivers who are witnesses of the death. From a secular perspective, the healing that may be experienced by the dying involves at least two important elements: a reframing of hope and reconciliation or healing of relationships. In this context, hope has been defined as the "positive expectation for meaning attached to life events."[36] "Hope lies in meaning that is attached to life, not in events themselves . . . As long as there is meaning, there is hope."[37] It is a loss of meaning and thus a loss of hope which often underlies requests for physician-assisted suicide. For hope to be reframed or redefined in the context of dying, it is crucial that the dying actually know that they are dying. The role of being a *sick* person hoping for a cure must transition to that of becoming a *dying* person with new sources of hope. Hospice can facilitate this transition by creating a new identity and point of reference for the dying patient. Hope can then be redefined in terms relevant to the new circumstances. There are several sources of hope for the dying person in this new context. The compassionate commitment of caregivers to never abandon their patients is a source of hope. Pain and other distressing symptoms will be controlled. The dying person will be remembered. Reconciliation and forgiveness can occur.

Preserving hope in the dying depends on relationships, especially with loved ones and caregivers. It is centered on finding meaning in

[35] Ibid.

[36] D. Parker-Oliver, "Redefining Hope for the Terminally Ill," *American Journal of Hospice Palliative Care* 19(2) (2002): 115–120.

[37] Ibid.

one's suffering. The search for meaning, in turn, is supported by excellent symptom control.

Reconciliation is at the heart of the healing that can be experienced in the relationships of dying persons. "Reconciliation is the most crucial thing for the dying irrespective of whether or not the person is religious or secular. Even as their bodies are disintegrating they are becoming whole."[38] Dr Ira Byock has identified reconciliation, the work of the dying, in very simple terms:

> "Forgive me."
> "I forgive you."
> "Thank you."
> "I love you."
> "Good-bye."[39]

Various authors have struggled to define healing that may occur without cure of the underlying fatal illness. One definition that may come close is "the personal experience of the transcendence of suffering."[40] Any healing associated with the dying process represents a fundamental paradox for the secular medical mind that is focused on cure. At the heart of the paradox is to have all pretense stripped away. One is presented with the opportunity to see the world as it really is and to see oneself without illusion. For some this may result in the discovery that the greatest source of meaning may be relational—to still be able to help, care for, and love other persons even up to the very end of one's life. The impact of this process of stripping away the detritus of one's existence should not be lost on the caregivers who witness the phenomenon. As noted above, there is a reciprocal character to healing. For healing to occur, it may be necessary only to experience or witness (be

[38]Sharon Burns, quoted by Vigen Guroian in *Life's Living Toward Dying* (Grand Rapids, MI: William B. Eerdman's Publishing Company, 1996), 87.

[39]I. Byock, quoted in D. Parker-Oliver, "Redefining Hope for the Terminally Ill," *American Journal of Hospice Palliative Care* 19(2) (2002): 115–120.

[40]T.R. Egnew, "The Meaning of Healing: Transcending Suffering" *Annals of Family Medicine* 3(3) (2005):255–262.

present for) the suffering of another or for the suffering one to experience the compassion and love of the caregiver.

The following story of a truly remarkable person may help illustrate the concept of healing as transcendence of suffering:

A 67-year-old man with advanced pancreatic cancer presented in a pain crisis with increasingly intense upper abdominal pain radiating through to his back. The pain was keeping him from his usual activity of preparing and distributing boxes of food for the poor in his neighborhood. He promptly resumed these activities once his pain was controlled and continued them up to the day before his death.

A secular medical understanding of spirituality in the care of suffering in advanced illness has developed rapidly. As this has occurred, there has been a tendency to seek the 'lowest common denominator' in an effort to create common ground independent of religious traditions and preferences. This approach has rapidly become normative within the medical literature and major textbooks of palliative care. This author has critiqued this trend in a recent article and suggested an alternate approach toward seeking common ground between health professionals of different faiths who are committed to caring for the suffering associated with advanced illnesses.

> Spirituality in western hospice and palliative care in recent years has been increasingly defined in secular terms that effectively dissociate it from the major faith traditions. This discontinuity limits the degree to which hospice and palliative care can be fully integrated holistically within a given faith tradition. It also limits the ability of hospice and palliative care providers to effectively address spiritual or existential issues related to their patients' suffering in as much as they are not prepared to fully understand their patients' spirituality in its full religious context. The major pioneers of hospice and palliative care in the mid-late twentieth century were from a common faith background, Western Christianity. They shared a common reverence for an even earlier and long standing Judeo-Christian tradition that informed their basic assumptions about

the nature of suffering and its relief. However, current practice and teaching regarding spirituality within hospice and palliative care is a reflection of the secular culture, largely a syncretistic mixture of ideas borrowed from eastern religions, the residual echoes of Judeo-Christian tradition in the west, and ideas taken from popular culture … Would not hospice and palliative care taught, developed, and practiced within a given faith tradition have unique characteristics that would not only inform attitudes and behaviors regarding controversial issues like physician-assisted death but also address the unique spiritual needs of adherents of the given faith tradition in a deeper and more profound manner?[41]

The remainder of this book will be devoted to articulating a traditional Christian vision and approach to the care of suffering in persons with advanced illnesses. This small effort is made in the hope that visible expressions of palliative care that are informed by a traditional Christian ethos may develop, and that they may in turn stimulate similar projects within other faith traditions. If such projects come to fruition, then a real dialogue can begin among palliative care providers from different faith traditions about the nature of suffering and its relief. This deeper level of discourse can then assist in the discovery of common ground based on a more profound mutual understanding and respect.

[41]D.B. Hinshaw, J.M. Carnahan, J. Breck, N. Mosoiu, and D. Mosoiu, "Spiritual Issues in Suffering: Creating a Dialogue between Clergy and Palliative Care Providers," *Progress in Palliative Care* 19(1) (2011): 7–14.

CHAPTER 10

A Traditional Christian Perspective
on Suffering and Death

THE ENGLISH ACADEMIC, writer, and great twentieth-century apologist for Christianity, C.S. Lewis, described the role of pain and suffering in the Divine economy this way: "God whispers to us in our pleasures, speaks in our conscience, but shouts in our pains: it is His megaphone to rouse a deaf world."[1] If pain and suffering are used by God to attract the attention of a deaf world, to what should the newly roused world attend? "As we rise daily, let us suppose that we shall not survive till evening, and again, as we prepare for sleep, let us consider that we shall not awaken. By its very nature our life is uncertain, and is meted out daily by Providence. If we think this way, and in this way live—daily—we will not sin."[2] St Antony the Great was not alone among the early fathers of the Church in admonishing Christians to remember their mortality. The pain and suffering that are such common features of the human experience are intimately connected to human mortality. It is the unique understanding of this problem and its resolution through the suffering and death of the Incarnate God that is the core of the Christian faith. In this chapter the traditional Christian teaching about suffering and death will be compared with the prevailing attitude toward these issues in popular culture, the relationship between suffering and the passions will be examined, and a traditional Christian response to suffering and death in the world will be proposed.

[1]C.S. Lewis, "Human Pain," ch. 6 in *The Problem of Pain* (New York: Macmillan Publishing Co., Inc., 1976), 93.
[2]St Athanasius, *The Life of Antony and the Letter to Marcellinus*, Classics of Western Spirituality (New York: Paulist Press, 1980), 45.

Recently, a gene was discovered that codes for a protein whose function is to transport and recycle metabolic byproducts.[3] Mutations of the gene in the fruit fly create a condition like fasting, doubling the life span of the fly. There is a human cognate of the gene which codes for a dicarboxylate transporter protein. The gene was affectionately named the 'Indy' gene in honor of the movie *Monty Python and the Holy Grail*, in which one of the characters declares emphatically, "I'm not dead yet!" when he is about to be thrown on a cart of corpses in a medieval town decimated by the Black Death. Caloric restriction has also been shown to increase longevity in small animals. This observation is not unlike the accounts of some of the great monastics who in their asceticism fasted extensively, practicing their own form of caloric restriction. Many of them were noted to live quite long lives, including St Antony who died at age 105. "I'm not dead yet"—could be the motto of every 'red blooded' man and woman desperately pursuing the Darwinian mandate to survive. This is in stark contrast with the traditional Christian teaching: "Remember your death!" Fundamentally, life has been defined by death. The fear of death has transformed human existence into a great struggle to survive, with sin and suffering as major outcomes of the struggle. "Death is a cosmic reality that is almost personalized—an objective reality in the world that also creates sinfulness. How does it create sinfulness? . . . It transforms the entire reality of the world into a desperate struggle for survival."[4]

For modern health care, which is wedded so closely to a biomedical reductionist model that is focused on the conquest of disease, death is just another biological problem to be solved. Indeed, denial of the reality of death may be even stronger in the culture of health care than among the dying themselves. This approach is very closely linked to the modern notion of progress: "It's just a matter of time before we conquer

[3]B. Rogina, R.A. Reenan, S.P. Nilsen, and S.L. Helfand, "Extended Life-Span Conferred by Cotransporter Gene Mutations in *Drosophila*," *Science* 290 (2000): 2137–2140.

[4]John Meyendorff, "Miracles: Medical, Psychological and Religious Reflections" in *Health and Faith: Medical, Psychological, and Religious Dimensions*, ed. J.T. Chirban, (Lanham, MD: University Press of America, 1991), 122.

aging, etc.!" In the meantime, while the 'problem' is being solved, we must be brave. Dying patients are frequently reassured with the comforting statement, "Death is a natural part of the world." Some advocates for hospice care in their efforts to comfort the dying insist with all sincerity that "you can have a beautiful death, if you only follow these easy steps." It's as if every death can be scripted like the text of a greeting card. For some, it seems the role of hospice is a dress rehearsal for the funeral home. All signs of suffering should be eliminated prior to death before the mortician's art can be fully exploited.

But for Christians, death is not natural or normal, it is not the way things are meant to be. "Christianity is not reconciliation with death. It is the revelation of death, and it reveals death because it is the revelation of Life. Christ is this Life. And only if Christ is Life, is death what Christianity proclaims it to be, namely the enemy to be destroyed, and not a "mystery" to be explained. Religion and secularism, by explaining death, give it a "status," a rationale, make it "normal." Only Christianity proclaims it to be abnormal and, therefore, truly horrible."[5]

Suffering is an inherent component of our mortal condition, it is a *dying*. In the fourth-century Nicene Creed of the ancient Church, there is no direct mention of Christ's death, "He was crucified under Pontius Pilate, suffered, and was buried."[6] Because suffering and death are so thoroughly interwoven together in the human experience, the presence of one implies the presence of the other. It is also important to remember that the origin of the word 'passion' comes from the Greek root that denotes suffering. *Pathos*, "that which is endured or experienced, suffering" was used extensively by the second-century church father, St Ignatius of Antioch, to mean 'suffering' (or specifically the Passion of Christ) and as a substitute for 'death'. It was also used by early Christian writers in reference to the passions (e.g., pride, lust, etc.).[7] Human

[5]Alexander Schmemann, *O Death, Where is Thy Sting?* (Crestwood, NY: St Vladimir's Seminary Press, 2003), 100.

[6]"The Nicene-Constantinopolitan Creed" in *Daily Prayers for Orthodox Christians: The Synekdemos*, ed. N.M. Vaporis (Brookline, MA: Holy Cross Orthodox Press, 1986), 61.

[7]Arndt and Gingrich.

suffering takes on various forms and patterns in the context of the passions. Each passion has its opposite virtue (e.g., pride versus humility), which is to be cultivated within the spiritual life of the Christian. God did not create the passions. They are distortions of gifts we were given as creatures. "God neither caused nor created evil and, therefore, those who assert that certain passions come naturally to the soul are quite wrong. What they fail to realize is that we have taken natural attributes of our own and turned them into passions ... Nature has provided us with anger as something to be turned against the serpent, but we have used it against our neighbor."[8] Thus, the particular passions that trouble each of us give the specific flavor or color to our suffering and can intensify it. If we struggle with anger, for example, it may be all the more difficult for us to control our anger when we may be suffering in severe pain. This, in turn, could make our suffering worse by wounding those we love with our anger and increasing our social isolation. Another example from St John Climacus (sixth century) will help to illustrate this further: "We have a natural urge to excel in virtue, but instead we compete in evil."[9] We are called in the spiritual life to resist the passions. Serious illness is not a vacation or holiday from the passions. Indeed, it may be the greatest time of testing by the passions in one's life. In spite of what may seem to be an overwhelming challenge and burden of suffering imposed by the passions, St John Climacus has some very encouraging words for those who are struggling. "An active soul is a provocation to the demons, yet the greater our conflicts the greater our rewards. There will be no crown for the man who has never been under attack, and the man who perseveres in spite of any failures will be glorified as a champion by the angels."[10] It is crucial for caregivers of those who suffer to recognize that each person has his or her own unique set of passions that not only affect the individual's experience of suffering but also may create unique challenges in providing care to them. The

[8]St John Climacus, *The Ladder of Divine Ascent*, trans. by C. Luibheid & N. Russell (New York: Paulist Press, 1982), 251.
[9]Ibid.
[10]Ibid.

palliative care provider's responsibility from a Christian perspective is first, to be empathic and not judge, and second, to use one's skills to relieve those aspects of the patient's experience (e.g., symptoms) that interact with the passions to harm the soul.

There is good news in the bad news of the passions. Although each human person must struggle with the passions, especially during times of intense personal suffering, there is a final respite from the passions. "Where are those who say that in this life there is a Sabbath, that is, repose from the passions? . . . Our Sabbath is the day of the grave; it is here that our nature truly keeps the Sabbath."[11] Many, of course, would hardly consider this comforting news. However, the hope of the Christian resides precisely in this Sabbath—our death.

Because of the incarnation, we know that God does not abandon us to suffer alone and without purpose. He has already entered fully into the experience of human suffering, embraced it completely even unto death, and thereby transformed it, making it a pathway to himself—to ultimate healing. God does not depart from us in our suffering. Indeed, it is in the depths of our greatest suffering where he approaches us most intimately. "God . . . will keep unsleeping watch over you; he will hold you in his almighty hand. Therefore, no sorrow or suffering will come to you except by his all-holy will, or with his permission, for your salvation."[12] Suffering can be transformed into an extraordinary opportunity to experience deep personal communion with the God who suffers with and on behalf of his creation. "The angels at the tomb identified the risen Lord as 'the Crucified One' . . . and the French Catholic philosopher Pascal echoed this message when he declared, 'Christ is in agony until the end of the world.' The Risen Lord remains forever the Crucified One. Those who are united to him, then, are united as well to his once-for-all crucifixion, whose meaning and power endure throughout the ages . . . Suffering, therefore, can become an effective

[11]St Isaac of Syria, "Homily 29" in *The Ascetical Homilies of Saint Isaac the Syrian*, (Boston: Holy Transfiguration Monastery, 1984), 143.

[12]Bp Ignatius Brianchaninov, *The Arena* (Jordanville, NY: Holy Trinity Monastery, 1997), 57.

means for creating a deep and intimate communion with Christ and with the afflicted members of his Body."[13]

Suffering on an individual or communal level can then become another sacrament or mystery of the kingdom, very much like baptism. For early Christians, martyrdom, a most extreme form of witness in suffering, was thought of as a baptism in one's blood, particularly for those who were still catechumens or unbaptized who professed belief in Christ and paid for their belief with their lives.

Is it even possible to understand illness and suffering as gifts from God? "For one to be ill is a divine visitation. Illness is the greatest gift from God. The only thing that man can give to God is pain."[14] This does not mean that we should seek out pain or that we should avoid relief of physical and other forms of distress when available. It does mean that suffering Christians can offer their pain in the same manner and spirit as the offering of Christ's Body and Blood which is made at each Eucharist. Our individual suffering is joined to his suffering. To be able to make an offering to God, we should be able to pray. For the Christian, the primary reason for good symptom relief is to enable us to pray. Thus, when all else has been stripped away from us by a terminal illness, our suffering, our death, remain always the one real gift we can offer back to God, being grateful in all things.

Unfortunately, for most persons nurtured in the materialism of the west, a strange dualism persists. While alive with the ability to use and consume the material world around them most westerners are thorough-going materialists. When confronted with death, there appears to be a rapid conversion to a form of Neoplatonism in which the body that was indulged for so long is now of no consequence and all hope resides in a spiritual, immaterial existence after death. This immaterial existence also seems to bear little or no relation to the material and

---

[13]J. Breck, *The Sacred Gift of Life* (Crestwood, NY: St Vladimir's Seminary Press, 1998), 221.

[14]Archimandrite Ioannikios, *An Athonite Gerontikon: Sayings of the Holy Fathers of Mount Athos*, trans. by Maria D. Mayson and Sister Theodora (Zion) (Thessaloniki, Greece: Publications of the Holy Monastery of St. Gregory Palamas, Kouphalia-Thessaloniki, Greece, 1997), 430.

is hoped to be the consummation of all the well wishes expressed in fine greeting cards. But, "Christ never spoke about the immortality of souls—He spoke about the resurrection of the dead!"[15] The person born and bred in the west is still confronted with the messy issue of the body. It is no wonder that cremation has become so popular.

> Christ is risen from the dead,
> trampling down death by death,
> and upon those in the tombs bestowing life![16]

For traditional Christians, precisely because of the incarnation of Christ, dead bodies do matter. To again quote St Gregory of Nazianzus, "For that which He has not assumed, He has not healed; but that which is united to His Godhead is also saved."[17] It is only because Christ assumed our entire nature, except for sin, and entered into death itself, that we can be healed. Because he died, was buried, descended into Hell, and overcame death, human nature has been restored. It is Christ's physical death that is crucial to his salvific act. Fr John Behr emphasizes the central character of this fact to all Christian faith and practice: "By his death, Christ conquers death—in no other way. By his most human action, an action which expresses all the weakness and impotence of our created nature, Christ shows himself to be God . . . we cannot look anywhere else to understand who and what God is; there is no other means to come to know God. Those who stand in this tradition must follow the apostle Paul in refusing to know anything else apart from Christ and him crucified."[18]

---

[15] A. Schmemann, *O Death, Where is Thy Sting?*, 26.

[16] "The Paschal Troparion," *The Paschal Service*, text prepared by J. Erickson, and P. Lazor, (Department of Religious Education, Orthodox Church in America, available from St Vladimir's Seminary Press, Yonkers, NY), 45.

[17] St Gregory of Nazianzus, Epistle 101 to Cledonius the Priest against Apollinarius, p. 440 in *Volume 7 of Nicene and Post-Nicene Fathers—Cyril of Jerusalem, Gregory Nazianzen*; edited by P. Schaff, and H. Wace (Peabody, MA: Hendrickson Publishers, Inc., 1994)

[18] J. Behr, *The Mystery of Christ: Life in Death* (Crestwood, NY: St Vladimir's Seminary Press, 2006), 32–33.

Why matter matters

During the iconoclast controversy in the Eastern Church, St John of Damascus in his defense of the use of icons in Christian worship emphasized the essential relationship between the incarnation and this aspect of the Church's faith and practice. There would be no veneration of icons without the incarnation of Christ in which matter has been transformed by the presence of the God-Man. "I worship the Creator of matter who became matter for my sake, who willed to take His abode in matter; who worked out my salvation through matter."[19] It is precisely because God became man that it is incumbent on Christians to give special care to the body. Each suffering body is now an icon of his Suffering Body. The centrality of Christ's physical death to the healing and salvation of the world is highlighted by a statement of Fr John Meyendorff regarding miracles. "The only true miracle that really matters is the miracle of Christ's overcoming death. It is a miracle in the sense that it is an intervention of God in this fallen world and a sign of His power, which can be shared. It is really, authentically the only true miracle. All the other events that we call miracles are only signs and point to this one miracle."[20]

"What Then Shall We Do"?[21]

What are the practical consequences, the applied theology that emanates from the traditional Christian understanding of Christ's incarnation, suffering, death, and resurrection? How are Christians to apply this not only personally in their own lives but also in their relationships with other human persons and the cosmos? As suffering defines culture, so also it defines ethics. The meaning and purpose associated with suffering will determine what responses to its presence are morally acceptable. Thus, for a compassionate secular humanist who sees

[19]St John of Damascus, *On the Divine Images*, trans. by D. Anderson (Crestwood, NY: St Vladimir's Seminary Press, 1983), 23.

[20]J. Meyendorff, "Miracles," 23.

[21]Luke 3.10.

no particular meaning in suffering but rather views it as the ultimate enemy to be eliminated or at least minimized whenever possible, any and all means available to end suffering may seem appropriate. Assuming one starts from the premise that suffering has no meaning or purpose, this is the most compelling argument for physician-assisted death (i.e., physician-assisted suicide and euthanasia). A very different ethical approach emerges from a Christian perspective where suffering is not the ultimate enemy. The individual suffering that Christians witness or experience is an opportunity to identify directly with the suffering of Christ both as co-sufferer and sufferer. Although the life of prayer and contemplation are exalted within the monastic as well as wider Christian tradition, there is still a powerful recognition that care of the sick and suffering may yield an even closer approach to Christ as is illustrated in this story from the Desert Fathers of fourth-century Egyptian monasticism. "A brother asked a certain old man, saying, 'There be two brothers, and one of them is quiet in his cell, and prolongs his fast for six days, and lays much travail on himself: but the other tends the sick. Whose work is more acceptable to God?' And the old man answered, 'If that brother who carries his fast for six days were to hang himself up by the nostrils, he could not equal the other, who does service to the sick.'"[22]

Not only has caring for the suffering of others become an opportunity for Christians to touch their Savior in the person of the suffering one, but the experience of the suffering individual is also changed by this reality. While the caregiver emulates Christ in relieving the pain and distress of the suffering one, the primary reason for good symptom relief from the afflicted Christian's perspective is to assist in preparation for death, where real healing will occur. "Pain control should be used not only to comfort the patient but to aid the patient in preparing for death ... The death to be feared is the one that comes suddenly, unanticipated, giving no opportunity for repentance."[23]

[22] *The Desert Fathers*, trans. by Helen Waddell (Ann Arbor, MI: Ann Arbor Paperbacks, The University of Michigan Press, 1957), 124.

[23] H. Tristram Engelhardt, Jr., *The Foundations of Christian Bioethics* (Lisse, The Netherlands: Swets & Zeitlinger Publishers, 2000), 326, 331.

Are Christians to seek to preserve life for as long as possible and at all costs? Although life is a holy gift from God, preservation of life for as long as possible is not the primary purpose of this precious gift. Rather than burying our talent in the ground we are to make use of it.[24] The real question relates to what we do with the gift we have been given, how we live the life given to us. "The appropriate focus is on a way of life, rather than just on saving or preserving life . . . Health care decision making should be focused on the ascetic turn from all that distracts so as to pursue the Kingdom of Heaven . . . As St Basil the Great warns, we should avoid 'Whatever requires an undue amount of thought or trouble or involves a large expenditure of effort and causes our whole life to revolve, as it were, around solicitation for the flesh.'"[25]

Sometimes the burden of suffering seems to be more than a person can bear. Even though a Christian should not seek human assistance in hastening the dying process, is it a sin to pray for death to come? In its prayers, the Eastern Church has recognized this dilemma for the dying Christian who is ready for death's approach but whose suffering persists without an apparent end in sight. "Yea, Master, Lord our God, hearken unto me a sinner and thine unworthy servant in this hour, and loose thy servant, N., from this intolerable sickness and the bitter impotency which holdeth him, and give him rest where the souls of the righteous dwell."[26] In situations of prolonged suffering, the priest, on behalf of the suffering person, may ask for divine intervention (not human) to bring an end to the suffering of the dying person.

How can Christians prepare themselves and their loved ones for this inevitable event? Advance care planning, especially the process of creating advance directives, can potentially be of considerable help to Christians as they prepare for their death. Advance directives usually consist of two components, a medical directive or living will and designation of a durable power of attorney for health care. The medical

[24]Matthew 25.14ff

[25]Engelhardt, 318, 317.

[26]"Prayer for one who has suffered long" from *Prayers for the Dying—An Abridged Euchologion* ed. by David F. Abramtsov (Thompson Ridge, NY: St. German's Chapel Press, 1971).

directive usually addresses, often in very explicit terms, specific wishes
a patient may have regarding types of health care and interventions at
or near the end of life. More often than not, a medical directive may
identify conditions under which a person would not want further
interventions directed at reversal of a condition, if that condition is not
reversible and the patient is by all accounts dying. Additional features
may also include a statement of one's goals for comfort and dignity at
the end of life which can be placed within the context of one's religious
faith or philosophical orientation. The designation of a durable power
of attorney for health care identifies the person or persons entrusted
with the responsibility to speak for the dying person when that individual has lost capacity for decision making. Of the two components of
advance directives, designating a durable power of attorney for health
care may be the more useful because it is very difficult, if not impossible, to anticipate every circumstance that might arise near the end of
life. Probably the most important feature of creating advance directives
is the process itself which implies a real and (one hopes) meaningful
discussion between persons executing the document and their loved
ones. If it is done truly with the mind of the Church in which Christians are admonished to "remember your death," the process can be an
opportunity for personal growth, greater understanding within a family, and even a powerful Christian witness of one's faith to the health
care team.[27] "In everything you do, remember your end, and you will
never sin."[28] "No one who has acquired the remembrance of death will
ever be able to sin."[29] When patients and families undergo the types of
discussions involved in the process of preparing an advance directive,
they can also be a helpful corrective, an antidote, at least to some extent,
to the denial which is so frequently an unhealthy coping mechanism

[27]There are Orthodox Christian advance directives available that reflect a traditional Christian perspective: "A Living Will and a Christian Death" (Liberty, TN: St.
John of Kronstadt Press Book Service, Rt.1, Box 205, Liberty, TN 37095; inquiries
to M.L. Sill, Rt. 2, Box 2343, Wayne, WV 25570).

[28]Sirach 7.36.

[29]Hesychius the Horebite, quoted by St John Climacus in *The Ladder of Divine
Ascent*, Classics of Western Spirituality (Mahwah, NJ: Paulist Press, 1982), 134.

seen when individuals are actually confronted with a terminal diagnosis. Unfortunately, less than a third of adults in the United States have executed an advance directive.[30]

The response of Christians to Christ's conquest of death does not end with advanced care planning. Christians as members of the crucified and resurrected Body of Christ are also called to be part of his healing presence in the world. We are not the healer. Christ, in us and through us, heals the world. With St John the Baptist we must also say, "He must increase, but I must decrease."[31] Humble obedient love, this is the key to being healed and becoming a healing presence.

What does it mean to co-suffer? Is it possible to carry the cross of another? We all—each of us— have our own unique suffering, our own personal cross or crosses of suffering to bear in our lives. But, in the same sense that we are members of each other as members of the Body of Christ, we are able to experience in a mysterious way the suffering of others, to co-suffer with them in their distress. Perhaps one of the most powerful literary examples of co-suffering comes from the twentieth-century classic *The Lord of the Rings* by J.R.R. Tolkien. In the trilogy, the struggle between good and evil in Middle Earth is centered on a terrible ring of power that must be destroyed through a long and arduous quest made by the most unlikely of heroes: two small and apparently insignificant but fundamentally good creatures known as hobbits. One hobbit, Frodo, receives and reluctantly accepts the unwanted task of being the ring-bearer. It is his unique cross to bear alone, even though the longer he carries it the weaker it makes him as it has its own desire or motion to return to its evil maker. Frodo's friend, Sam Gamgee agonizes over how he can help his friend carry his burden as they journey through many trials to take the ring to be destroyed in the fires of the mountain where it was created. Finally, when Frodo is too weak to go further up Mount Doom and collapses near the end of their quest, Sam

[30]The George H. Gallup International Institute, *Spiritual Beliefs and the Dying Process*, A Report of a National Survey Conducted for the Nathan Cummings Foundation and Fetzer Institute, October, 1997, p. 47.

[31]John 3.30.

realizes how he can help Frodo with his burden." 'Come Mr. Frodo!' he cried. 'I can't carry it for you, but I can carry you and it as well.'"[32] This is the challenge for those who would respond to the call to co-suffer with the suffering of others. The opportunity and the means of co-suffering may not be readily apparent, but by grace they eventually manifest themselves to those who faithfully accompany those who are suffering. St Maria of Paris, a saint of the twentieth century who was martyred at Ravensbruck concentration camp for helping Jews in Nazi-occupied Paris, understood co-suffering in very personal, if stark terms. "Our neighbor's cross should be a sword that pierces our soul. To co-participate, co-feel, co-suffer with our neighbor's destiny—this is love."[33] Shared suffering can be a source of intimate union between persons. Without this element of co-suffering, however, merely witnessing the suffering of others could become a macabre form of voyeurism. With an intimate co-participation in another's suffering even unto the death of the other person, those who co-suffer may experience a foretaste of their own death. "There is no meeting more meaningful than that which takes place in the sharing of suffering unless it be in the sharing of death itself when we touch immortality."[34]

Is caring for human suffering and in particular, the suffering of the dying, a unique vocation for Christians? The historical answer from the Church's experience has certainly been a resounding "Yes!" especially when considering the evidence of Christ's healing ministry within the Gospels and the work of early church fathers like St Basil the Great of Caesarea. In the current era when the denial of death within the popular culture is so strong and suffering can be eliminated legally by physician-assisted death in many locales, is there not even a greater need for Christians to respond to this vocation?

[32]Sam Gamgee, quoted in J.R.R. Tolkien, *The Return of the King* (Boston: Houghton Mifflin Co., 1994), 919.

[33]St. Maria of Paris and Ravensbruck, "On the Imitation of the Mother of God" in *Mother Maria Skobtsova: Essential Writings*, trans. by R. Pevear and L. Volokhonsky (Maryknoll, NY: Orbis Books, 2003), 71.

[34]Matthew the Poor, *The Communion of Love* (Crestwood, NY: St Vladimir's Seminary Press, 1989), 123.

A new form of philanthropic organization, even a new expression of Christian vocation, seems required today, if the Church is to provide a genuine alternative to physician-assisted suicide. True "aid-in-dying" could be furnished by specially trained Christian lay persons or medical professionals . . . Orthodox hospice programs . . . should be ranked as high priorities among the many pastoral tasks the Church is called to assume.[35]

Healing in the Sacramental Life of the Church

"Whatever you do that is in accordance with the flesh is spiritual, for you do everything in Jesus Christ."[36] For the Christian there is no dualistic dichotomy between the material and spiritual. For in essence, St Ignatius of Antioch is saying that in the person of Christ, the spiritual and material have been reconciled. When the Word of God became flesh, the spiritual was united to the material. This reality forms the basis for the sacramental life of Christians within the Church. The mysteries or sacraments of the Church all have material forms or expressions that are infused with spiritual realities. The heart, the core reality of all the sacraments is the healing power of the death and resurrection of Christ that is actualized in the life and death of each Christian believer. "The whole life of the Church is in a way the sacrament of our death, because all of it is the proclamation of the Lord's death, the confession of His resurrection."[37]

Baptism is the entrance of each Christian into the living and suffering Body of Christ through sacramental participation in his passion. Christians have already died with Christ in the mystery of baptism before their physical death.". . . Unless we willingly choose to die through him in his passion, his life is not in us."[38] Although Christ did not need

[35]J. Breck, *The Sacred Gift of Life—Orthodox Christianity and Bioethics* (Crestwood, NY: St Vladimir's Seminary Press, 1998), 239.

[36]St Ignatius of Antioch, "Ephesians," 8:2, Alistair Stewart, tr. and ed., *St Ignatius of Antioch: The Letters*, Popular Patristics Series no. 49 (Yonkers, NY: St Vladimir's Seminary Press, forthcoming).

[37]A. Schmemann, *O Death, Where is Thy Sting?* 109–110.

[38]St Ignatius of Antioch, Letter to the Magnesians 5:2, *Apostolic Fathers* vol. 2,

to be baptized, he submitted to the ritual mystery, transforming the material world by his contact with the water into a source of healing.

> My spirit is devoted to the cross, which is an offence to unbelievers, but to us salvation and eternal life. 'Where is the wise? Where is the disputer?' Where is the boasting of those who are called prudent? For our God, Jesus the Christ, was conceived by Mary by the dispensation of God, 'as well of the seed of David' as of the Holy Spirit: he was born and was baptized, that by himself submitting [perhaps better translated, "by his suffering" Greek: *pathos*)] he might purify the water.[39]

Water is not only a symbol of life, it is the sine qua non of biological life. Christ's baptism in water was a prefiguring of his life-giving death, burial, and resurrection. The Suffering One was also, in effect, cleansing and healing the whole of creation by his baptism in the Jordan River. The water of our own baptisms was and is fundamentally different because of his being baptized. Our healing begins with baptism in which we enter a new life in Christ. "Do you not know that all of us who have been baptized into Christ Jesus were baptized into his death? We were buried therefore with him by baptism into death, so that as Christ was raised from the dead by the glory of the Father, we too might walk in newness of life."[40]

Confession extends the healing of baptism to the realities of sinful life after baptism. "Confess your sins to one another, and pray for one another, that you may be healed. The prayer of a righteous man has great power in its effects."[41] Accountability to the other, and ultimately to the Other, is a healing act of humility, a necessary and often painful condition for real change and repentance. When one bares one's soul to at least one other person then real accountability and potential for

trans. by Kirsopp Lake, Loeb Classical Library no. 24 (Cambridge, MA: Harvard University Press, 1912, repr. 1985), 201.

[39]St Ignatius of Antioch, Letter to the Ephesians 18:1–2, *Apostolic Fathers* vol. 2, 193.

[40]Romans 6.3.

[41]James 5.16.

change can occur. This is very different from the therapeutic use of patient biography described earlier in this book.

The medicine par excellence is the Eucharist in which the Christian touches, consumes, and is nourished by Christ himself. To quote St Ignatius of Antioch once again, "Breaking one bread, which is the medicine of immortality, the antidote that we should not die, yet enables us to live at all times in Jesus Christ."[42] Whereas Western Christians have debated the nature of the Real Presence, the Eastern Church has preferred to observe silence in the face of an ineffable mystery realizing that in the eucharistic metaphor and symbolism is the very real offer of God to dwell within each of his children—to achieve spiritual union through material means, a further extension of the healing initiated by his baptism in the Jordan. Where God is, there is real health and wholeness. For the disciples on the road to Emmaus, the striking observation was that they only recognized the risen Lord in the blessing and breaking of the bread. "When he was at table with them, he took the bread and blessed, and broke it, and gave it to them. And their eyes were opened, and they recognized him . . . 'Did not our hearts burn within us . . . ?' He was known to them in the breaking of the bread."[43] In some sense, every shared, blessed meal is also a source of healing inasmuch as it is also an icon of the Eucharist. Christ gives himself to us as our ultimate medicine, an incomprehensible mystery of his desire to be with us, in us, healing us but also the world through us. The Eucharist should never be the last option for the seriously ill Christian. It should be the foundation for all therapy.

"Is anyone among you sick? Let him call for the elders of the church, and let them pray over him, anointing him with oil in the name of the Lord; and the prayer of faith will save the sick man, and the Lord will raise him up; and if he has committed sins, he will be forgiven."[44] This passage in the letter of St James is the foundation

[42]St Ignatius of Antioch, "Ephesians," 20: 2, *Apostolic Fathers* vol. 2, 195.
[43]Luke 24.30ff.
[44]James 5.14–15. The Greek word *presbyteroi* is translated as "elder" in this translation. But *presbyter* is the source from which the English word "priest" is ultimately derived, and in this context *presbyteroi* might be better rendered as "priests."

for the healing service of the Eastern Church.[45] In ancient times the healing rite was performed in private homes. It was designed ideally to have seven priests present for the seven Gospel readings, seven accompanying prayers, and seven anointings. Now, it is rare that seven priests are able to be present, and the service is almost always performed in church. The seven prayers that are read by the priests before the seven anointings of the sick have a strong emphasis on repentance and forgiveness of sin, an emphasis that highlights the powerful linkage between sin and physical illness in Christian theology.

Even after death the healing ministry of the Church continues for deceased Christians and their bereaved loved ones. Each burial and memorial service is a small recapitulation of Holy Week and Pascha (Easter). Great emphasis is placed on care of the whole person who has died. The body is still very much reflective of the person, so it is treated with great respect. Orthodox Christians do not cremate. The body sown in the grave will be resurrected at the second coming of Christ, consistent with every Christian's Paschal hope, a hope that has been confirmed by Christ's bodily resurrection. In the burial service, the priest carries on a dialogue at times between (on behalf of) the deceased and God: "Your creative command was my origin and existence . . . I lament and shudder when I think about death and see our beauty, created in the image of God, lying in the tomb disfigured, bereft of glory and form . . . How have we been given over to corruption and wedded to death?"[46] But it continues in hope: "Your death, O Lord, became the cause of eternity, if You did not lie in the tomb, Paradise would not have been opened; wherefore, since You love mankind, give rest to the departed."[47] Memory eternal! If God remembers us, we live, whether we have died or not.

[45]For a complete description of the service with a new translation of the liturgical prayers, see P. Meyendorff, *The Anointing of the Sick* (Crestwood, NY: St Vladimir's Seminary Press, 2009).

[46]Quoted from "Funeral Service," *Orthodox Service Book*, prepared by Fr Peter Costarakis (San Bernardino, CA: Mount of Olives Press, 1991), 110.

[47]Ibid.

Although we appropriately grieve for our deceased loved ones, the late Metropolitan Anthony Bloom (+2003) has reminded us that we must not forget the birth of the deceased into eternal life. "We have no right, if we are Christ's own people, to allow ourselves to overlook the birth into eternity of the departing one because we ourselves are so deeply wounded by our bereavement and overcome by our earthly loneliness. There is in death a power of life that reaches out to us."[48]

---

[48]Metropolitan Anthony [Bloom] of Sourozh, *Death and Bereavement* (Oxford: St. Stephen's Press, 2002), 11.

Essential Elements of Healing

"I will go as far as I can, and break open my life, Lord, at Your feet like an alabaster jar."[1]

T HIS FINAL CHAPTER will explore eight elements that are essential in healing in the traditional Christian context. These include transformation of suffering; reconciliation; cooperation; silence; acquaintance with one's death; gratitude; worship; and communion.

Transformation of Suffering

For Christians the issue is not whether suffering has ceased, been eliminated, or even transcended; rather it has been transformed—it has become a source of healing. "In Christ suffering is not 'removed'; it is transformed into victory. The defeat itself becomes victory, a way, an entrance into the kingdom, and this is the only true healing."[2] By virtue of the incarnation, individual human persons, especially members of the Body of Christ, can participate in the redemptive suffering of the Crucified One. Relief of pain and other forms of distress (i.e., symptoms) does not end suffering. However, good symptom relief makes it easier to explore fully and address the deeper spiritual issues that underlie one's suffering. The meaning of suffering for Christians is fully realized to the degree that the suffering draws one into a closer relationship with God. "And why have I given myself up to death, to fire, to the sword, to wild beasts? Because near the sword is near to God; with the

---

[1]B. Pasternak, "Magdalene," from *Selected Poems*, trans. by J. Stallworthy, and P. France (London: Penguin Books, 984), 137.

[2]A. Schmemann, *O Death, Where is Thy Sting?* (Crestwood, NY: St Vladimir's Seminary Press, 2003), 107.

wild beasts is with God; in the name of Jesus Christ alone am I endur-
ing all things, that I may suffer with him, and the perfect man himself
gives me strength."[3]

Reconciliation

Cure relates to disease, whereas healing relates to persons. A person
isn't fully a person except in community. Just as sin and suffering affect
the entire Body of Christ, healing is not an individual or private phenomenon but is also experienced within the entire Body. The trinitar-
ian nature of God is the foundation for understanding reconciliation
within the Body of Christ. "God's mode of being . . . love . . . is offered
to created beings and developed in them as a gift of the three Persons
of the Holy Trinity."[4] God is a community or communion of love. The
Trinity is the model for our relationships with others. Forgiveness is a
precondition for Christian reconciliation. Forgiveness in the Christian
context embraces and extends the secular concept of reconciliation. In
Christian practice, we can't fully receive forgiveness until we realize our
utter helplessness to alter our condition without God's help. Neither
can we live forgiven lives, if we have not forgiven (been reconciled to)
others. "And forgive us our debts, as we also have forgiven our debtors
. . . For if you forgive men their trespasses, your heavenly Father also
will forgive you; but if you do not forgive men their trespasses, neither
will your Father forgive your trespasses."[5] In Christ's parable of the
Prodigal Son, it is the Prodigal's Father who defies all human logic
and wisdom (witness the older brother's reaction), continually seeking
and then rejoicing in the return of his prodigal son, even though the
son clearly hasn't proven his worthiness for such love or trust. This is
our model for forgiveness, without preconditions, and with unlimited

---

[3]St Ignatius of Antioch, Letter to the Smyrneans 4:2, *Apostolic Fathers* vol. 2,
trans. by Kirsopp Lake, Loeb Classical Library, vol. 24 (Cambridge, MA: Harvard
University Press, 1912, repr. 1985), 257.

[4]A.G. Keselopoulos, *Man and the Environment*, trans. by E. Theokritoff (Crestwood, NY: St Vladimir's Seminary Press, 2001), 21.

[5]Matthew 6.12, 14 & 15.

love. Repentance for one's role in all broken relationships must be pursued by the Christian to achieve reconciliation, especially when death approaches. Metropolitan Anthony Bloom emphasizes "the necessity for preparing for death through a stern and liberating process of coming to terms with life, making one's peace with everyone, with oneself, with one's conscience, with one's circumstances, with the present and the past, with events and with people—and indeed with the future, the coming of death itself. . . . One cannot enter into eternity tied and fettered by hatred."[6]

Cooperation

We must *want* to get well (to be healed). Christ specifically asked the paralyzed man at the pool of Bethesda, "Do you want to be made well?"[7] God won't force healing on us. There are some who may actually prefer their illness, physical, psychological, or spiritual, to being made whole, especially if they realize the radical change that they may need to undergo for real healing to occur. There must also be cooperation on the level of belief and trust in the healer. "And he could do no mighty work there, except that he laid his hands upon a few sick people and healed them. And he marveled because of their unbelief."[8] With reference to Mark 6:5, St Gregory of Nazianzus comments, "Something essential for healing is required on both sides—faith on the part of the patients, power on that of the healer. So one side without its counterpart 'could not,' so to speak, perform them. As this can be seen in medical care, it can also be seen in moral transformation."[9] Even those with a vocation to suffer must continually seek real healing in their suffering (e.g., St Pimen the Much-Ailing, August 7).

---

[6]Metropolitan Anthony [Bloom] of Sourozh, *Death and Bereavement* (Oxford: St. Stephen's Press, 2002), 42.

[7]John 5.6.

[8]Mark 6.5–6.

[9]St. Gregory of Nazianzus, Oration 30, On the Son 10, quoted in Thomas C. Oden and Christopher A. Hall, *Mark* (Revised), Ancient Christian Commentary on Scripture NT 2 (Downers Grove, IL: InterVarsity Press, 1998), 75.

He was sickly from his youth, and from his youth desired monasticism. Brought to the Monastery of the Caves for healing, he remained there till his death. He prayed more for sickness than for health. One night, angels appeared to him and tonsured him a monk, telling him at the same time that he would be sick until his death, and would be healed at that moment. And so it was; he lay sick for twenty years, working wonders even during his lifetime and being possessed of a rare gift of discernment. At the time of his death, he got up from his bed completely healed, immediately prepared his grave and entered into rest in the Lord, in the year 1110.[10]

Silence

One of the passages from the Old Testament Scriptures that is read during the liturgy on Holy Saturday—the day before Pascha or Easter, in the Orthodox Church—is from the book of Exodus. Like the other passages from the Old Testament, it represents a prefiguring of the saving act of God in the passage of his Son from death to life. It initially describes the fear and terror of the Israelites when they reach the apparent barrier of the Red Sea and are being chased by Pharoah and his army. In this moment of crisis in which their very survival is threatened, they are told by Moses: "The Lord will fight for you, and you have only to be still."[11] Their terror is not unlike that of patients facing the diagnosis of a terminal illness. This silence or stillness (Gk—hesychia) that is to be cultivated is as necessary for the healer as for the patient. We both must wait for God to act. "By your patience, possess your souls."[12] It is important in this context to remember also the distinction between hearing and listening. Whereas both hearing and listening can have similar meanings of giving one's attention, the secondary meanings of listening

[10]St Nikolai Velimirovic "Our Holy Father Pimen the Much-Ailing," in Part 3 of The Prologue from Ochrid, trans. by Mother Maria (Birmingham, UK: Lazarica Press, 1986), 166.
[11]Exodus 14.14. The Greek verb used here is sigaō, which has the root meaning of to be quiet, to keep silence."
[12]Luke 21.19.

(i.e., paying attention with the intent to obey or waiting attentively)[13] is crucial to understanding the practical implications of *hesychia*. As Christians, whether ill or not, we are to be continually aware of our mortal nature, not in a morbid sense, but a realistic perception grounded in the hope of the resurrection. This reality is at the heart of the ancient Christian precept, "Remember your death!" Understanding this, living this understanding, can then be our kenosis, the stripping away of the 'noise' so that real silence—*hesychia*—can be experienced once our full trust has been placed in the Person who has conquered death. With this as a foundation, then we can really begin to listen. If we are finally prepared to listen, where do we encounter God?

Two examples from the Scriptures, one from the Old and one from the New Testament, help identify the conditions conducive to the encounter with the Divine.

> "They seek my life to take it away." And he said, "Go forth, and stand upon the mount before the Lord." And behold, the Lord passed by, and a great and strong wind rent the mountains, and broke in pieces the rocks before the Lord, but the Lord was not in the wind; and after the wind an earthquake, but the Lord was not in the earthquake; and after the earthquake a fire, but the Lord was not in the fire; and after the fire *a still small voice*.[14]

> He entered a village; and a woman named Martha received him into her house. And she had a sister called Mary, who sat at the Lord's feet and listened to his teaching. But Martha was distracted with much serving; and she went to him and said, "Lord, do you not care that my sister has left me to serve alone? Tell her then to help me." But the Lord answered her, "Martha, Martha, you are anxious and troubled about many things; *one thing is needful*. Mary has chosen the good portion, which shall not be taken away from her."[15]

[13] *Webster's New Universal Unabridged Dictionary* (New York: Barnes & Noble Publishing, Inc., 2003).

[14] 1 Kings 19.10 ff.

[15] Luke 10.38 ff.

Human beings are not particularly good at identifying priorities in the realm of the spiritual life or committing to them. The noisy or dramatic often more easily capture our attention and preempt our ability to recognize "the still small voice" of God and to attend to it. As members of modern society we may be plagued by even more distractions and responsibilities, in which the assumption of good intentions, as with Martha, prevents our discovery of "the one needful thing." In effect, both of these stories identify necessary features of a vital prayer life. There must be sufficient stillness or silence in the soul to make it possible to really listen eagerly and obediently for the voice of God in the experience of our lives; we must seek this one needful thing as our highest priority.

For the learned and intellectuals there is another barrier to finding true *hesychia*.

> Two philosophers came to an elder and asked him to say something beneficial to them. The elder remained silent. Again the philosophers spoke: "Will you not answer us, father?" The elder said to them: "That you are skilled in the use of words I am fully aware, but I do testify to you that you are not truly lovers of wisdom. How long will you cultivate the art of speech, you who have no understanding of what it is to speak? *Let the object of your philosophy be always to contemplate death, possessing yourselves in silence and tranquility.*"[16]

True silence of the soul seeking communion with God is not possible without humility. This is the great secret blessing hidden within the awareness of our mortality. A real and honest contemplation of our death will be the antidote to pride, the silencer of all noise and distractions, and the teacher who will lead us to "the one needful thing." Ultimately, we are called as Christians to a healing encounter with the deepest mysteries of God which are hidden in his silence. "And the virginity of Mary, and her giving birth, were hidden from the Prince of

---

[16]John Moschos, *The Spiritual Meadow*, trans. by J. Wortley (Kalamazoo, MI: Cistercian Publications, 1992), 129–130.

this world, as was also the death of the Lord. Three mysteries of crying out were performed in the quietness of God."[17]

Acquaintance with One's Death

"Ah, how afraid I am of death, and how sinful that is!"[18] This unholy fear of death has many adverse consequences. For the patient with a terminal illness to know the diagnosis is critical. Although the diagnosis may be devastating (e.g., metastatic cancer), not knowing it robs patients of the ability to confront directly the evil facing them and to respond to this last opportunity for repentance. It may ultimately add to their suffering, particularly as unresolved spiritual distress accumulates and is not addressed. The early fathers of the Church made no real distinction between the importance of recognizing physical and spiritual illness, in their ultimate healing. Thus, the same is true for spiritual evil (sin)—half the battle is being able to clearly see and acknowledge our sin before we can be healed of it. "The sick one who is familiar with his illness is easily cured, and the one who acknowledges his pain is close to healing."[19] But, unfortunately, there is the great temptation to lie to patients and loved ones about bad news so as not to rob them of hope. "Even in our most decent society, you meet with the wish to lie with the purpose of making your neighbor happy, for we all suffer from this unrestraint of the heart."[20] This unrestraint of the heart effectively robs dying patients of the true source of their hope, their death. To know the truth of one's condition can be the only true foundation for healing. "You will know the truth, and the truth will make you free."[21]

How can the Christian overcome the fear of death? The faith that is central to the hope of Christians is the recognition of Christ's conquest

[17]St Ignatius of Antioch, "Letter to the Ephesians," 19:1, *Apostolic Fathers* vol. 2, 193.

[18]F. Dostoevsky, *The Adolescent*, trans. by R. Pevear, and L. Volokhonsky (New York: Vintage Classics, 2003), 192.

[19]St. Isaac of Syria (Nineveh), "Second Discourse," *St Isaac of Nineveh On Ascetical Life* (Crestwood, NY: St Vladimir's Seminary Press, 1989), 33.

[20]F. Dostoevsky, *The Adolescent*, 205.

[21]John 8.32.

of death and that his resurrection is the first fruits, the guarantee, of the universal resurrection of all human beings at the end of time. "In order to be able to face death one must be anchored in the certainty, an experiential and not only theoretical certainty, of eternal life ... there is in this possession of eternal life a certainty that reduces to nought the fear of death—not the pain of separation, not the regret that death exists, but the fear."[22]

There is another aspect to becoming acquainted with one's death. Just as suffering is experienced by persons in community, so also death, the full ripening and culmination of suffering in a person's life, can be an opportunity for learning for those who witness the process as they accompany the dying person on the journey. Each death we experience in this life is a preparation, a 'dress rehearsal' for our own death. Grief can educate. The key is the lens through which we observe and reflect upon our experience of grief. Witnessing the deaths of loved ones whose hope and trust have been placed in the Crucified One is our apprenticeship in dying. Metropolitan Anthony has some very comforting words for bereaved Christians. "If we can truly, sincerely say that the person who has departed this life was a treasure to us, then where our treasure is there our heart should be, and we should, together with this person who has entered into eternity, live as completely, as deeply as possible in eternity ... as more and more beloved ones leave this earthly pilgrimage and enter into the stability and peace of life eternal, we should feel that we belong more and more to that world, ever more completely, ever more perfectly, that its values increasingly become ours."[23]

Gratitude and Worship

For traditional Christians, healing also includes giving glory and thanks to God—it is doxological and eucharistic. Giving glory or worship cannot be described apart from giving thanks, the eucharistic element that is at the heart of Christian worship. Christ *cured* ten lepers of their

---

[22]Metropolitan Anthony, *Death and Bereavement*, 19.
[23]Ibid. p.31

leprosy in the account recorded in Luke 17.11–19, and one (the Samaritan) who glorified God and gave thanks was *healed*. Our worship is a source of healing, if it gives glory and thanksgiving to God regardless of our condition and the apparent outcome. For it is in giving glory and thanksgiving to God that the proper relationship between the human person and God is restored. Is it really possible to give thanks and glory to God when there is no apparent cure or even hope of one? "Naked I came from my mother's womb, and naked shall I return; the Lord gave, and the Lord has taken away; blessed be the name of the Lord."[24] Job's statement is a reflection of complete trust in God even when the reason for one's misery is not forthcoming. St Paul very succinctly states the hope of every believing Christian, even in the face of great suffering. "For to me to live is Christ, and to die is gain."[25] Christ and his suffering are the answers Job was seeking for his own suffering. St Paul can in turn rejoice and give thanks for his own participation in the sufferings of Christ as he hopes to participate also in the resurrection glory of the Crucified Lord.

Communion

Healing is ultimately centered in communion (Greek: *koinonia*) or fellowship—a deep, intimate relationship of love, faith, and trust—with God and our neighbor. "Love one another as I have loved you,"[26] and "Your faith has made you well."[27] Whether Christ forgives our sins or cures our diseases, they are complementary aspects of the same phenomenon—healing! It may be helpful to remember that the Greek word for sin—*hamartia*—means 'missing the mark' or failing in one's purpose. Physical diseases as well as evil thoughts or deeds both represent different aspects of this same failure to be the way things should be. In essence, they reflect a breaking of communion between God and his creatures. Full or complete healing is centered in restoring communion

[24]Job 1.21.
[25]Philippians 1.21.
[26]John 15.12.
[27]Luke 17.19.

with God. Eric Cassell has identified the locus of human suffering as being centered in the individual person with its primary manifestation being a threat to the 'intactness' of the person.[28] From the Christian perspective there is a communal or transpersonal aspect to suffering— a *koinonia* or fellowship of suffering that is hidden within the mysteries of the Church. This is most particularly true of the Eucharist, in which praise and thanksgiving emerge as a collective experience from the participation in the passion of Christ both liturgically and extra-liturgically. Whether aware or not of a threat to one's intactness as a person, individual members of the Body of Christ as the Body of Christ suffer or co-suffer with all those who are suffering or have suffered in the world, to the extent that their suffering is in the image and likeness of the suffering of the Crucified One. Thus, in a mysterious manner, all the *pathemata*—bad events/suffering—that have happened within human and cosmic experience, have been swallowed up or assimilated within the great mysteries of the Church, e.g.., baptism, anointing of the sick, marriage, the burial service, and most specifically eucharistic communion. Suffering in the Christian sense is not only personal but is also a collective experience shared by the entire creation. Rather than being centered only in individual persons, suffering is primarily centered in relationships. Just as suffering is centered in relationships and is transpersonal, so also is healing. A dramatic and explicit instance of this transpersonal character to healing is given in the Gospel account of the healing of the paralytic: "And they came, bringing to him a paralytic carried by four men. And when they could not get near him because of the crowd, they removed the roof above him; and when they had made an opening, they let down the pallet on which the paralytic lay. And when Jesus saw their faith, he said to the paralytic, 'My son, your sins are forgiven . . .'"[29] Note "when Jesus saw *their* faith." Not only does their faith make it possible for his sins to be forgiven but also for his physical cure to be effected, in other words complete holistic healing.

[28]E.J. Cassell, "The Nature of Suffering and the Goals of Medicine," *New England Journal of Medicine* 306 (1982): 639–645.

[29]Mark 2.3–5.

Real healing in the Christian sense occurs in community, the community of the faithful, not in isolation.

Communion in the Christian sense is an intimacy between persons modeled on and animated by the continuous love flowing between the persons of the Holy Trinity. There are two aspects of the person that warrant further exploration in the context of Christian communion. In Greek, *to prosopon* means 'face'. It also means person. In seeing someone's face, there is the potential of encountering the person. Not only do we need to listen rather than merely hear, so also we must search out more than the face: the person behind what we see when we look at another human being. There is also great power in a name. Having a name means you are a person and in some sense it is your identity, who you are as a person. The rich man in the parable of the Rich Man and Lazarus did not have a name. He was not a real person, but a mere shell of humanity eaten up by the passions. In contrast to human names, we can never know the Name of God, because the Ineffable One cannot be circumscribed by a name. *But*, because of the incarnation, we can know Jesus, the Son of God: "He who has seen Me has seen the Father."[30]

Interestingly, the faith that brings healing may not be that of the one apparently performing the healing. Indeed, the faith of others operating through an unbeliever may not only bring healing to the subject of the healing activity but also to the unbeliever through whom the healing takes place. Faith has a communal quality rooted in love that can transcend and transform the individual's relationship of faith (or lack of faith) with God, through the Body of Christ. The following story from the early monastic tradition of the Church illustrates this principle in a dramatic fashion.

> In Egypt, the robber chief Flavian, intending to rob a certain women's convent, put on the monastic habit and went to the convent. The nuns took him for one of the holy Fathers, conducted him to the church and asked him to offer prayers for them to God, which Flavian did against his will and to his own amazement. Then food was

[30]John 14.9.

set before him. After finishing his meal, the nuns washed his feet. In the convent one of the sisters was blind and deaf. The nuns brought her and gave her some of the water to drink with which the stranger's feet had been washed. The patient was immediately healed. The nuns glorified God and the holy life of the strange monk, and they spread the news of the miracle that had taken place. The grace of God descended upon the robber chief. He offered repentance, and was changed from a chief of robbers into a renowned father.[31]

How do we live in healing communion with God and our neighbor? St Paul's admonition for all Christians—which is also at the heart of the monastic vocation—is, "Pray without ceasing."[32] But, how is this possible? The monastic tradition within the Church has answered this question by emphasizing the absolute necessity of practicing the continual awareness of God and making all that one is and does prayer; i.e., become prayer. The invocation of the name of Jesus, especially in the ancient form of the Jesus Prayer ("Lord Jesus Christ, Son of God, have mercy on me a sinner"), or other shorter variants, has aided many Christians over the centuries to develop and maintain the continual awareness of God, so that, armed with the all-powerful name of Jesus even in the midst of terrible suffering, one can say with the twentieth-century monk, St Silouan of Athos, "Keep thy mind in hell, and despair not."[33]

The Jesus Prayer is a concise vision of the healing act of God in the incarnation.[34] It is a ladder of Divine condescension to the human

[31]Bp. Ignatius Brianchaninov, *The Arena* (Jordanville, NY: Holy Trinity Monastery, 1997), 46.

[32]1 Thess 5.17.

[33]Archimandrite Sophrony, *St. Silouan the Athonite* (Crestwood, NY: St Vladimir's Seminary Press, 1999), 212.

[34]The Jesus Prayer is an ancient prayer of the Church that is rooted in Scripture. It originates with the prayer of the tax collector in Christ's parable about prayer recorded in Luke 18.13, "God, be merciful to me a sinner!" The historical roots of the Jesus prayer and its use in the prayer life of Eastern Christians have been recently highlighted in a DVD entitled "Mysteries of the Jesus Prayer," and in an accompanying book of the same title by Norris J. Chumley (New York: Harper One/Harper

condition, each word/phrase being a rung on the ladder by which God comes to his creatures in need of healing and those same rungs of the ladder being our means of ascent to the Divine.

- *Lord*—the 'shorthand' expression for the unnamed God, 'the One who is' (Greek—*ho ōn*);

- *Jesus Christ*—God who cannot be contained, in his humility accepts being circumscribed by a name—the 'Anointed Savior' (the anointing a material act experienced by Pure Spirit who has united himself to his material creation);

- *Son of God*—is the further condescension of the Divine humility in which the Word of God as the Son in obedience to the Father enters into human relationships which are thereby blessed as a means of healing;

- *have mercy*—the essential act of the God who is Love (and when God has mercy, he heals, he restores that which has been broken);

- *on me*— the mercies of God are experienced personally, by individual persons;

- *a sinner*—the nature of the malady upon which the infinite mercies of God are showered. He who came down even into Hades also came back up drawing all with him. This is at least part of the meaning, the incarnational truth embedded within this ancient prayer of the Church.

Also, hidden within the mystery of this prayer is the role of the Virgin Mary, the 'Mother of God' (Greek— *Theotokos*) in the miracle of the incarnation and her ongoing role in support of the faithful. She is the ladder that the Old Testament patriarch Jacob perceived in his dream.[35]

Collins Publishers, 2011). Also, many western readers are familiar with the anonymous 19th century Russian classic of spirituality, *The Way of the Pilgrim*, that features the Jesus Prayer in the story of the Russian pilgrim's spiritual journey across Russia.

[35]Genesis 28.12ff. A good example of the many patristic references to Mary as the ladder upon which the "angels of God were ascending and descending" is from

It was her complete "yes" to God ("Behold, I am the handmaid of the Lord; let it be to me according to your word"[36]) that made possible the 'enfleshment' of the Word of God. "Rejoice, heavenly ladder by which God descended; rejoice, bridge leading us from earth to heaven!"[37] St Isaac of Syria speaks encouragingly of the fruits of this labor of prayer of each Christian that is joined to the prayers of all the faithful ('the Cloud of Witnesses') in the communion of the saints, the foremost of whom is the Virgin Mary:

> Be at peace with your soul and heaven and earth will be at peace with you. Endeavor to enter the treasury within you and you will see that treasury which is in heaven. The former and the latter are one and through a single entrance you will see both of them. The ladder of that kingdom is hidden within you, within your soul. Dive away from sin into yourself and there you will find the steps by which you may ascend.[38]

God is the Good Samaritan who descends the ladder of his kenosis and condescension as Christ and shows mercy to us to which we can respond (ascend back to him) by showing mercy to him in others who are suffering. The 'rungs' of the ladder of God's condescension to us in our fallen state ('on me a sinner') now become spokes emanating from a hub, our recreated self (our new humanity in Christ), reaching out

St Andrew of Crete, "Homily III, On the Dormition of Our Most Holy Lady, the Mother of God," from *On the Dormition of Mary: Early Patristic Homilies*, trans. Brian E. Daley, S.J. (Crestwood, NY: St Vladimir's Seminary Press, 1998), 147–148: "Behold, the ladder that Jacob saw in a moment of divine revelation, on which he saw God's angels moving up and down (Genesis 28.12; cf. Jn 1.51)—whatever that ascent and descent signified. This is the gate of heaven, of which Jacob said, 'How awe-inspiring is this place! It is nothing other than God's dwelling—it is itself the gate of heaven!'" (Genesis 28.17).

[36]Luke 1.38.

[37]Ikos II from the "Akathistos Hymn in Praise of the Theotokos," *A Manual of Prayer and Praise to the Theotokos* (Otego, NY: Holy Myrrhbearers Monastery, Otego, 1995), 30.

[38]St Isaac of Syria [Nineveh], "Second Discourse," *St. Isaac of Nineveh On Ascetical Life* (Crestwood, NY: St Vladimir's Seminary Press, 1989), 34.

in all directions to embrace the entire cosmos. We can become a true 'mikrokosmos', a microcosm of the Divine Love. Our model is the humility of Christ. We must also be humble, recognize our incredible need, and then desire with our whole being to be healed (e.g., John 5), not only for our own healing but also if we are to become healing agents of God's mercy and grace in the world.

Prayer leads to knowledge of God in an ever deepening relationship. Indeed, to know God (and most importantly to be known by him) is eternal life. "And this is eternal life, that they know Thee the only true God, and Jesus Christ whom Thou hast sent."[39] How do we come to know God? "That I may know him and the power of his resurrection, and the fellowship of his sufferings, being conformed to his death."[40] We can only come to know him fully in "the fellowship of his sufferings."

Within the ancient tradition of the Church, the life of Moses has been held up as a model for understanding the spiritual life. "The Lord used to speak to Moses face to face, as a man speaks to his friend."[41] God also says to Moses, "I know you by name."[42] Moses is the friend of God. With reference to Moses as the Christian's model for becoming the friend of God, St Gregory of Nyssa, says, "We regard falling from God's friendship as the only thing dreadful and we consider becoming God's friend the only thing worthy of honor and desire. This . . . is the perfection of life."[43] Friendship with God—this is the knowledge that heals, whether we *live* or *die*. For the friend of God will live forever. The fearful word to hear will be the word spoken to the foolish virgins: "I do not know you."[44]

"When we attain to love, we attain to God. Our way is ended and we have passed unto the isle that lies beyond the world, where is the Father,

[39]John 17.3.
[40]Philippians 3.10.
[41]Exodus 33.11.
[42]Exodus 33.17.
[43]St Gregory of Nyssa, *Life of Moses*, trans. by E. Ferguson and A.J. Malherbe (New York: Paulist Press, 1978), 137.
[44]Matthew 25.12.

and the Son, and the Holy Spirit to Whom be glory and dominion, and may He make us worthy of His glory and His love through the fear of Him. Amen"[45]

---

[45]St Isaac of Syria, "Homily 46" in *The Ascetical Homilies of Saint Isaac the Syrian* (Boston: Holy Transfiguration Monastery, 1984), 225.